SUFISM

Misconceptions and the Reality

SHAYKH HUMAYUN HANIF MUJADDIDI

Special thanks to my Shaykh Mowlana Shamsur Rehman Al Abbasi with whose dua, support and guidance this work has been compiled. Special thanks to all the scholars, whose literary work is cited. May Allah shower His blessings upon them. Due consideration is taken to cite the work, however, intext referencing is kept to minimum to keep the flow for the reader. The text is referenced following the Turabian Sixth edition rules. The cover page and the calligraphy is designed by the Egyptian designer Marwa Abbas.

All rights reserved by Maktaba Islahenafs, aside from fair use, meaning a few pages or less for non-profit educational purposes, review, or scholarly citation. No part of this publication maybe reproduced, stored in a retrieval system or transmitted in any form or means, electronic, online, mechanical, photocopying, recording or otherwise, without the prior permission of the copyright owner.

SUFISM: MISCONCEPTIONS AND THE REALITY

First Edition: 2022
Publisher: Maktaba Islahenafs, Karachi, Pakistan
www.islahenafs.org
Email: info@islahenafs.org
Phone: +92 321 2172484

AVAILABLE IN PAKISTAN

MAKTABA ISLAHENAFS
Email: info@islahenafs.org
Phone: +92 321 2172484

AVAILABLE ON AMAZON

USA, CANADA, UNITED KINGDOM
AUSTRALIA, FRANCE, ITALY, SWEDEN
NETHERLANDS, POLAND, SPAIN, DENMARK

ALSO AVAILABLE IN USA & CANADA

Ha-Meem Store
www.hameemstore.com
Email: orders@hameemstore.com
Phone: +1 416 8792545

آنہا کہ طلبکار خدائید خدائید | بیرون زشمانیست شمائید شمائید
جیزی کہ نکردید گم از بہر چہ جوئید | واندر طلب گم نشدہ بہر چہ جرائید
اسمید و حروفید و کلامید و کتابید | جبریل امینید و رسولان سمائید
در خانہ نشینید و مگردید بہرسوی | زیرا کہ شما خانہ و ہم خانہ خدائید
ذاتید و صفاتید گہی عرش گہی فرش | در عین بقائید و منزہ ز فنائید
خواہید کہ ببینید رخ اندر رخ معشوق | زنگار ز آئینہ بصیقل بزدائید

The thing you seek, you are, you are
You who seek God apart, apart

Why then search for what you have not lost?
Searching for what's not lost, distrust!

You are the letters, names and the book
Prophets and angels, your word undertook

Just sit still, let this futile search go
You are the house, master and foe

Essence and form, celestial and terrestrial
Always eternal, in death and at birth

Mowlana Rumi
Divan-i Shams-i Tabrizi

INDEX

About the Author	1
Foreword	4
Chapter 1: THE PROPHETIC MISSION	**7**
Definition of Sufism or Tasawwuf	12
Chapter 2: MISCONCETIONS REGARDING SUFISM	**20**
Sufism and Monasticism	20
Modern Sufism	22
Sufism and Ahmadiyat (Qadiyaniat)	25
Sufi versus Yogi	27
Are Sufis part of the Mainstream Society?	28
Is Tassawuf a Reprehensible Innovation (Bid'a)?	30
Chapter 3: ELEMENTS OF TASAWWUF	**37**
The Internal State	37
Significance of Heart	43
Purification of the Carnal Self (Tazkiyah e Nafs)	45
Path (Tariqa)	49
Definition of Suluk	52
Chapter 4: THE GUIDE-SHAYKH	**56**
Following a Teacher (Ittiba)	58
Attributes of the Shaykh	63
Fake Sufis	68
Reality of the Pledge (Bayá)	72
Connection (Tálluq)	76
Communication (Raabta)	80
Etiquettes with the Shaykh (Adab)	82
Attention (Tawajjuh)	88
Affinity (Nisbah)	91
Benefit from One's Shaykh (Tauheed e Matlab)	94
Succession (Khilafah)	95
Women on the Path	96

Chapter 5: ARTICLES OF FAITH (AQAID)	**99**
Belief in Allah ﷻ	99
Belief in Angels	104
Belief in Scriptures	105
Belief in the Messengers	106
Belief in the Day of Judgement	110
Belief in Predestination (Qadr)	114
Life of the Prophet ﷺ after Death (Hayat un-Nabi)	115
Chpater 6: REMEMBRANCE (DHIKR)	**119**
Assemblies of Dhikr (Halqah)	125
Silent Dhikr	128
Chapter 7: PURIFICATION OF THE SOUL (TAZKIYAH)	**129**
Lack of Sincerity (Riya)	129
Pride	131
Unnecessary Talking	132
Unrestrained Glances	134
Backbiting (Ghiba)	135
Envy	136
Anger	136
Gluttony	138
Bad Company	139
Stinginess	141
Chapter 8: JOURNEY OF THE SEEKER	**143**
Three Essentials	145
Love of Allah	148
Fear of Allah (Taqwa)	151
Hope in Allah	154
Reliance on Allah (Tawakkul)	155
Love of the Beloved Prophet ﷺ	156
Virtuous Character (Ikhlaq)	162
Repentance (Tawba)	163
Striving (Mujahida)	166
Gratitude (*Shukr*)	167

Patience (Sabr)	170
Abstinence (Tabattul)	171
Generosity (Sakha)	171
Chastity	173
Preach (Tableegh)	174
Humility (Tawadu)	175
Contentment (Qaná)	177
Lawful Sustenance	178
Time Management	180

Chapter 9: DIVINE LAW AND THE REALITY — 182

The Concept of Ihsan	182
Divine Law and The Reality (Shariáh and Haqiqa)	186
Maárfa	190
Level of Certitude	194
Walaya	198
True Knowledge (Ilm e Haqeeqi)	202
Bestowed Knowledge (Ilm al-Ladunni)	203
Fana fil-Shaykh, Fana fir-Rasool and Fana Fillah	205
Journey towards Allah (Sair I'lallah and Sair Fillah)	208

Chapter 10: MYSTICAL STATES AND STATIONS — 209

Contraction and Elation (Qabd and Bast)	214
Awe and Intimacy (Hayba and Uns)	216
Ecstatic Behaviour, Rapture and Ecstatic Finding	217
Unification and Separation (Jam and Farq)	220
Unification of Unification (jam al-jamá)	221
Annihilation and Subsistence (Faná and Baqá)	222
Absence and Presence (Ghayba and Hudur)	224
Tasting and Drinking (Dhawq and Shurb)	225
Sobriety and drunkenness (Sahw and Sukr)	226
Erasure and affirmation (Mahw and Ithbat)	227
Concealment and Manifestation (Satr and Tajalli)	229
Presence, Unveiling and Witnessing	229
Proximity and Distance (Qurb and Buád)	230
Concept of Unity of Perception and Unity of Being	232

Chapter 11: GENERAL MISCONCEPTIONS	**240**
Use of Musical Instruments	240
Conveying the Reward of Actions	242
Visiting the Graves of Awliya	245
Chapter 12: THE ORDERS-SILSILA	**248**
Chishtiya Order	249
Qadiriya Order	251
Shadhili Order	252
Sohrevardi Order	253
Chapter 13: NAQSHBANDI ORDER	**254**
Chapter 14: NAQSHBANDI PRINCIPLES	**291**
Conscious Breathing (Hosh dar Dam)	291
Watch the Step (Nazar bar Qadam)	291
Journey Homeward (Safar dar Watan)	293
Solitude en masse (Khalwat dar Anjuman)	293
Remembrance (Yad Kard)	294
Resonate (Baaz Gasht)	294
Diligence (Nigah Dasht)	295
Recollection (Yad Dasht)	295
Awareness of Time (Wuqoof e Zamani)	295
Awareness of Number (Wuqoof e Adadi)	296
Awareness of Heart (Wuqoof e Qalbi)	296
Chapter 15: SUBTLETIES AND MANIFESTATIONS	**297**
Chapter 16: DAILY ROUTINES IN THE NAQSHBANDI ORDER	**302**
Remembrance (Tasbeehat)	302
Meditation (Muraqabah in the Naqshbandi Order)	302
Envisage (Tasawwur-e-Shaykh)	304
Hierarchy of the Spiritual Order (Shajrah)	308
Chapter 17: LESSONS OF THE NAQSHBANDI ORDER	**315**
Works Cited	**338**
Section Index	**342**

About the Author

The author of the book, Shaykh Mohammad Ali Humayun Hanif Naqshbandi Mujaddidi was born in Karachi in November, 1962. After his O levels from Karachi Grammar school, Shaykh Mohammad Ali Humayun Hanif studied business and joined the family industry of Textiles. His father, Mohammad Hanif Dost Mohammad was a successful industrialist and a renowned philanthropist, the founder and president of the Federation of Pakistan Chambers of Commerce and Industries as well as All Pakistan Textile Mills Association.

Over last thirty years, Shaykh Mohammad Ali Humayun Hanif has been a patron and amongst the Board of Governors for Liaquat National Hospital in Karachi. Throughout these years, with all his commitments with his family, business and the charity projects, his unbounding desire for the love of Allah and the Last Prophetﷺ never overshadowed.

In 1989, Shaykh Mohammad Ali Humayun Hanif started attending *Dhikr* gatherings conducted by Hazrat Mowlana Shamsur Rehman Al Abbasi who further nurtured his yearning for the Love of Allah. In 1991, Hazrat Shaykh Mohammad Ali Humayun Hanif entered into Bayá (oath) with Mowlana Shamsur Rehman Al Abbasi. By the Grace of Allahﷻ, in 1994, Hazrat Mowlana Shamsur Rehman Al Abbasi authorised him as a Shaykh. Shaykh Humayun Hanif was appointed as the first *Khalifa* (spiritual successor) of Mowlana Shamsur Rehman Al Abbasi and he gave *'ijazah'* (permission) to conduct *Dhikr* gatherings and guide others.

He has travelled widely across the globe and spent time in the company of many renowned scholars and *Awliya*. Shaykh Mohammad Ali Humayun Hanif is also authorised by Dr. Ismail Memon Madni; Khalifa of Shaykh al-Hadith Mowlana Mohammad Zakariya Kandhalvi﷫ in *Naqshbandia, Chistiya, Qadiriya* and *Soharwardiya* Orders. Hazrat Mowlana Ishaq Sajid, Khalifa of Mowlana Ali Murtaza﷫ of Gadei Shareef also authorised Shaykh Mohammad Ali Humayun Hanif دامت بركاتهم in the *Naqshbandia, Chistiya, Qadiriya, Soharwardiya and Shadhiliya* Orders.

Shaykh Humayun Hanif's vision is to purify and connect the individuals to Allahﷻ by following the path of His Last Prophetﷺ. He corroborates Islam as a *Deen*; a way of life and not just a set of rituals. Through his own practical example, he demonstrates to follow Shariáh, encompassing faith and action, behaviour, and morals, bringing together the practical and the spiritual aspects of human life as determined by Allah's Messengerﷺ.

His students come from all walks of life and he encourages them to stay in contact with him for guidance. Shaykh Humayun Hanif endeavours to bring a positive change in every sphere of their lives. He emphasises upon his students to become 'Active Muslims', both in their spiritual life and worldly matters. To achieve the desired outcome in the seekers, weekly *Dhikr* gatherings and lectures on *Tasawwuf* are conducted at *Khanqah e Shamsia* located in Karachi, Pakistan. The Khanqah also has a separate Shariah compliant arrangement for ladies.

Lectures available on:

You Tube: Islahenafs-Shaykh Humayun Hanif

Website: www.islahenafs.org

Other Publications by the Author:

- ❖ Umrah and Hajj-Inner Dimensions of the Journey to Love [Eng- Published 2022]
- ❖ Umrah aur Hajj-Ba Nigah e Ruh, Ishq se Qurb ka Safar [Urdu- Published 2022]
- ❖ *Duroos Maktoobat*-Imam Rabbani Hazrat Mujaddid Alf Thani ؒ [Urdu-Published 2021]
- ❖ *Umrah-Ahle Dil ki Nazar Se* [Urdu- Published 2016]

Publications under the Tutelage of the Author:

- ❖ Rehmatulil Aalameen-The Last Prophet Muhammad ﷺ [Eng- Published 2022]
- ❖ Jamal e Mustafa ﷺ [Urdu- Published 2021]

PREFACE

Praise be to Allah, the First and the Last, who created everything according to their measures and guided them, whose Mercy is infinite. May Allah's blessings be bestowed upon His Prophet Muhammadﷺ-the chosen one, who was created the first and was sent as the Last Prophet; the highest in ranks amongst all His creations:

> "And if you would count Allah's favours, you will not be able to count them." [Qurán Surah-An-Nahl,16:18]

I have neither the forte nor the strength, to enumerate the blessings of Allahﷻ as they are beyond comprehension. It is only by Allah'sﷻ infinite blessings with which He enabled us to say His Name. May we be able to recognise the Divine Love which was the centre and cause for all creations. It is with the *dua* and guidance of my Shaykh Mowlana Shamsur Rehman Al Abbasi that this low servant has been able to compile few words. My special *dua* for Atiya Gilani who assisted in compiling this work.

If we compare our society with the social order established by Allah's Messengerﷺ, we can hardly see any resemblance. We must remind ourselves, whether it is the lack of knowledge or lack of practice which has brought us to this point where we can hardly find any remnants of the Islamic society. The individuals are in pursuit of their own desires, following the ideals which do not match Qurán and Sunnah. Muslim Ummah is a body as a whole and the act of each one of us impacts this in a negative or a positive way. We can see how our actions are affecting the society where values are on a decline and morals are deteriorating.

The reason being that some believe that Islam merely consists in the practice of outward piety without inward contemplation hence disregard the Internal aspect of the religion, while others presume that the outer aspects of faith and Islamic jurisprudence do not hold value. If it was only for the external aspects of religion, then we have more religious schools and books than ever, but our society in general is deteriorating and moral and social standards worsening by the day. The behaviour and patterns of a society are built upon by its members but by losing the inward aspects of Islam, the soul of the Islamic society is fading. Greed, jealousy, hatred, rage and other negative feelings are not part of the Islamic society. The Islamic society is built upon love, care and respect and that was how the first Islamic society in Madinah was established.

Even on an individual basis, depression, tension and anxiety are very common in every age group. Marriage breakdowns and family feuds are a common theme. If we analyse these issues, they do not form a part of our belief system; we believe that our Lord loves us more than seventy mothers, He is the One who provides us with countless bounties and holds our destiny, so what is the reason behind the anxiety and depression?

Qurán clearly defines the expectations from an individual within a society and we have been shown the way by our Beloved Prophetﷺ. In such dire times, there is a need to apply the knowledge and practice the inner aspects of Sunnah; the state of the heart which created the Islamic society where the Companions were eager to share all their possessions with their brethren in faith.

Purity is the characteristic of Abu Bakr Siddique؏. *Tasawwuf* has a root and a branch: its root being the severance of the heart from 'others' (*Ghair*) and its branch that the heart be void of the deceitful world. Both are the characteristics of Abu Bakr؏ whose heart was devoid of this world. He gave away everything, clad himself in a rough woollen garment and came to the Beloved Prophetﷺ, who asked him as to what he had left behind for his family and Abu Bakr؏ replied, "Only Allahﷻ and His Apostleﷺ." *Tasawwuf* is the way of Ali؏; who is the leader of this path, as he was the one who loved Allahﷻ and His Prophetﷺ and Allahﷻ and His Prophetﷺ loved him. Allah's Prophetﷺ said, "I am the house of wisdom, and Ali؏ is its door." [Tirmidhi]

The Westernised orientalists portrayed the concept of Modern Sufism which is remote to the true discipline, then to top it up the fake Sufis added the Hindu spiritual concepts which created a concoction of fake ideologies around *Tasawwuf and Sufis*. There arises a need to answer the questions as to what is the inner aspect of Islam and what is the place of *Tasawwuf* in traditional Islam in the light of Hadith and Qurán?

Chapter One

THE PROPHETIC MISSION

At the time Abrahamﷺ built Ka'ba, he supplicated and requested Allahﷻ to send a Messenger amongst them, who would teach them the book and purify them:

'Our Lord, and send among them a messenger from themselves who will recite to them Your verses and teach them the Book and wisdom and purify (Tazkiyah) them. Indeed, You are the Exalted in Might, the Wise.'

[Qurán, al Baqarah 2:129]

Allahﷻ answered his prayers and sent His Last Prophetﷺ with the mission:

'Just as We have sent among you a Messenger from yourselves reciting to you Our verses and purifying (Tazkiyah) you and teaching you the Book and wisdom and teaching you that which you did not know.'

[Qurán, al Baqarah 2:151]

Allahﷻ explicitly mentions four tasks of the mission for His Last Prophetﷺ. Reciting the Qurán, teaching the Book, wisdom and purifying constitutes the primary objectives of the Prophetic mission. They form the foundation upon which the Islamic law, code of conduct and governance are based upon. The ones who adjoined the company of the Beloved

Prophetﷺ had the opportunity to learn from him and the Beloved Prophetﷺ testified on their behalf as he said, "The best mankind is my generation." [Bukhari]

The companions of the Beloved Prophetﷺ had the best morals and they excelled in this world and the hereafter. They loved for the sake of Allahﷻ and hated for the sake of Allahﷻ, their end goal was to please Allahﷻ and they definitely succeeded in that mission. That was the outcome of the Prophetic teaching and purification. Even after the Beloved Prophetﷺ left this world, the Companions continued his mission till the end of their lives.

As Muslims, we believe that all four objectives of the Prophetic mission are important, hence purification holds a strong significance in the mission. The question arises as to what *'Yuzakkihim'* (Purify) means and how to achieve it? Referring to the first objective of the mission, which is to 'recite the verses of Qurán and teach the Book', it is obvious that Qurán had to be taught. Even though the Arabs were fluent in the Arabic language and known for their eloquence, yet the verses were explained and the meanings taught by the Beloved Prophetﷺ.

Allah's Messengerﷺ imparted the knowledge of Qurán to the Companions and then the Companions taught the *Tábiyeen* (the ones who followed the Companions) and the *Tábiyeen* educated the *Tába Tábiyeen* (the ones who followed the followers of the Companions); thus, the process continued. When it comes to the other objective of Prophetic mission which is *'Yuzakkihim',* we believe that the Beloved Prophetﷺ performed that task himself, on his Companions; hence, the Companions reached the level of excellence which no other human can achieve till the end of time. The word *'Yuzakkihim'* means 'to purify them'. The purification in the literal term means 'to follow Shariáh', lead the life according to Sunnah, get rid of the evils and attain the true state of heart. Allah's Messenger ﷺ led by his own example of the best morals, the Companions followed him in each and every aspect and taught those ethics or *Khulq* to their followers and so on.

When the objectives of reciting the verses and teaching the Qurán were carried forward by the Companions of the Beloved Prophet ﷺ, the other tasks of the mission such as teaching wisdom and purification were also taken over by them. Hence, the process continued just as the first and the second objective of the mission. The Prophetic mission of *Yuzakkihim*, as explained by the scholars clearly entails the importance of purification. Allah ﷻ mentions the four objectives of the mission as a blessing to the believers, as in Qur'an:

> *'Allah has truly blessed the believers, for He has sent them a messenger from themselves, who recites His signs to them and purifies them, and teaches them the Book and the Wisdom'*
>
> [Qur'an, Ale Imran 3:164]

In simple words, *'Tasawwuf'* is the branch of knowledge, dealing with the Prophetic mission of *'Yuzakkihim'*. The knowledge of the Qurán and Sunnah does not suffice till the time it is applied. The practical approach to the knowledge of Qur'an and Sunnah is to be learnt from those who led their lives in the light of that knowledge. This knowledge is then to be implemented in one's life by practice and under the guidance of the one who himself has the knowledge. Another common question arises about the need for purification to which Qurán clearly answers in the verse:

'Gardens of perpetual residence beneath which rivers flow, wherein they abide eternally. And that is the reward of one who purifies (Tazkiyah) himself.'

[Qurán, Taha 20:76]

One may think that purification may only be required for a place in paradise as an eternal abode. Although, each one of us desires that, yet we still want to lead a happy, content and a successful life in this world. This human desire is also addressed as Qurán gives the glad tidings of success to the one who purifies himself:

'He who purifies (Tazkiyah) himself has certainly succeeded'

[Qurán, al-A'la, 87:14]

Whether it is the eternal life or the transient life, it is evident that the way to success is through purification. Some may think that it is just an option and Allah has not made it mandatory to achieve a state where the self is cleansed of the blameworthy traits. The answer is in the verse, where Allah commands the believers to rid the inner self of all evils and purify it:

'And whoever purifies himself does so for the benefit of his soul; and the destination (of all) is to Allah' [Qurán al-Fatir 35:18]

The believers are ordered using a commanding verb which is a directive, to fear the Lord as He deserves and this is the state of purity called *Taqwa*:

'O believers! Fear Allah in the way He deserves'

[Qurán, Aal e Imran 3:102]

Just as there are haram or forbidden acts in Islamic Fiqh (Islamic Jurisprudence), there are forbidden inner states like jealousy, greed, pride and hypocrisy. The one who is pure is closer to Allah than others, as Allah's Messenger said;

"Allah ﷻ does not look at the external outward appearance or the wealth, He looks at your heart and deeds." [Muslim 2564]

The causes and remedies for the forbidden states are discussed by scholars such as Imam al-Ghazali ﷺ in Ihya' 'ulum al-din [The Revival of the Religious Sciences], Imam al-Rabbani ﷺ in his *Maktoobat* [Letters], al-Suhrawardi ﷺ in his *'Awarif al-Ma'arif* [The knowledges of the illuminates] and other classic works, which also discuss the inner states. These are the books of Islamic jurisprudence, which deal with the inner state of a Muslim, according to the Prophetic Sunnah.[1]

Definition of Sufism or Tasawwuf

Tasawwuf is the complete submission to Allah with the physical body and the spiritual heart, for the heart it is in the cognizance of Allah and for the body it is in the acts of obedience in accordance with Shariáh. The cognizance of Allah cannot be achieved in a heart which has the ailments, neither can it be achieved with the '*ghair*' in it. The '*ghair*' or the other is anything and everything except for Allah. For the physical body, complete submission demands having the right '*Aqida*' or creed and following the law of Islamic Jurisprudence. If there is an error in '*Aqida*', then no matter how many good deeds one performs, Allah's cognizance and pleasure cannot be attained.

The reality of *Tasawwuf* is based upon the Hadith where it is narrated that the Prophet appeared before the public one day when a man came to him and said, "O Messenger of Allah, what is 'Iman' (faith)?" The Prophet said, "Iman (Faith) is to believe in Allah, His Angels, His Books, meeting with Him, His messengers and to believe in the resurrection in the Hereafter."

He said, "O Messenger of Allah, what is Islam?" The Prophet said, "Islam is to worship Allah alone without associating anything with Him, to establish the prescribed prayer, to give obligatory charity and to fast the month of Ramadan." He said, "What is 'Ihsan' (excellence)?" The Prophet said, "Ihsan (Excellence) is to worship Allah as if you see Him. Verily, He sees you although you do not see Him...." The Hadith Continues, then the man left and the Prophet asked his Companions to call him back, but they could not see him.

The Prophetﷺ said, "That was Gibrael؏ who came to teach the people their religion." Abu 'Abdullah؇ said: 'He (the Prophetﷺ) considered all that as part of faith.' [Bukhari:50, Muslim:9]

This is a *sahih* Hadith, described by Imam Nawawi؇ as one of the Hadiths upon which the Islamic religion is based. The use of *deen* in the last words of it, "came to you to teach you your *'religion'*" entails that the religion of Islam is composed of the three fundamentals mentioned in the Hadith: *Islam*, or external compliance with what Allah؇ asks of us; *Iman*, or the belief in the unseen that the Prophets have informed us of; and *Ihsan*, or to worship Allah؇ as though one sees Him. The level of *iman* or faith is the *Aqida* or 'tenets of faith'; Islam is the Shari'ah or 'Sacred Law' and its ancillary disciplines; and the level of *Ihsan*, "to worship Allah؇ as though you see Him," is *'Tasawwuf'*.

The concept is explained by Shaykh Abd al-Qadir Gilani؇ in *Futuh-al-Ghaib*, 'The Revelations of the Unseen'. The first discourse covers the concept of life for a Muslim in faith, belief and actions encouraging him to engage with mind body and soul and this is the precise definition of a Sufi;

"Three things are indispensable for a believer in all conditions of life: First, he should keep the commandments of Allah؇. Second, he should abstain from the forbidden things and third, he should be pleased with the decree of Providence. Thus, the least that is expected of a believer is that he should not be without these three, so he should make up his mind for these and talk to himself about these and keep his organs engaged in them.'[2]

For a believer, the fundamental of *Tasawwuf* is in strengthening the faith by following the way of the Prophetﷺ in his actions

The Prophetic Mission

and deeds and following his example in the inner state of the heart. The question may arise in many minds that the Beloved Prophet's ﷺ status in unequalled and unmatched even amongst the Prophets, so how can it be possible to follow his example in the external and internal Sunnah. The answer is simple, referring back to the verse where Allah ﷻ mentions in Qurán:

> *'Allah has truly blessed the believers, for He has sent them a Messenger from themselves, who recites His signs to them and purifies them, and teaches them the Book and the Wisdom'*
>
> [Qurán, Ale-Imran 3:164]

Allah ﷻ sent a Messenger from ourselves so we can follow him in his deeds and actions whether external or Internal, *Tasawwuf* is the path to attain the Divine love of Allah ﷻ by following the path of Allah's Last Prophet ﷺ. *Tasawwuf* is not just in the abstinence or denial of worldly pleasures. It entails that the person leads his life according to Sunnah, strive to curtail the negative feelings associated with the worldly desires as lust, greed, jealousy, anger and perform the rituals and practices of Deen without these evils in his heart. The journey of *Tasawwuf* begins by purifying intentions and the destination is the constant cognizance of Allah ﷻ which keeps on increasing as it is limitless and boundless.[3]

Some people may say that the term *Tasawwuf* did not exist in the times of the Beloved Prophet ﷺ; the same goes for the other Islamic disciplines such as *Uṣul al-fiqh* (jurisprudence), *Tafsir* (exegesis), *kalam* (theology), and *Uṣul al-ḥadith* (principles of hadith). The term *Tasawwuf* like many other Islamic disciplines, came into origin after the first generation of Muslims. The historian Ibn Khaldun writes in his book *Muqaddimah*;

"The science of *Tasawwuf* belongs to the sciences of the religious law that originated in Islam. Sufism is based on (the assumption that) the method of those people (who later on came to be called Sufis) had always been considered by the important early Muslims, the men around the Last Prophet Muhammad ﷺ and the men of the second generation, as well as those who came after them, as the path of truth and right guidance.

The (Sufi) approach is based upon constant application to Divine worship, complete devotion to Allah ﷻ, aversion to the false splendour of the world, abstinence from the pleasure, property and position to which the great mass aspires, and retirement from the world into solitude for Divine worship.

These things were general among the men around Allah's Last Apostle Muhammad ﷺ and the early Muslims. Then, worldly aspirations increased in the second [eighth] century and after and people inclined more towards worldly affairs. At that time, the special name of Sufis (Sufiyah and Mutasawwifah) was given to those who aspired to Divine worship."[4]

The basic foundation of Islam is held in the beliefs, then there is also a system of morality, which concerns man's relationship with other humans and creatures, which is expressed in social, civil and criminal laws. Worship is the physical aspect of man's relationship with Allah ﷻ which constitutes the basics of all other systems, may it be moral, social or legal. If the heart accepts and believes the truth, the body follows it in worship in proportion to the extent of the faith. If the inner aspect of faith becomes weak, the outward form of worship becomes soulless. It is the human's direct relationship with his Creator which is the life of religion and this relationship is cultivated through *Tasawwuf*.[5]

The Prophetic Mission

The origin of the word 'Sufi' was also discussed by the great scholar, Ali Ibn Uthman al-Hujwiri﷽ known as 'Data Gunj Baksh', in his book *Kashf al-Mahjub*:

"Some assert that the Sufi is so called because he wears a woollen garment (*jama'i suf*); others that he is so called because he is in the first rank (*saff-i awwal*); others say it is because the Sufis claim to belong to the Ashab-al-Suffa (Companions living in the veranda of Masjid e Nabwi), Others, again, declare that the name is derived from Safa (purity)."[6]

There is a hype that *Tasawwuf* is not an Islamic discipline or is isolated from Islam which is part of the *fitna* (temptation/trial) of our times. *Tasawwuf* can be called the spiritual aspect or the inner state of Islam. Ideas and practices which are foreign to Islam, more so antagonistic to it have entered the mainstream faith, but disease does not prove the non-existence of health. Despite the corrupting influences and their adverse effects, *Tasawwuf* has existed throughout the Islamic history. *Tasawwuf* is the inner aspect of Deen and to promulgate that *Tasawwuf* is not part of Islam is to take the soul out of our religion.

This controversy is created out of thin air and the fake Sufis or pretenders have caused great harm to the concept of *Tasawwuf* as they are using the term for their worldly desires and bringing disrepute to this discipline. Consider the example of a doctor who is incompetent and unskilled, but does that mean all doctors are incompetent and we should stop seeking medical advice because there is no one in the profession who is trustworthy and competent?

Just as there exists good and bad in every walk of life, the same stands for Sufis. There are those who only stand for their own benefits and desires and pretend to be Sufis and bring disgrace to the word of *Tasawwuf*. Then, there are those great Sufis who spent their lives to reform the society as Imam al-Ghazali﷽, Imam al-Rabbani Mujaddid Alf Thani﷽, Ali Hujwiri﷽, Bulleh Shah ﷽.

Another misconception or *fitna*, undermining the deed and the action is that the intention should be pure and sincerity of the heart is enough. Some claim that they are very sincere in their heart, therefore, they do not need to perform Salah or for that matter any other deed as per Shariáh because the deeds are just external actions. Remember, these are the people deceived by the devil and lost in the darkness as the internal aspect of an action cannot take place without its external counterpart.

A man may keep his heart earnest throughout his entire life, yet there is no sincerity until it is combined with action; although he may perform external actions throughout his life, his actions do not become acts of devotion until they are combined with sincerity. So, for every internal action there has to be an external action and the value in that external action is achieved by the internal aspect.

The Messengerﷺ said; "The true emigrant is a person who leaves behind everything that Allahﷻ has forbidden" [Bukhari : 6484, Abu Dawood : 2481]

It is evident from the Hadith that the true migrant is the one who abandons everything which Allahﷻ has forbidden. Nonetheless, no one should assume from the Hadith that the outward practices of Islam are without value, in fact Allahﷻ has created for every inner meaning an external form and without performing the external deed, the inner significance is impossible.

It is narrated that Malik bin Dinarﷺ who was a companion of Hasan al-Basraﷺ spent the evening in a party. When his friends were all asleep, a voice came from a lute which they had been playing: "O Malik! why don't you repent?" Upon hearing that, Malikﷺ abandoned his evil ways and went to Hasanﷺ and showed himself steadfast in repentance. He attained the status that once during a voyage, he was suspected of stealing a jewel, he looked at the sky and a school of fish came to the surface, each carrying a jewel in its mouth. Malikﷺ took one of the jewels and gave it to the man whose jewel was missing, then he set foot on the sea and walked until he reached the shore. It is related that he said: "Sincerity (*Ikhlas*) in the deeds is what I love the most."

The Companions practiced constant vigilance of the heart, as soon as they discerned changes to that condition, they made adjustments immediately. It is narrated that one of the Companions, Abu Talhaﷺ was performing Salah in his orchard, a bird flew in and could not find a way out as the orchard was quite dense. Abu Talha'sﷺ eyes followed the bird and when he turned his attention back to Salah, he forgot the number of *raka'a*, he then went to the Beloved Prophetﷺ and gave his orchard in the name of Allahﷻ. [Muwatta Imam Malik]

Ibne Sina, in his famous book *'Kitab al-Isharat wa al-Tanbihat'* explains, "The man who is devoted to absolute abstinence of worldly pleasures is called *'Zahid'* and the man who keeps almost every moment of his life devoted to worship is called *'Aabid'*. The man who keeps his attention perennially focussed towards Qudoos-e-Jabroot (The Holy Omnipotent) and expects every moment the Manifestation of Divine Light in his inner self to illuminate every spectrum of his life as a whole, is recognised and adored with the ever-shining title of

'Aarif'. In the opinion of Ibne Sina such an exceptional human amongst the countless creatures of Allahﷻ is worthy of being honoured by the title of Sufi and venerated as the vicegerent of Allah."⁷

In the sight of a Sufi the deliverance from the hellfire or being admitted to the Garden of Paradise is not vital, his heart and mind is immersed in the Dhikr or remembrance of Allahﷻ and his heart finds pleasure in seeking the Love of Almighty. A Sufi is not concerned about the trees and the jewels of the paradise or fears Allahﷻ out of the fear of hellfire, he is the one who beholds the love of Allahﷻ over everything and anything. It is quoted from Rabia Basri﷫ that she prayed to Allahﷻ, 'O Allah ﷻ! If I worship you out of the fear of hellfire, then throw me into the fire and if I worship you in return for Paradise then deprive me of that and if I worship you with the hope of your Grand Visage then do not deprive me of that Vision."⁸

Those who take the path dedicate every breath of their existence to gain the Divine Love which is the essence of the vicegerent of Allahﷻ on earth. Imam Ghazali﷫ explained the reality of *Tasawwuf* as; "The first step on the path of *Tasawwuf* is that the seeker should undertake hard work, get rid of evil deeds, remove extraneous relations or associations and bend all his energy towards concentration of Divine Manifestation mirroring the Entity of Almighty Allahﷻ. When the seeker attains the noble perfection, then Allahﷻ Himself becomes the Guardian and Protector of the heart of the servant and provides guidance from the Divine treasures of enlightenment."

Chapter Two

MISCONCETIONS REGARDING SUFISM
Sufism and Monasticism

Islam is a complete code of conduct and does not allow one to lead a life of monasticism. There is a major difference between a monk and a Sufi. The purpose of creation as mentioned by Allahﷻ is to worship Him;

'And I (Allah) have not created the jinn and mankind except that they should worship Me (alone)'

[Qurán, Adh-Dhariyat 51:56]

Allahﷻ has also entrusted the believers with their families and Allah's Messengerﷺ said that the one who is best loved by Allahﷻ is the one who is best towards his dependents. The seeker is to be compassionate, generous and loving towards Allah's creations. *Tasawwuf* promotes living a complete life as a functional member of the society; a good son, a good father, a good husband, neighbour, employee, businessman or for that matter any other aspect of human life.

Tasawwuf does not promote abstinence from the worldly affairs rather it promotes to perform all those affairs with the best effort and the best practice as defined by Islam and following the Messengerﷺ as the example. A true believer is the one who follows in the footsteps of the Beloved Prophetﷺ in all aspects of life. The definition of true believers as mentioned in Qurán is:

'These are the true believing Muslims whom the merchandise, the business transactions cause no negligence in the remembrance of Allah.'

[Qurán an Nur 24:37]

In *Tasawwuf* there is no abhorrence to a balanced normal life, within the boundaries of Shariáh. The seeker is not barred from having children or run a successful business and be a contributing member of society. The lives of the Companions are a testament to this as they fulfilled their responsibilities in every aspect of life. *Tasawwuf* entails that the life be spent according to Shariáh in the path of the Beloved Prophetﷺ and his Companions and their way was not about denying the rights of the body or avoiding worldly affairs. They did earn their living, got married and supported families.

Throughout the journey, the important factor is to follow the path of the Shariáh, the money is to be earned through permissible means and spent on halal things. The family be raised in accordance with the teachings of Islam, so the children become useful members of the Islamic society. Allah's Messengerﷺ said, "Verily, the most complete of believers in faith are those with the best character and who are most kind to their families." [Sunan al-Tirmidhi:2612]

Islam is a religion which promotes the relationship between man and his Lord, human being's relation with himself and with the fellow men. Hence, it is expected that the person fulfils all requirements of the society according to Shariáh. Allah's Messengerﷺ said, "The merciful will be shown mercy by the Most Merciful. Be merciful to those on the earth and the One in the Heavens will have mercy upon you." [Sunan al-Tirmidhi : 1924].

As authenticated by the Hadith narrated by Abdullah ibn 'Amr ibn al Aas؆,"Allah's Messengerﷺ said to me, "Am I not told that you fast all day and pray all night?" and I replied, "Indeed, O Allah's Messengerﷺ. He said, "Then don't. Fast, but also leave it; pray, but also sleep. For verily your body has a right over you, and your guest has a right over you. Verily, it suffices you to fast three days a month, for you are rewarded for each good deed ten the like of it, so to do only that is to perpetually fast." [Bukhari : 1975. S]

For a Muslim, Allahﷻ has given great ease, his sleep time, the time he spends with his family, his parents or earning a livelihood is part of his spiritual path, only if done with the intention to please Allahﷻ. It is narrated that Allah's Messengerﷺ said, "Asceticism or *Zuhd* does not mean forbidding what is permitted, or squandering wealth, rather *Zuhd* means not thinking what you have in your hand is more reliable than what is in Allah'sﷻ Hand and it means feeling that the reward for a calamity that befalls you is greater than that which the calamity makes you miss out on." [Sunan Ibn Majah : 4100]

The realities of asceticism '*Zuhd*' and *Tawakkul (meaning trust in Allah*ﷻ) are two desired qualities which are inseparable. This Hadith eliminates the misconception and describes *Zuhd* as having faith in Allahﷻ and bearing the suffering with patience. Being a seeker does not mean that one should abandon the world, neither perform his duties nor participate in its affairs and retire to a corner doing nothing. The Beloved Prophetﷺ said, "Indeed the most wholesome of what you consume is from your earnings, and indeed your children are from your earnings." [Jamí at-Tirmidhi : 1358]

Modern Sufism

The concept of so-called modern Sufism or the western orientalism that anyone can be a Sufi, regardless of his faith or religion, is completely incorrect. If a person does not believe in any of the basic tenets of faith for example '*Wahdaniyat*' or Oneness of Allahﷻ, and associates partners in His being or attributes or in His acts, that person is completely lost and astray. Same goes for any other tenet of Islam as believing in the Prophet Muhammad ﷺ as the last Prophet or Allah's Books or Angels or other prophets. If one does not truly believe in any of the fundamental tenets, he cannot be a Muslim.

This is proved by the Hadith that Salmah bin Yazeed ؓ along with his brother went to the Beloved Prophet ﷺ and told him about their mother who was kind and generous but died without accepting Islam. They asked the Beloved Prophet ﷺ if she would be rewarded for her good deeds in the hereafter, to which the Beloved Prophet ﷺ replied in negative. [Musnad Ahmad: 119]

Modern Sufism: the term created by orientalists is as fake as it could be, the concept is as Allah ﷻ describes:

'Deaf, dumb and blind, that they do not comprehend'

[Qurán, al Baqarah 2:171]

The belief often held in the West that Sufism is universal and a person from any religion can be a Sufi, is a delusion. To set out on the path of Sufism, it is absolutely necessary to be a Muslim, for Sufism is the way of excellence in Deen, excellence in *Iman* and *yaqin*. Without *Shahdah*, correct belief, following the Shariáh and the Prophetic Sunnah, no one can attain the pleasure of Allah ﷻ. Ahmad Zarruq ؒ, the fifteenth century Hadith scholar, states, "So there is no Sufism except through comprehension of Sacred Law or Shariáh and there is no comprehension of Sacred Law or Shariáh without Sufism, for works are nothing without the sincerity of approach." As expressed in the words of Imam Malik ؒ, 'He who practices Sufism without learning Sacred Law or Shariáh corrupts his faith, while he who learns Sacred Law or Shariáh without practicing Sufism corrupts himself. Only he who combines the two proves true.'[1]

As mentioned in Qurán, the deliverance from hellfire is only through faith (*Iman*) and action (*amal*). Faith without action and action without faith is fruitless and barren. If one does not have *Iman* and performs good deeds, his deeds are not acceptable. Adi bin Hatam؇ asked Allah's Prophet؇ if his father Hatam Tai who was known for his generosity would get any reward in the hereafter, to which the Prophet؇ replied that he was granted what he desired (i.e., Fame) [Musnad Ahmad:120]. And again, referring to Hadith where Salmah bin Yazeed؇ and his brother asked the Beloved Prophet؇ about their mother who died without accepting Islam, whether she would be rewarded for her good deeds. The Beloved Prophet؇ replied in negative. [Musnad Ahmad:119]

Therefore, without faith and action (*Iman* or *amal*), one cannot reach the state of excellence which is *Ihsan*. However, once the person comes in the folds of Islam, all his good deeds even though performed before accepting Islam, would be rewarded. As authenticated by the Hadith, Hakeem bin Hazam؇ who was a generous man, after he accepted Islam, once asked the Beloved Prophet؇ if he would be rewarded for the deeds he performed as a disbeliever. The Beloved Prophet؇ replied, "You have entered the folds of Islam with the good deeds you had performed earlier." [Musnad Ahmad: 121] It is obvious from the above narrations that faith forms the basis of action. Good deeds performed before one accepted Islam would be carried over and Allah ؇ would reward those, whereas deeds performed without *Iman* have no reward in hereafter.

Mowlana Ashraf Ali Thanvi؇ wrote, "With regards to the misconception that there is no need to adhere to the Shariáh in *Tasawwuf*, it is mentioned in Al-Futuhat al-Makkiyya: "*Tasawwuf* that is against the Shariáh is irreligious and rejected. Whoever says that there is a path to Allah؇ different to what the Shariáh has outlined, then he is a liar. Hence, a person who has no *adab* (prescribed Islamic etiquette) cannot be a Shaykh. We have no path to Allah﷾ except that which has come by way of Shariáh, and we have no path to Allah﷾ except that which the Shariáh has shown."[2]

Tasawwuf or true Sufism is a branch of knowledge just as Islamic Jurisprudence, or Fiqh, the knowledge of Hadith or Tafsir. As each branch of knowledge has its roots within the bounds of Qurán and Hadith, so does *Tasawwuf*. The modern Sufism promulgates the concept of the universal validity of all religions, which is completely against the concept of true Sufism. Islam is the final religion and the fundamental concepts of *Tawheed* and articles of faith cannot be compromised, *Tasawwuf* does not exist without *Shahadah* and Shariáh. Therefore, "Do not follow anyone whose Shariáh leaves him, even if he brings you the tidings from Allah﷾ Himself." [*Al Futuhat al-Makkiyya*[48], 2.364]

Sufism and Ahmadiyat (Qadiyaniat)

"The Ahmadiya religion was founded in 1889 by Mirza Ghulam Ahmad who claimed to have received revelations that in his person Imam Mahdi had become present and that he was also the Promised Messiah and was indeed the Prophet whose advent had been foretold in the principal religions of the world."[3] The Lahori Group is an offshoot of the Ahmadiya Movement, and separated shortly after Mirza Ghulam Ahmed died in 1908. "They do not accept [Mirza Ghulam Ahmed's] prophethood but they do adhere to his views regarding Jihad and the death of Christ and are always included in the legislation directed at the Ahmadis."[4]

If one does not truly believe in any of the fundamental tenets of Islam, he cannot be a Muslim. Ahmadi or Qadiyani are not Muslims as they refute the basic tenets of faith. Muslims believe in the finality of Prophethood and the ending of Revelation with the Last Messenger Muhammad ﷺ, whereas the Ahmadis or Qadiyanis negate the fact. Mirza Ghulam Ahmad Qadiyani in his books falsely claimed, 'God's words have come upon me in such abundance that if written that would compile not less than twenty juz.' [*Roohani Khazain: Haqeeqat ul Wahi, pg. 407*]

In his book *Tazkirah*, page 77, he claimed 'Qurán is God's book and the talk of my mouth.' He also claimed to be the son of God and then God himself. He wrote, 'In one of the revelations God addressed me and said, 'O Mirza! To me, you are just like my son.' [*Majmua Wahi O Ilhamat pg.442*]

He claimed himself not only the son of God, the prophet, Imam Mehdi, Messiah but also as God himself. He wrote, 'I dreamt that I myself am God and I believed in this that I am God." [*Roohani Khazain, Vol V, pg.564*]

Mirza said, "It is a fact that Muhammad ﷺ worked only three thousand miracles... My Miracles exceed one million in numbers." [*Ijaz-e-Ahmadi, pg.79, Tadhkira tul Shahadatain, pg.41*]

Another false claim, "It is possible for a man to attain a spiritual position higher than any other man; if any man wishes, he can rise even above Muhammad ﷺ." [*Daily Al-Fadl, Jul 17. 1992, Mirza Basheer al-Din Mahmud Qadiyani*]

Mirza also said, "I swear by God in whose hand lies my existence and say that it is He who has reputed me and called me a Prophet and the Messiah." [*Haqiqat-ul-Wahi, Appendix, Pg. 68*]

Mirza Ghulam's ideology refutes the basic tenets of Islam. Hence, Ahmadis or Qadiyanis are declared non-Muslims by law and *Tasawwuf* or Sufism without *'iman'* is a baseless idea. The Beloved Prophetﷺ told the Ummah about the liars who would falsely claim to be prophets, "In my ummah there will be twenty-seven liars and dajjals, among whom are four women, (but) I am the seal of the Prophets, there is no prophet after me". [*Musnad Ahmad ibn Hanbal:22747; at-Tabarani, Mújam al-Awsat: 5596, Mújam al-Kabir:2957; at-Tahawi, Mushkil al-Athar:2493*]

None of Allah's Messengers or Prophets claimed to be God or semi-god. Allahﷻ mentions in Qurán:

'Allah has not taken a son for Himself, nor is there a god with Him. Otherwise, each god would have taken away what he creates, and some of them would surely have nominated over the others. Allah is above all what they attribute to Him.' [Qurán al Mominun 23:91]

Sufi versus Yogi

The concept of *Tasawwuf* is completely opposite to the concept of the Hindu Yogi. Islam promotes a healthy and wholesome life; self-abnegation or complete solitude is not accepted at all. The Beloved Prophetﷺ showed through his Sunnah the concept of a complete life, living as a leader, husband, father and a teacher.

As a fundamental rule, *Tasawwuf* does not exist without *Shahadah* and Shariáh. A Sufi aims to find Allahﷻ whilst the Yogi detracts from the very Existence of Allahﷻ with the aim of achieving Nirvana. *Tasawwuf* is reaching the excellence in *Iman* which is the state of *Ihsan* whereas the Yogi is a disbeliever. In one of his letters written to a seeker, Mowlana Ashraf Ali Thanvi﷫ wrote, "Purification is dependent on Shariáh. The success which is defined as *"Verily, the person who purifies himself will truly succeed"* [Quran 87:14] is defined only within the bounds of *Tawheed* and Shariáh, therefore, purification of a Hindu Yogi is not deemed as purification. If there is dust on the mirror, it has to be cleaned with water, if someone tries to clean it with urine, it will be impure and unacceptable."[5]

Some assert that the rigor and exercises which a Sufi goes through are similar to those of Hindu Yogi. This assertion is completely fake as the training and rigor which the Sufi goes has its origin only from Islam. The Beloved Prophetﷺ spent time in the cave of Hira and never ate to the fill. The custom of less eating, less sleeping and less talking has no connection with the Hindu Yogi rather it is the Sunnah of the Prophetﷺ.

Are Sufis part of the Mainstream Society?

To assume that *Tasawwuf* becomes a hindrance in achieving other targets of life is a misconception. The one who follows the path of *Tasawwuf*, follows the Sunnah of the Beloved Prophetﷺ and the life of the Beloved Prophetﷺ was the best code of practice according to Qurán. He led his life as a merchant, a family man and the greatest leader ever. Each and every aspect of his life guides us through our own everyday lives and this is to be reflected in the life of the seeker.

It is true that the seeker is trained to achieve constant cognizance of Allahﷻ and he goes through arduous training to achieve this goal. As the seeker progresses through the stages the heart becomes void of the worldly desires and the mind stays focussed towards the end objective. The great mystics in Islamic history were the most learned scholars of their respective times. History reveals that some of the great Sufi Shaykhs played active roles in spreading the word of Allahﷻ and bringing revolution to the society. Syed Ahmad

Shaheed﷼ fought the forces of Maharaja Ranjit Singh at Balakot. The nation of Mongol Tatars accepted Islam through the influence of the Sufi Shaykh Saád ad Din al-Himawi﷼.

The letters of Mujaddid Alf Thani﷼ are the source of guidance till eternity. Mujaddid Ahmad al Faruqi al-Sirhindi﷼ (1564–1624) was a great scholar and known as Mujaddid or "reviver". It was the time of great trial as the Mughal king Akbar created a religion called din e ilahi based on Jainism, Hinduism, Christianity and many other ideologies, proclaimed himself to be the god and demanded everyone to prostrate before him. Muslim scholars were not allowed to express their views against the newly created religion and most were tortured to death. Innovations were made in the tenets of faith and belief, many Islamic practices as Salah, fasting and slaughtering the cow were forbidden. During that time, the letters Mujaddid Alf Thani﷼ wrote to his disciples became a movement and brought the much-needed revolution.

It was a revolution where instead of swords, it was the power of Mujaddid Alf Thani's﷼ knowledge, that brought the change. His letters to his disciples enlightened by the Divine light, became a non-military gazette and brought the change from within the society. It is said that these letters have addressed the forthcoming trials or *fitnas* and provided solutions to the next generation Muslims. The concepts of spirituality are elaborated with an intention of purification of hearts and souls. He culminated the false notion of the pretentious Sufis who claimed to be above the Shariáh law as he repeatedly emphasised that the only way to the achieve the Divine love is through Qurán and Sunnah. Hence, *Tasawwuf* is about following the Sunnah of the Beloved Prophetﷺ and his life was not of seclusion.

Misconcetions regarding Sufism

It is a misconception that the Sufi Shaykhs are not part of the mainstream Islam, whereas the great Sufis (mystics, devotees) were the most learned men of their times, who not only possessed the knowledge of Qurán and Hadith but also gained the true understanding of that knowledge. Abd al-Qadir Gilaniﷺ, Moeen ud din Ajmeriﷺ, Shahab ud din Suhurwardiﷺ, Bahaud din Naqshbandﷺ, Mujaddid alf Thaniﷺ, were the men known for their understanding of the Islamic Jurisprudence(Shariáh Law) and the Divine knowledge *(uloom e Maárfat)*.

Is Tassawuf a Reprehensible Innovation (Bid'a)?

The concept of *Tasawwuf* has been subject to many objections and opposition just like any other discipline or creed. The pretentious Sufis (so-called Peers) and their outward mantled negative elements caused great harm to the concept of true *Tasawwuf*. There has been an objection that the concept of *Tasawwuf* is *Bidá* and does not belong to Islam as it is not inscribed in Qurán or Hadith. This is however, not true as many other disciplines were developed in later years.

Some say aren't the Quran and Sunnah enough? The superiority of the Qurán and Sunnah is not what is at stake here. Rather, the essence of all substantive prescriptions of Qurán and the Sunnah lies in human attitude toward the Divine. For example, there is no question that the best of the speech is the word of Allahﷻ, the Qurán. But, if a non-Muslim were to recite the Qurán from beginning to end, it would not be beneficial to him. Instead, it would be beneficial to him if he recites *Shahdah* or Testification of Islam once, with conviction. Reason being, that he is standing in front of a particular door, to which he needs the key of *iman* or faith in Allahﷻ and His Messenger ﷺ. Nothing else will do, no matter how superior in itself.

Throughout Islamic history, Sufism has been taught and understood as an Islamic discipline, like *Tafsir* or Quránic exegesis, Hadith, Tajwid or Qurán recital, tenets of faith or any other Islamic science which preserved some particular aspect of the religion of Islam. The terminology of these disciplines was unknown to the first generation of Muslims, but they were not considered *Bidá* by the scholars of Shariáh, because for them, *Bidá* did not pertain to means, but rather to ends. To illustrate this point, we may note that the Beloved Prophetﷺ never in his life rode a car to Masjid or went for Hajj in the aeroplane. Neither did he ascertain the times for prayers from a watch or mobile phone application. These are merely a means to carry out the command.

Books of detailed interpretation of the Qurán, verse by verse and Surah by Surah, were not known to the first generation of Muslims, nor was the term *tafsir* current among them. However, in preserving and understanding the Quran, when the *tafsir* literature came into being, it was acknowledged to serve an end endorsed by the Shariáh and was not condemned as Bid'a. The same is true for most of the Islamic sciences, such as *ilm al-tawhid*, "the science of tenets of Islamic faith", and other disciplines essential to the Shariáh. In this connection, Imam Shafi'i said, "Anything which has a support (*mustanad*) from the Shariáh is not Bid'a, even if the early Muslims did not do it" [*Ahmad al-Ghimari, Tashnif al-adhan, Cairo: Maktaba al-Khanji, n.d., 133*].

Similarly, *Tasawwuf* or the science of Sufism came into being to preserve and transmit a particular aspect of the Shariáh which deals with the internal aspect of sincerity. It was recognized that the Sunnah of the Beloved Prophetﷺ was not only words and actions, but also states of being. For example, the Shariáh in many Quránic verses and Hadith commands one, to fear Allah, to have sincerity toward Him, to be so certain in one's knowledge of Allahﷻ that one worships Him as if one sees Him, to love the Prophetﷺ more than any other human being, to show love and respect to all fellow Muslims, to show mercy, and to have many other states of the heart. It likewise forbids us such inward states as envy, malice, pride, arrogance, love of this world, anger for the sake of one's ego, and so on. If we reflect upon these states, they result in a human change so profound that the Qur'an in many verses terms it as purification;

"He has succeeded who purifies himself"

[Qur'an, Surah al A'la 87:14]

Shariáh commands us to bring this change, which is the aim of the Islamic science of Sufism, hence it cannot be a reprehensible innovation or *Bi'da*. At the practical level, the nature of this science of purifying the heart requires that the knowledge be taken from those who possess it. Throughout history students or seekers had gathered around Shaykhs to learn the discipline of Sufism. The way or Tariqa may have been slightly different; however, some features are common; such as learning knowledge from a teacher by precept and example and then methodically increasing ones *iman* or faith by applying this knowledge through performing obligatory and supererogatory works of worship, among the greatest of latter being remembrance of Allah.

Islamic scholars have acknowledged that *ilm* or Sacred Knowledge is not sufficient in itself, but also entails *amal* or application of that knowledge as well as the resultant *hal* or praiseworthy spiritual state termed as purification. Many of the Islamic scholars to whom Allahﷻ gave success in their work were Sufis. These men included such scholars as Imam Muhammad Amin Ibn Abidin﷫, Imam Ibn Daqiq﷫, Shaykh al-Nabulsi؜, Imam al-Ghazali؜, Imam al-Nawawi؜, the hadith master (hafiz, someone with 100,000 Hadiths by memory) Abd al-Adhim al-Mundhiri؜, the Hadith master Murtada al-Zabidi؜, the Hadith master Abd al-Rauf al-Manawi؜, the Hadith master Jalal al-Din al-Suyuti؜ and many others.

The allegations against Tasawwuf made by Ibn Taymiya and Ibn al-Jawziyya were not directed against Tasawwuf in principle, but to specific groups and individuals. The proof of which is the books by the same authors that showed their understanding of Tasawwuf as a Shariáh science. Ibn Taymiya؜ devoted volumes ten and eleven of his *Majmu al-fatawa* to Sufism, while his student Ibn Qayyim al-Jawziyya؜ wrote his three-volume *Madarij al-salikin* as a detailed commentary on Abdullah al-Ansari's *Manazil al-sairin* [Guide to the spiritual stations of the Sufi path].[6]

Imam al-Nawawi's؜ attitude towards Sufism is evident from his work *Bustan al-arifin* [The grove of the knowers of Allah] on the subject, as well as his references to Qushayri's famous Sufi manual, *Risala al-Qushayriyya* throughout his own *Kitab al-adhkar* [Book of the Remembrance of Allah]. The Muslim scholars knew the value of Sufism as an ancillary Shariáh discipline needed to purify the heart, and this was the reason that Sufism was not judged as a Bid'a through the ages of Islamic civilization, but rather recognized as the science of *ikhlas* or sincerity, needed by every Muslim as Qurán mentions:

> 'a day when wealth will not avail, nor sons, but only him who brings Allah a sound heart'
>
> [Qur'an, Surah ash Shuára 26:88]

Imam Abu Hanifaﷺ, the great Hanafi Jurist, is the Imam of Imams and the exemplar of the Sunnites. He is one of the greatest Muslims theologian and Jurist as well as an authority on the principles of Sufism. At first, he wished to go into seclusion and abandon the society as his heart was devoid of the worldly desires. One night, however, he dreamt that he was collecting the bones of the Messengerﷺ from the tomb, choosing some and discarding others. He awoke in terror and asked one of the pupils of Muhammad ibn Sirinﷺ to interpret the dream. The scholar said to him: "You will attain a high rank in knowledge of the Apostleﷺ and in preserving his ordinance (*Sunnah*), you will sift what is genuine from what is spurious." Another time Abu Hanifaﷺ dreamt that the Apostleﷺ said to him: "You have been created for the purpose of reviving my ordinance." Imam Abu Hanifaﷺ, spent all his life in compiling Hadith and he was the master of many great Sufi Shaykhs as Ibrahim ibn Adhamﷺ, Fudayl ibn `Iyad ﷺ, Dawud Ta'Iﷺ and Bishr Hafiﷺ.

Some people question about the supplications, if they are reprehensible innovation or not? The Beloved Prophetﷺ himself encouraged us doing *duas* or supplications which were not part of the Sunnah, as authenticated by the Hadith, Buraydaﷺ said, "I entered the Masjid with the Messengerﷺ, where a man was supplicating; "O Allahﷻ, I ask you by the fact that I testify, You are Allahﷻ, there is no god but You, the One, the Ultimate, who did not beget and was not begotten, and to whom no one is equal," and the Prophetﷺ said, "By Him in whose hands is my soul, he has asked Allahﷻ by His Greatest name, which if He is asked by it He gives, and if supplicated, He answers." [Ibn Hibban]

The Prophetﷺ not only taught the Companions supplications but also encouraged their own supplications and accorded them with highest acceptance. The Companions, their students

(Tábiín), their students *(Taba Tabiín)* and the great scholars as Imam Sakhawiﷺ, Abd al-Qadir Gilaniﷺ and Hasan al-Shadhiliﷺ composed their own litanies of *Dhikr* and supplications as *Dalail ul Khairat* or *Hizb al Bahr*. The scholars believe that supplications in one's own time and one's own way does not become a *Bídá* or reprehensible innovation unless it competes against a specific Sunnah legislated for that time and place. For example, reciting any other *dua* after coming out of the toilet, instead of the specified *dua*, '*Ghufranaká*', would constitutes *Bídá*, however, after reciting the specified *dua* for the time and place one can continue with other supplications.

The respect and veneration for Sufism is evident when reading the words and life of Imam Ahmad ibn Hanbalﷺ. Shaykh 'Abdul Hafiz al Makki discusses Imam Ahmad'sﷺ positive opinion of *Tasawwuf* and Sufism in his book which is dedicated to Imam Ahmadﷺ. He narrates, Imam Ahmadﷺ was once asked regarding the seeker who takes the path of *Tasawwuf*, he replied, "The seeker should remain with Allahﷻ as Allahﷻ wishes and he should leave all which he himself desires for what Allahﷻ desires…" Imam Ahmadﷺ gave great importance to the Sufis and honoured them. He was once asked regarding Sufis and was told that they sat in mosques. He replied: "Knowledge is with those who sit with them the most."[7]

Another question is posed about spending limited time in seclusion. In Tariqa, many Sufi masters have adopted the practice of remaining in seclusion for forty days and Allahﷻ bestowed upon them the divine knowledge and the truths. The basis for this act is the Hadith that the Beloved Prophetﷺ said, *'Whoever worships Allahﷻ for forty days with sincerity, fountains of wisdom shall gush forth from his heart and from his tongue"* [*Musnad ash-Shihab 1:285*]

Misconcetions regarding Sufism

Another Hadith as narrated by the Mother of the believers Ayesha؛ that before the revelation commenced, Messenger؛ became attached to seclusion in the cave of Hira and engaged in worship for several nights in succession without going back to his family. [Bukari:3]

Mostly those who engage in remembrance of Allah؛ use counters or Tasbih to count their litanies. Some people object to Tasbih or the counting beads, the following Hadith is the basis for the counters, the string is merely used to keep the beads together. Saffiyah؛ the Mother of the believers, narrated that the Messenger؛ came to her when she had in front of her four thousand date pits which she was using [as counters] for glorification of Allah؛. [Tirmidhi : 3554]

Chapter 3

ELEMENTS OF TASAWWUF

The Internal State

Ali؈ narrated that: "There is no [real] benefit in recitation of the Qur'an in which there is no reflection, nor in any act of worship in which there is no cognition." [Ad-Daylami, al-Firdaws: 1/135]

In Islam, the action and the deed are extremely important and the value to those deeds is added through the sincerity of intention. As the body is nothing without a soul and a soul is immaterial without a body. Hence, the external or the outer aspect of the deed and the inner aspect of the deed are interrelated, an action only becomes an action in virtue of its sincerity. Sincerity has the same relation to an action as the soul to the body. A body without a soul is called dead and an action without sincerity is worthless.

The Islamic Jurisprudence or *Fiqh* governs the regulations and determines the conditions of the deeds whereas, *Tasawwuf* is the discipline which gives the profound meaning to that deed; the pure intention and the cognizance of Allah؈. Some regard knowledge superior to action, while others regard action more important, however both are integral. Prayer or Salah for example, is not really Salah until performed with purification, intention (*Niyah*), direction towards *Qibla*; it is an action but if not performed with knowledge, it will lose its essence. As Quran mentions:

'Successful indeed are the believers; those who humble themselves in the prayers.'

[Quran, al-Múminun 23:1-2]

Thus, humility in *Salah* is subject to performing the *Salah*, if someone does not even perform *Salah*, how could he claim humility. Similarly, knowledge without action has no reward. If someone has the knowledge of how to perform *Salah*, the direction of *Qibla*, the rules for purification but does not perform the actions of *Salah*, then how would he expect the reward as he has not performed the action. Thus, the attributes of an action lay in the performance of that action. The details of faith and action combined with the pure state of the heart have been explicitly shown to us by the Prophetﷺ, through his own life, as an example. On the day of judgement, Allahﷻ will decide on the sincerity of the deed. Consider the first Hadith of Sahih Bukhari;

"The reward of the deeds depends upon the intention" *[Bukhari-1]*

Just as the body comprises of the material and the immaterial which is the physical body and the soul, there is an external aspect and an internal aspect of every action; the intention with which the deed is performed for whom it is performed and why is it performed-the motive behind that deed. Soul does not need words; it has a silent language of its own, linked to the inner state of the heart which decides the destiny of a deed. For a deed to be accepted on the Day of Judgement, the criterion is;

> The deed must be the actions that Allah ﷻ declared as good deeds,
> The deed must be performed according to the method outlined by Shariáh-the Islamic Jurisprudence, and
> The deed must be done purely for Allahﷻ.

Elements of Tasawwuf

The third condition which is 'purely for Allahﷻ' is the concept which deals with the inner aspect of the deed which has to be practised and *Tasawwuf* is the practice of those disciplines. Consider the Hadith related in Muslim that:

"The first person judged on Resurrection Day will be a man martyred in battle. He will be brought forth, Allah ﷻ will reacquaint him with His blessings upon him and the man will acknowledge them, whereupon Allah ﷻ will say, "What have you done with them?". The man will respond, "I fought to the death for You."

Allahﷻ will reply, "You lie. You fought in order to be called a hero, and it has already been said." Then, he will be sentenced and dragged away on his face and flung into the fire.

Next, a man will be brought forward who learnt the Sacred Knowledge, taught it to others and recited the Qur'an. Allahﷻ will remind him of His gifts to him and the man will acknowledge them. Then, Allahﷻ will say, "What have you done with them?" The man will answer, "I acquired Sacred Knowledge, taught it and recited the Qur'an, for Your sake."

Allahﷻ will say, "You lie. You learnt so as to be called a scholar, read the Qur'an so as to be called a reciter, and it has already been said." Then, the man will be sentenced and dragged away on his face to be flung into the fire.

Next, a man will be brought forward whom Allahﷻ generously provided for, giving him various kinds of wealth. Allahﷻ will recall to him the benefits given and the man will acknowledge them, to which Allahﷻ will say, "And what have you done with them?" The man will answer, "I have not left a single expense You love to see made, except that I have spent it for Your sake."

Allahﷻ will say, "You lie. You did it so to be called generous, and it has already been said." Then, he will be sentenced and dragged away on his face to be flung into the fire. [Sahih Muslim, 3.1514: Hadith 1905]

The Hadith gives an in depth understanding of the sincerity and the worth of intention behind a deed, even when one willingly gives away his life or his wealth. Without a pure and sincere intention, the deed is not accepted by Allahﷻ. The scholar acquired and taught sacred knowledge, martyr gave his life and the altruistic gave his money but the intention was not pure so nothing was accepted.

Another Hadith emphasises the importance of sincerity as is narrated by Abdullah bin Umarﷺ that the Beloved Prophetﷺ said, "Three men from among those who were [from a nation] before you, set out together till they reached a cave at night and entered it. A big rock rolled down the mountain and closed the mouth of the cave. They said (to each other), 'Nothing could save you from this rock but to invoke Allahﷻ by giving reference to the righteous deed which you have done (for Allah's sake only).'

So, one of them said, 'O Allahﷻ! I had old parents and I never provided my family (wife, children etc.) with milk before them. One day, by chance I was delayed, and I came late (at night) while they had slept. I milked the sheep for them and took the milk to them, but I found them sleeping. I disliked providing my family with the milk before them. I waited for them, and the bowl of milk was in my hand and I kept on waiting for them to get up till the day dawned. Then, they got up and drank the milk. O Allahﷻ! If I did that for Your Sake only, please relieve us from our critical situation caused by this rock.' So, the rock shifted a little, but they could not get out."

The Prophet ﷺ added, "The second man said, 'O Allah! I had a cousin who was the dearest of all people to me and I wanted to have sexual relations with her, but she refused. Later, she had a hard time in a famine year and came to me. I gave her one-hundred-and-twenty Dinars on the condition that she would not resist my desire and she agreed. When I was about to fulfill my desire, she said: 'It is illegal for you to outrage my chastity except by legitimate marriage.' So, I thought it a sin to have sexual intercourse with her and left her though she was the dearest of all the people to me and I also left the gold which I had given her. O Allah ﷻ! If I did that for Your Sake only, please relieve us from the present calamity.' So, the rock shifted a little more but still they could not get out from there."

The Prophet ﷺ added, "Then, the third man said, "O Allah ﷻ! I employed few laborers and paid them their wages with the exception of one man who did not take his wages and went away. I invested his wages and got much property thereby. Later, he came and said to me: 'O Allah's slave! Pay me my wages.' I said to him: 'All the camels, cows, sheep and slaves you see, are yours.' He said: 'O Allah's slave! Don't make fun of me.' I said: 'I am not mocking at you.' So, he took all the herd and drove them away and left nothing. O Allah ﷻ! If I did that for Your Sake only, please relieve us from the present suffering. So, that rock shifted completely and they got out." [Sahih al-Bukhari : 2272]

The Qurán commands to 'perform *Salah* and give alms' and at the same time the Muslims are to 'be patient' and 'be thankful'. Of course, as Muslims we must follow all the commandments, Qurán censures the one who 'does not pay the due share of alms' and also condemns the one who is 'prideful' or 'contemptuous. We are to follow all the commandments of Allahﷻ, there is no picking and choosing. The Messengerﷺ said: "The true emigrant is a person who leaves behind everything that Allah has forbidden. [Bukhari:6484]

The Hadith proves that external form is of no value unless it is accompanied by inner significance. Thus, the true object of our deeds is their inner significance or reality. From the Hadith above it is evident that the migrant is the one who abandons all that is contrary to the pleasure of Allahﷻ. Nonetheless, no one should assume from the above Hadith that external actions are without value. The proper way to approach the matter is to realise that Allahﷻ has created for every inner meaning a corresponding external form and without that form the acquisition of inner significance is impossible.

In another Hadith, the importance of inner state is clearly indicated as a part of a lengthy narration that Allah's Prophetﷺ said, "For sure, it is not your bodies or forms which concern Allahﷻ, but your hearts and your deeds. Piety (*Taqwa*) is here! Piety is here! Piety is here!" And he pointed to his chest. [Bukhari, Muslim, Abu Dawud, Tirmidhi]

Once a man questioned Shaykh al-Hadith Zakriya﷫ about *Tasawwuf*. Shaykh Zakriya's﷫ answer was plain and clear, "The beginning of *Tasawwuf* is the Hadith that 'deeds are dependent upon their intentions' (*Innamul a'mal o binnyat*) and the epitome is that you worship Allah ﷻ as you see Him (*Ihsan*)"

Significance of Heart

Allahﷻ created man to recognise his Lord and this cognizance is not bound by time, age or space. It is a connection for all times not restricted to the mosque or prayers. The inner state of the heart has to be practiced and developed as it is not taught by the books. The path of *Tasawwuf* is a journey to reform the inner self and rid the heart from the ailments, as the Beloved Prophetﷺ said; "There is a piece of flesh in the body, if it becomes virtuous, the whole body becomes good but if it is ruined the whole body gets ruined and that is the heart. [Bukhari: 52]

For the purpose of understanding, the Arabic word *'Qalb'* has two meanings: the biological and the spiritual. The biological heart, as in anatomy, is placed in the chest which is the centre for circulation of blood. Another connotation is the spiritual heart which is also called *Qalb*; a subtle element which finds unison with Allahﷻ. The heart as mentioned in Hadith is not the biological heart but the connection or the unseen energy to the material heart which connects the believer to Allahﷻ.

The word *Qalb* in Qur'an and Hadith is used to express mind, thoughts, perception, as well as the physical heart itself. Qurán describes the heart as a 'living entity' and refers to it with many attributes; a Divine gift, locus of faith and piety, centre for belief, a place for mercy and compassion. It can be enlightened, contented, peaceful, the point where Divine light descends and the subtle faculty through which human beings attain their humanity. *Qalb* is the locus for discernment, feeling and knowledge. According to Qurán it represents the relationship between the human being and the Lord. In the words of Qurán it holds *tadabbur* meaning contemplation and *tazzakur* meaning remembrance. When the spiritual heart is immersed in the love of Allahﷻ the body being the slave follows the Shariáh and the soul submits to the Lord. It is also denoted as the source of diseased morality, disbelief, disdain or blindness as in the verse:

> 'In their hearts is sickness' [Qurán, al Baqarah 2:10]

Or as in the verse:

> 'It is rather the hearts in the chests that are blind'
> [Qurán, al Hajj 22:46]

The ailments of the heart not only consume the person from within but also retards his abilities. Due to the ailment of the *Qalb*, a Muslim may not be able to perform to the best of his capabilities, which in turn affects the families and the overall society. This gives a brief understanding of the heart- the subtle faculty which finds unison with Allahﷻ. Qurán also mentions the term *Qalb e Saleem;*

> 'When he came to His Lord with a sound heart'
> [Qurán, As Saafat 37:84]

In another verse, Qurán mentions:

> 'The Day when there will be no benefit from wealth or sons, but only one who comes to Allah with a pure heart.'
> [Qurán, Ash Shuára 26:88-89]

According to scholars as Ibn e Abbas؄, Ibne Sireen؄ and al Alusi؄, *'Qalb e Saleem'* is a pure heart free from disbelief, hypocrisy, pride or jealousy, filled with faith and sincerity. Al Razi؄ in his book *'Mafatih al ghayb'* describes *Qalb e Saleem* as the one free from disbelief and rebellion. Imam Ghazali؄, at the pinnacle of his career, left for ten years and spent time with the great Sufis of his time and only with that illumination he wrote his masterpiece *Ihya' 'ulum al-din* [The revival of the religious sciences] and described the heart as the locus of the knowledge of Allahﷻ and wrote, "Ignorance of Allahﷻ is a deadly poison and disobedience its disease. Knowledge of Allahﷻ is its antidote and obedience its medicine; there is no other way to heal the heart without medicine.[1]

The Messenger of Allahﷺ said, "Whenever a servant commits an act of wrongdoing, a black spot appears on his heart and when he desists, and seeks forgiveness, and repents, his heart will become clear. But, if he again commits the same wrongs, more and more black marks will accumulate until they overshadow his heart. This is the rust which the Almighty speaks of in the Qur'an. [Qur'an 83:4]" [Tirmidhi: 3334, Ibn Majah: 4244]

Purification of the Carnal Self (Tazkiyah e Nafs)

In Qurán, Arabic *al-Nafs* has been used with two meanings, one is to indicate 'self':

'And remember your Rabb inside your-self'

[Qurán, al Aáraf 7:205]

Secondly, the word '*Nafs*' has been referred as a specific part of our self which represents worldly desire, lust, anger, greed, ego and other blameworthy traits. Even though, it is not part of our physical body, the *Nafs* is part of our physical self. Some scholars refer to it as the carnal self or the egotistic self, as Allahﷻ mentions:

'Verily the self ever commands to do evil'

[Qur'an, Yusuf 12:53]

The *Nafs* carries the blameworthy traits as anger, pride, envy, greed, discontent and when it divulges in darkness and surrenders to the devil, is called *Nafs e Ammara* as in:

> 'Indeed, the self is a persistent enjoiner of evil 'Nafs e Ammara"
>
> [Qurán, Yusuf 12:53]

The carnal self or *Nafs e Ammara*, takes command and joins Satan in evil; hence, it is heedless and disobedient to Allah. Nowadays, it is a common practice to say, 'Do as you please or do whatever you feel like doing or whatever makes you happy'. This is not the way of Islam, it is the way of the followers of *Nafs e Ammara*, which indulges in the worldly pleasures and takes the man to the valley of desires which is tempting yet barren. Shaykh al-Niffari said, "The *Nafs* is innately disposed to bad manners, while the servant is commanded to have good manners. Thus, the *Nafs* by its nature takes along the path of disobedience and the servant turns its back by all his might."[2]

The second type of *Nafs* is imperfect but rebukes for neglecting the Divine duties, it is called the self-accusing or 'Nafs e Lawwamah'. 'Lawwam' means to self-incriminate and reproach. This is the *Nafs* that may bring a person to do sin, but then it incriminates itself and repents, eventually making it possible for the person to stop from that sin altogether. The sign of this *Nafs* is that it is remorseful and repentant and fights a battle, which it may lose or win.

Allah mentions *Nafs e Lawwamah* as:

> 'And I swear by the reproaching self'
>
> [Qurán, al Qiyamah 75:2]

The third is '*Nafs e Mutmai'n*', this *Nafs* is content in the obedience of Allahﷻ and finds its epiphany performing the acts of devotion. *Nafs e Mutmain* finds peace in unison with Allahﷻ and the heart becomes the epicentre for sincerity and reaches a state of serenity. This *Nafs* does not divulge in its desires rather finds peace in obedience to Allahﷻ and in return Allahﷻ is pleased with this *Nafs*:

> "To the righteous it will be said "oh reassured soul, return to your Lord well pleased, and pleasing to Him"
>
> [Qurán, Al Fajr 89:27-28]

Striving against one's desires is referred to greater *jihad* or battle in *Tasawwuf* and the term is established from the Hadith, that the Beloved Prophetﷺ said, "A Mujahid is the one who strives against his desires to obey Allahﷻ." [Shuáb al-Iman,1123-Bayhaqi]

The Hadith, means that the perfect *mujahid or the* warrior is the one who struggles with his desires. *Nafs e Ammara* can be subdued by constant rebuke and rigor. In the first stage the carnal self is uncontrolled, restless and lacks conscience. Through systematic course of training and rigor, it develops the sense of self inculpation and repents if it slips the right course, hence, becomes *Nafs e Lawammah*. With constant training and rebuke, eventually it turns into *Nafs e Mutmain*. Imam Ghazali﷫ describes the process as, "The first step in this path is that the seeker should undertake '*mujahida*' or rigor, destroy and get rid of all the evil deeds and bend all his energy towards concentration of Divine Manifestation, when the seeker attains this noble perfection, then Allahﷻ Himself becomes the Guardian and Protector of the heart of His servant and provides light and guidance from the Divine treasures of enlightenment."[3]

The Beloved Prophetﷺ said, "No man ever filled a vessel worse than his stomach. It is sufficient for a human being to eat few bites that keep his back upright. But, if need be, then a third for his food, a third for his drink and a third for him to breathe." [Tirmidhi 2537]

The ego or the *Nafs* constantly asks for more, without any care for haram or halal. The earlier Sufis believed in mortifying the *Nafs* through extreme rigors of sleeplessness or hunger. The way to restrain is through constant effort, where we allow it what it wants within the boundaries of Shariáh and make it serve us. As an example, the *Nafs* wants to sleep, we give it a little sleep and then rise at night to pray, or it wants lavish foods, we eat just enough food according to the Sunnah and do our duties as assigned by Allahﷻ. It is narrated that in his dream, Abu Yazid Bustamiﷺ, asked Allahﷻ the way to Divine Love. The reply was, "Discard yourself and come to Me.", Abu Yazid Bustamiﷺ said, "Then, I got out of myself as a snake gets out of its slough."[4]

Once, the *Nafs* surrenders, a complete sense of peace and rectitude is achieved and the *Nafs* becomes *Nafs e mutmai'n*, completely absorbed by the love of Allahﷻ. When *'Nafs e Mutmai'n'* is achieved through complete obedience to the command of Allahﷻ and following the path of Sunnah, the person disconnects from pride and surrenders to Allahﷻ. For those who put their *Nafs* through rigor in this world, Paradise is promised as a refuge:

"But as for he who feared the position of his Lord and prevented the self from inclination, then indeed, paradise will be his refuge"

[Qurán, An Nazíat 79: 40-41]

Tazkiyah is a term for cleansing the carnal self from the worldly evils; it involves cleansing of thoughts and deeds, the heart and the soul. The exertion and worship of the seeker finally leads to a "state" that is the result of his exertion and when it is firmly rooted becomes a "station" for him or may demonstrate as an attribute affecting the soul, such as joy or calmness.

Shah Shabbir Ahmed Kakakhel explained *Tazkiyah e Nafs* as, "The purification of the Qalb or the spiritual heart is achieved through *Dhikr* or remembrance of Allah ﷻ, as heart is the abode of feelings, emotions and where spiritual states or stations are conserved. Once, the darkness of the heart, created by sins, is cleansed through regular *Dhikr* or remembrance of Allah ﷻ, then the incessant purity is to be attained through rectification of the *Nafs*, which is achieved through rigor." [Seerah Majlis, 4Jan, 2021]

Path (Tariqa)

A common term used in *Tasawwuf* is '*Tariqa*', which may be characterized as following the way of the Beloved Prophet ﷺ:

'Say, 'if you all love Allah, then follow me, and Allah will love you and forgive your sins; and Allah is all-fearing, all-compassionate'

[Qurán, Aal e Imran 3:31]

Tariqa is to take the path to transform the soul, the way of the *Tariqa* may differ but mostly it consists of uprooting the blameworthy traits of the *Nafs*, cleansing of the heart so it is pure to reach the state of *Ihsan*. In the words of Shaykh Nuh, a true seeker focuses on what he may do, his adoration of his Lord and that is his progress. Otherwise, Allah ﷻ often keeps the prideful waiting until they lose some. The spiritual *'enemies'* of sincerity remains enemies and, *taqwa* means keeping them at arm's length throughout one's life. Whosoever, sides with me, myself and I and enjoys assertion and notice is thus far in its grip.

The seeker sublimates the *Nafs* by Dhikr, humility to Allahﷻ, thinking of the fewness of our mortal days, low profile spiritual works, the *Muraqabah*, lessons of the Tariqa and submitting to the Shaykh. One is helped in this by sincere *istighfar* or asking Allah's forgiveness and by not siding with *Nafs* but always asking Allah'sﷻ help against it.[5]

As explained by Shaykh Abd al-Qadirﷺ in the thirty sixth discourse, "Look at yourself with mercy and choose for yourself that is better, keep away from disobedient associates and make the Book of Allahﷻ and the Sunnah your guide. Look at these two authorities with contemplation and meditation and act on them and do not be deceived by mere talks and greed. As mentioned in Qurán: *'Whatever the Messenger gives you, accept it, and whatever he forbids you abstain and keep your duty to Allah.'* (Qurán 57:27) Accordingly, Allahﷻ kept His Prophetﷺ away from falsehood, thus Allahﷻ says; *'Nor does he speak out of desire. It is not but revelation that is revealed.'* (Qurán 53:34).

Meaning, that whatever the Beloved Prophetﷺ said it is from Allahﷻ and not from his own desire or self, so every word he uttered is the commandment of Allahﷻ and then Allahﷻ mentions in Qurán; *'Say, if you love Allah, then follow me: Allah will love you'* (Qurán 3:30') It is obvious that the path of love is to follow the Beloved Prophetﷺ in word and deed- his practice and state. Safety is in the Book of Allahﷻ and the practice of the Sunnah of the Beloved Prophetﷺ and whatever is beside these two is destruction and only by following the Qurán and Sunnah can the servant progress towards the state of Awliya Allah."[6]

The work of the *Tariqa* lies in belief, which is belief (*Iman*), Tenets of faith (*Aqaid*), Practice (*Mamoolat*) and character (*Khulq*). When the seeker takes the path, small incremental change comes from within and with due practice the seeker can control his *Nafs*, even if the *Nafs* or Satan tries to tempt him, the seeker can either control the urge or seek forgiveness of Allahﷻ. There may be some by the special favour or *inaya* of Allahﷻ who are born Wali or travel the path swiftly but mostly it is a journey which is done through purifying the *Nafs* and remembrance of Allahﷻ.

A common saying for the seekers is *'Istiqama fauq ul karamah'* meaning being steadfast is better than miracles. The Beloved Prophetﷺ said, "The good deed, most loved by Allahﷻ, is the one that is less but continuous. [Bukhari:32; Muslim]

Tariqa is the path of Shariáh and Sunnah, to love what the Prophetﷺ loved, to hate what the Prophetﷺ hated. In one of his letters to his disciple Mujaddid Alf Thani﷦ writes, "Attainment of every kind of perfection and achievements is dependent on the obedience of the Prophetﷺ and rightly guided caliphs (*Khulafa' al-Rashidin*), they are the stars of guidance and the suns of Walaya. Whosoever followed them was guided and whosoever disobeyed, is misguided."[7]

At times people ask if the Islamic scholars followed the *Tariqa*; in fact, most of the great scholars of Qurán and Hadith followed the path of Tariqa, Abd al-Qadir Gilani﷦, Imam Ghazali﷦, Rumi﷦ al-Nawawi﷦, al-Suyuti﷦, Mujaddid Alf Thani﷦, Abd al Haqq Muhaddis Dehlwi ﷦, Shah Wali Allah﷦, and the great scholars of recent times kept the tradition. Mowlana Yaqub﷦, Mowlana Qasim Nanutawi﷦, Mowlana Madni﷦, Mowlana Ashraf Ali Thanvi﷦ Mufti Taqi Usmani are few of the noble scholars who not only followed the path but also provided guidance to hundreds of thousands of people on the path.

Definition of Suluk

Suluk means to constantly keep the body and the heart occupied in the obedience of Allahﷻ. This should be done in accordance with the *Shari'ah* and the Sunnah of Allah's Messengerﷺ to such a degree that it becomes second nature. There are two paths in *Tasawwuf*; the path of *Suluk* and the path of *jadhb*. The path of *Suluk* takes one towards Allahﷻ through spiritual exertions and devotions. Once the seeker traverses the path and becomes consistent in his devotion, he attains the affinity with Allahﷻ. The path of *jadhb* means that a person attains the affinity with Allahﷻ without effort or will. The way of *jadhb* is through Allah's special bestowal of heightened spiritual states. This can affect the senses and intellect, consequently, the person may lose his senses in the ordinary meaning and maybe mistaken as insane. Those who are chosen for this path are called *Majdhub*.

Suluk is to follow the Sunnah in actions and habits as the external and internal of the Messenger of Allahﷺ were most perfect. The effect is such that one starts to despise the blameworthy traits and the praiseworthy traits are attained. For the believer, following the Shariáh becomes second nature, the heart finds peace in the obedience of Allahﷻ and the acts of worship become easy to perform.

Hafiz ibne Qayyim﷫ said, "Allahﷻ revealed to these respected individuals the way of the pure Sunnah. One of the blessings of the noble Sunnah is that Satan has very little opportunity to interfere with the seeker's path. It is clear that if a person was to diligently perform those actions that the Prophetﷺ did, such as offering Salah with congregation etc., and if a person was to stringently offer the *fard, wajib* and sunnah *al-muákkadah* (emphasized sunnah) prayers, then he would not experience devilish insinuations. The person would not consider himself as a *wali* and others will also not consider him as the perfect pious."

The benefit of taking the path of Suluk is that it removes indolence and makes it easy to follow Shariáh. The purpose is not to view unseen images, forms, lights or colours as these are all useless entertainment. The tangible forms, unseen forms and lights are all created; they are signs bearing witness to Allah's existence. The mere objective is acquiring the state of *ihsan* and the spiritual exercises prescribed by the Sufis have been devised for the ailments of the heart just as the doctors prescribe medication for physical ailments.

Ibn Taymiyyah, in his book *Al-Tuhfah al-'Iraqiyyah fi 'l-'Amal al-Qalbiyyah*, explains the true stations and spiritual states of the heart as; "These are a few words explaining the states of the heart, which are defined as stations and spiritual states. They are from among the fundamentals and foundations of faith and religion, for example the love of Allah and His Prophet, trust in Allah sincerity, gratitude, patience, fear and hope in Allah. The *imams* have agreed that all of these actions are incumbent upon the entire creation."

Hafiz Ibn Qayyim wrote *Madarij al-Salikin* [Ranks of the Divine Seekers] which deals with the topic of *Tasawwuf*, he writes, "The servitude of the man is divided over the heart, the tongue and the remaining limbs of the body. The issues dealing with the heart are sincerity, trust, love, patience, penitence, fear, hope, firm belief and true intention. The consensus is that these actions of the heart are incumbent. There are two types of actions from which one should abstain; disbelief and disobedience. Examples of disbelief include having doubts, hypocrisy, and polytheism etc. Disobedience can be major or minor- major disobedience is lack of sincerity(*riya*), vanity (*'ujub*), pride (*kibr*), boasting (*fakhr*), haughtiness (*khuyala*), feeling hopeless [of the mercy of Allah] (*qunut*), to not fear the punishment of Allahﷻ, feeling pleasure when a Muslim is harmed, expression of joy when a Muslim is afflicted with trouble, to spread indecency among Muslims, to be jealous of Muslims, and other such sins that are worse than adultery and drinking wine etc. If the heart is not cleansed then it will become foul, which will affect the entire body. The rectification of the heart comes before the rectification of the limbs. If the purification of the heart is ignored, it will be diseased."[8]

Shaykh Mirati﷫ in his book, *Tadhkirat al-Rashid* quotes that he found a written script by Shaykh Rashid Ahmad Gangohi﷫ which described the attributes of the one on the path of Suluk;

"*Tasawwuf* is the strength of belief and internal and external knowledge of *Deen*. The way of the Sufis is in the perfection of morals and perpetual absorption in Allahﷻ. The essence of *Tasawwuf* is to be embellished with the meanings of the attributes of Allahﷻ [as humanly as possible], elimination of the carnal self and achieving a constant desire to please Allahﷻ. The morals of the Sufis are the same as the morals of the Blessed Prophet'sﷺ, as mentioned in the Qurán: "And you are surely on an excellent standard of character" [Qurán 68:4]. All that is mentioned in the Hadith is also inclusive of the morals of the Sufis. Below is a succinct description of those morals:

> Think lowly of oneself and this is the opposite of arrogance,

Be compassionate to the creation of Allah ﷻ and overlook the transgressions of the creation against oneself,
Avoid anger and treat others with kindness and warmth,
Be sympathetic to others and prefer them over oneself; to favour the rights of others over one's own rights,
Be generous and forgive others and overlook their mistakes,
Be optimistic and cheerful,
Be soft-spoken and modest
Avoid ostentation, jealousy and haterd
Spend without stinginess and avoid overspending such that one becomes needy,
Be reliant on the Creator and be content with the possessions of the material world,
Avoid arguments or criticism unless it is with truth,
Fulfill promises,
Be insightful, Love the fellow Muslims and have good relations with them. Be grateful when someone does a favour and be of service to other Muslims [9]

Chapter Four

THE GUIDE~SHAYKH

When the person is lost in the web of worldly desires, he becomes an instrument for Satan and Satan then, uses the worldly desires and lust to lure that person in the trap to forget his Lord. The reality is forgotten and the mirage of this world becomes the objective. Allah ﷻ describes *Nafs* as 'ever prompting to do wrong', [Qurán, 12:53] and it never surrenders unless trained to submit. *Nafs* never agrees that it has any ailment, rather tries to hide behind self-praise. The submission of the *Nafs* cannot be achieved by mere reading of the books, in fact, knowledge can harbour pride as we notice many whose learning is tarnished by arrogance. Iblees was the teacher of the angels, yet his pride and arrogance made him accursed.

To identify and cure the ailments of the *Nafs*, one needs to seek guidance from someone who has travelled the path himself and has been trained by a teacher to guide others. A true Shaykh is the one who has been on the journey of *Tasawwuf* under the guidance of his Shaykh and has the knowledge and understanding of both Islamic Jurisprudence and the discipline of *Tasawwuf*. The Shaykh takes the seeker to follow the Beloved Prophet ﷺ and adjoins him to Allah ﷻ. In *Tasawwuf*, the purpose of the Shaykh is to help the seeker get rid of the spiritual ailments, assist in the fight against *Nafs* and guide him through to the path of true love which is *Ihsan* (spiritual excellence).

The Guide-Shaykh

The seeker takes the path and by special favours of Allahﷻ, Shaykh's training and *dua* the journey begins. A true Shaykh always ensures that the seeker follows the way of Shariáh and the Prophetic Sunnah. A Shaykh loves his students because he is assigned the duty of purifying them and they are the means of his worship by guiding them to the path. Shaykh is the guide who takes one to the path of Allahﷻ and takes him through the journey of love. The path is for anyone who wants to take it but each individual has his own pace. If the seeker is steadfast and the intentions are pure, the journey is faster. One of the main factors determining the pace is the *adab* or etiquettes with the Shaykh. One major hindrance is when the seeker compares the Shaykh's judgement on the merits of his own.

As for the learning of *Fiqh*, Islamic Jurisprudence, we seek knowledge from those with traditional Islamic education and who are the followers of one of the four Sunni Schools of Fiqh; Hanafi, Maliki, Sháfíí or Hanbali. Whilst university degrees, acclaims and published work are great achievements yet they cannot replace the learning from an unbroken line of teachers extending back to the Beloved Prophetﷺ. Same goes for *Tasawwuf* as the matters of the soul and the heart are beyond the capacity of the human brain to comprehend.

For a bodily disease or ailment, one would never consult a self-proclaimed doctor who has read a few books on medicine, so how can one consider to receive any benefit in the spiritual path from a person who is a self-proclaimed Sufi. The true *Tasawwuf* has to be learnt and practiced under the guidance of someone who has learnt and received it by another Shaykh linking the chain back to the Companions and ultimately to Allah's Last Prophetﷺ.

Following a Teacher (Ittiba)

Tasawwuf is not information, it is knowledge that has to be learnt in the company with the means of *ittiba*, the following. It is evident that the function of following a teacher did not end after the first generation of Muslims, Allahﷻ explicitly confirms in His injunction:

> "And follow the path of him who turns unto Me"
> [Qur'an, Luqman 31:15]

The word used in this verse is *'ittiba'* meaning 'follow', implying to follow as in keeping the company and following the example of the teacher which is the fundamental method of teaching in *Tasawwuf*. The companions followed the Prophetﷺ in every aspect whether external or Internal and continued the Prophetic mission of *'Yuzakkihim'* meaning 'to purify them' so they became the guiding stars for the next generation Muslims and the chain continued.[1]

Only by following the ones who are linked to the chain can one reach the ultimate goal which is the love of Allahﷻ. 'Purifying' is the Sunnah of the Prophetﷺ carried on by the Companions and being purified is the Sunnah of the Companions who reached the ultimate station of *'Radhi Allah'* meaning Allah is pleased with them. Though, many pious and truthful men may have performed great deeds in the history of mankind however, there is no doubt that after the Prophets, the status of the Companions of the Beloved Prophetﷺ is the most exalted. This status was awarded to them not because of their deeds but only because of the blessed company of the Beloved Prophetﷺ which illuminated their hearts and they received the title of *Radhi Allah*. The station of *'Radhi Allah'* only belongs to the Companions of the Prophetﷺ,

even if they spent a few moments in his blessed company and besides them no one can attain that station. As mentioned in Qurán:

> 'And the first forerunners among the Migrants and the Helpers and those who followed them with good conduct-Allah is pleased with them and they are pleased with Him, and He has prepared for them gardens beneath which rivers flow, wherein they will abide forever. That is the great attainment.'
>
> [Qurán, at Tawbah 9:100]

One sight of the Beloved Prophet's ﷺ was enough to cleanse the hearts of the believers. Although, we do not have that privilege, yet we can enjoin the company of those who held the chain and performed the journey. The company is called *'Suhba'* in *Tasawwuf* and the Beloved Prophet ﷺ said, "The example of good company in comparison to a bad one is that of a musk seller and the bellows of the Blacksmith; from the first you would either buy musk or enjoy the good smell while the bellow would either burn your clothes or your house, or your clothes would stink." [Bukhari: 2101]

Qurán commands the Muslims to follow the truthful. *'Sadiq'* was the quality of Abu Bakr ؓ and he was unquestionably the true most follower of the Beloved Prophet ﷺ. Some assert that it is not possible to find a true Shaykh in this time and era. There is a misunderstanding that the pious only existed in the past and piety is a word lost in history. This is a misconception as Allah ﷻ commands the believers to be with *'Sadiqeen'*, therefore, true guides will exist till the believers exist. The verse implies that *'Sadiqeen'* or the truthful will exist till the end, as the command of Qurán is for all times and generations. This perception that the true Sufis do not exist anymore is baseless, Allah ﷻ mentioned in Qurán:

"O, you who believed! fear Allah and be with those who are truthful"
[Surah al Taubah 9:119]

The verse very well orders the believers to fear Allahﷻ and be with those who are truthful, and the word used for truthful is *'Sadiqeen'* (The most truthful). As Allahﷻ has ordered the Muslims to be fearful of Allah and be with the truthful, that implies that such men will exist till the End. It is a matter of finding those who are truthful and follow Allah's Messengerﷺ in the true spirit as those are the ones who can lead us to the true path of *Tasawwuf*. The company of a person who possesses these qualities is an elixir. If the seeker cannot identify these qualities in a person, then he must look for the person whom most of the pious people of his time consider to be righteous. When one attends the company of such men, the heart shifts away from evil and inclines towards good.

There have been many fake Sufis who have tarnished the concept of *Tasawwuf*, therefore one has to be very diligent when looking for a Shaykh. As for the one in whom evil qualities are observed, one shall not follow him as Allahﷻ mentions in Qurán:

'Do not obey from among them a sinner or disbeliever'
[Qurán Surah Al Dahar-24]

The qualities of the person who should be chosen as a guide are elaborated in the Hadith as the Beloved Prophetﷺ said, "Luqman؏ said to his son: 'O my son! Impose on yourself to sit in the company of the scholars and to listen to the talks of those who possess wisdom because Allahﷻ revives a dead heart with the light of wisdom just as He revives a dead land with continuous rain."

The Beloved Prophet ﷺ taught the believers the importance

of the company of those who remember Allahﷻ as he said, "Should I not teach you something on which a (major) portion of faith rests and through which you can acquire the good of this world and the Hereafter? Hold on firmly to the assemblies of the people of Allah's remembrance. When you are in solitude, keep your tongue occupied in Allah'sﷻ remembrance as much as you can. Love solely for Allah'sﷻ sake and detest solely for Allah's sake." [Shaib al Emaan, Bayhaqi:8608]

Allah's Messenger ﷺ said: "If you see a person endowed with abstinence in this world and the trait of speaking less, stay close to him for he is bestowed with wisdom [from Allah]." [Shu'ab al-Iman: 4985] The sort of knowledge alluded to in the Hadith is the bestowed knowledge which may be gifted to the closest servants of Allahﷻ.

Tasawwuf is not the path of seclusion as some believe, it is a path where one keeps the company of those who have achieved the Divine love. The good fragrance of the Divine love from those who had a sip from the amphora of Maárfa is enough to give passionate longing. In the path of *Tasawwuf*, keeping the company is of immense importance, it is a saying that a breath spent other than the company of the pious men, *Dhikr* or prayers is spent in vain. Shaykh Sa'di ؓ described the effects of company in a parable, *"I picked up a sweet-smelling lump of soil. I asked it whether it was musk or ambergris. It replied that it was plain sand; however, the company of a sweet-smelling rose left its impression on it."*

Some have even said that, whoever, has no Shaykh, but travels the path alone has the Satan as his Shaykh. Another saying is that a person is like a tree growing in the wild, if not trimmed and pruned, it becomes a scrub. However, one has to ensure to find the company of the righteous as the company or association with a sinful or heedless is worse than that of a disbeliever. The *kufr* of the disbeliever is obvious whereas the heedless will corrupt the heart of his associates.

Mujaddid Alf Thani ﷺ reiterated in his letter, 'In this path, the benefit depends on the company, saying and writing is not enough. The honourable 'Khawja Naqshband ﷺ said that the path is through company, due to the company with the best of the persons (*Khair-ul-Bashr* ﷺ), the noble Companions ﷺ are superior over the friends of Allah (Awliya) of the nation, that none of the friend of Allah (Wali) can reach the rank of any Companion of the Beloved Prophet ﷺ even if he is Owais Qarni ﷺ."[2]

For most of us, the inner ailments remain unnoticed and undetected, therefore, it is hard to cure them. Only an accomplished Shaykh can recognise and diagnose such spiritual maladies and then prescribe appropriate cure through spiritual exercises and disciplines, such as *Dhikr* and *Muraqbah*. The disciple has to adhere to the inner and outer aspects of Shariáh and engage in constant remembrance as the essence of the path is not to waste a breath without the remembrance of Allah ﷻ. Baba Bulleh Shah ﷺ the great Sufi poet said, "My Master taught me the lesson; any moment of negligence [from remembrance of Allah ﷻ] is a moment spent in denial of Allah ﷻ."

Mujaddid Alf Thani ﷺ wrote, "Allah's friends (*Awliya*) are such people that their associates are never wretched and those who sit in their company are never deprived. When they are seen, one is reminded of Allah ﷻ, their sight is medicine, their words cure. Their company is light and effulgence. They are such people that those who only look at their outward aspect are deprived and lose hope, but those who gaze at their inner aspect become Allah's friends themselves."³

Abul Hasan Ali Nadwi☺ quoted in his book, "Imam Ghazali☺ was of the opinion that Sufis are indeed the ones traversing Allah's☺ path. Their ways are the best ways and their path is the most straight. Their character is the most nurtured and correct. If the intelligence of the intellectuals, the wisdom of the sages and the knowledge of the experts in Shariáh were combined to surpass the ways and character of the Sufis, it would still be impossible. The reason being that their external and internal is based on the light from Prophethood and every other source of light is nothing as compared to the light of Prophethood.⁴

Attributes of the Shaykh

Someone asked the Beloved Prophet☺, "Allah's Messenger☺! Who is the best person in whose company we should sit?" The Beloved Prophet☺ replied, "[Sit in the company of the one] Who when you merely look at, he reminds you of Allah☺ whose speech increases you in knowledge, and whose actions remind you of the Hereafter." [Abu Ya'li: 2437, al-Muntakhab: 630]

An authentic Shaykh is of the calibre that he possesses the knowledge of Shariáh (Islamic Jurisprudence) and *Tariqa* (Mystic aspects of Shariáh). It is important that one must follow a Shaykh who has knowledge of the Book and Sunnah. It does not mean that he must possess a formal degree from a religious school, rather it suffices one to have studied

Qur'anic exegesis. He is not required to have memorised the Qur'an, neither is he required to have studied principles of jurisprudence, theology and hypothetical matters related to *fiqh* and *fatwa*. The objective of the pledge is to command the lawful and prohibit the unlawful, remove blameworthy traits and practice praiseworthy traits, therefore, the Shaykh should have enough knowledge of *Deen* to guide the seeker.

One of the important attributes is that the Shaykh is associated with the pious and always refers to Qurán and Hadith for guidance. The Shaykh should be following the Sunnah to the best, abstain from major sins and shall not persist in minor sins. His heart be void of the worldly affairs and firmly attached with Allahﷻ and His Last Prophetﷺ. He should command the lawful, prohibit the unlawful and not be obstinate, characterless and unmanly. He should be wise and intelligent so that he can be relied upon in what he commands and prohibits. It is not a pre-requisite that he should manifest extraordinary acts and supernatural feats nor is it necessary that he should not earn a livelihood. One should not be deluded by those who claim supernatural feats as those can be manifested by the disbelievers as well. The Shaykh who fulfils these conditions, will not ask his disciples or others to do anything which is not permissible in Islam. The Shaykh as a true guide does not desire the seekers to follow him, in fact he ensures that his disciples follow the life of the Beloved Prophetﷺ to achieve the love and the closeness of Allahﷻ (*Maárfa*). Some basic conditions for a true Shaykh are:

> Being a Sunni Muslim with valid tenets of faith (Aqida) and follower of one of the four Sunni schools of Fiqh; Hanafi, Maliki, Shafi'i, Hanbali,
> Being aware of the Shariáh law; to be able to answer

> the questions of the seekers or humble enough to ask the scholars when he does not know,
> Being a male as a Shaykh is an heir,
> Have been publicly authorised by a true Shaykh, connecting him through an unbroken chain of authorisation back to the Prophet ﷺ,
> Being worthy of the position to be taken as an example,
> Has travelled the path under the guidance of his Shaykh,[5]

Few of the attributes as described by the scholars; and I have been blessed to witness these signs and many more in my Shaykh, Mowlana Shamsur Rehman:

> Firstly, a true Shaykh does not seek this world by his religious learning. He is someone cognizant of this world's wretchedness. He is aware of the next world's permanence and the triviality of this world,
> His deeds do not belie his words and he does not tell anyone to do something without doing it himself,
> He is devoted to the knowledge of the hereafter, which increases the desire for worship,
> He is declined to luxury in worldly affairs,
> His main concern is the knowledge of the inward and keeping the eye on the path to hereafter. He combats his ego, keeps a vigil on the heart and perpetually strives to deepen his certitude which leads to beholding the Divine light,
> He is somber and subdued, his mien bespeaking his works; the awe of the Divine being plain in his manners, dress, speech and silence. No one sees him without being reminded of Allah ﷻ.[6]

Hafiz Ibn Qayyim﷫ has mentioned the prerequisites of the Shaykh as, "When a person intends to follow a man then let him see: Is he from among the people of remembrance (*Dhikr*) or the people of heedlessness? Whether his desires control him or Revelation? If his desires control him and he is heedless then his behaviour has exceeded the limits. It is therefore, advised to observe the Shaykh, his exemplar and followers. If he is found to be heedless, then one should stay away from him. If he is one of those who remember Allahﷻ, follow the Sunnah and prudent in his matters, then hold on to him. The only difference between the alive and the dead is by *Dhikr*; the one who remembers his Cherisher is alive and the one who does not is dead."⁷

A Shaykh does not have to be one who has denounced and abandoned the world. It is not a pre requisite for a Shaykh to not have a family or earn a living. Rather, it is the way of the Beloved Prophetﷺ to have a family, earn the living yet keep the worldly desires at bay. Shaykh is the spiritual father for the seeker, he takes the raw materials and shapes the seeker to achieve a higher plane of consciousness. My Shaykh Mowlana Shamsur Rehman stays in the state of ablution at all times. Ablution for him is a state of readiness and this was the habit of the Beloved Prophetﷺ who said, *"No one remains upon ablution but a true believer" [Ibn Hibban1037.s]*

I had the favour of Allahﷻ to join my Shaykh on one of his visits for *Umrah* (lesser pilgrimage). When we went to Madinah and checked in to our hotel rooms, the fellows called out in excitement as they could view the tomb of the Masjid al Nabwi from the window. My Shaykh, even though he was already in the state of ablution, renewed it to have the view of the Masjid al-Nabwi.

Most of my Shaykh's family is settled in Madinah and we were invited for dinner by his family members. By the time we returned to our hotel room, it was past midnight and it is his routine in summer to be up by 3 am. Finally, we retired but he had to use the toilet, so he got up and afterwards thoroughly performed his wudu, dressed up, tied his head dress (*amama*) and performed two rakaa's of *Tahayat ul Wudu* as he would do at any other time. I have always witnessed him follow the same routine, may it be cold winter nights or long travels.

Once at a gathering, he looked very upset, when I asked him about the matter, he told me that he forgot his *siwak* at home (teeth cleaning twig as per Sunnah). He therefore, had to perform wudu without the *siwak* and this bothered him, as he had never missed the Sunnah, over years. He is one of those whose obedience to Allah is perpetual. Once there was a discussion about attendance at the *Masjid* before the first *takbeer* (Adhan) and a person was being praised for not having missed his first *takbeer* for few years. Out of curiosity, I asked my Shaykh if he had missed any, to which he replied, "You know! I just manage to reach in time". I knew that he had never missed the first *takbeer,* yet he concealed the fact out of true humility.

His scrupulousness and *taqwa* (piety) is to the degree that he had never missed his *tahajjud* or before dawn prayers, even as a child. As a young boy, before coming of age he used to perform his *tahajjud* prayers in the Masjid. Once, he saw a strange light and got scared and only after that he would perform his *tahajjud* prayers in his room. As a child, instead of playing with other boys, he dedicated his time to invoking the name of Allah and sending the blessings to the Prophet.

Recently, he went through major heart surgery which lasted about six or seven hours and only finished by evening. The same evening of his heart surgery, as soon as he regained some consciousness, he performed his *isha* prayers. I have been blessed to be a disciple and be in his company for over thirty years, yet never witnessed anything except adherence to Sunnah. I have seen in him a learned man who has learnt the Divine command, holds it at the centre of his life and lives it in every aspect. His humility and modesty sometimes surprise me, but this is what each one of those before him in the chain have possessed and passed on to the next- Love and absolute surrender to the Lord. As in Qurán;

'Lo, Verily the friends of Allah, never need they be feared for, nor shall they grieve: Those who believe, and are ever Godfearing. Theirs are the great good tidings in this life and the next: There is no changing the words of Allah; That is the mighty triumph'

[Qurán, Yunus 10:62-64]

Fake Sufis

As in any other jurisdiction, there have been those who have tainted the concept of *Tasawwuf* by false ideas. The misconception that *Tasawwuf* is above the Shariáh law, or the one on the path does not need to follow the rules of the Islamic Jurisprudence is complete heresy and such false ideas have no place in Islam. Each Muslim and especially those who desire to achieve piety need to be even more cautious in following the rulings of the Shariáh law. Anything and everything which is forbidden in Shariáh is forbidden for every Muslim and there are no exceptions to this. People have to be wary of such pretenders and it is the responsibility of the seeker to ensure that the person he is taking as Shaykh has the attributes of a true Shaykh. As Allahﷻ says,

> *"By no means follow the way of those who do not know"*
> [Qurán, Yunus 10:89]

Some pretenders boast they are the successors of such acclaimed masters or pledged to a certain Sufi order where they do not need to follow Shariáh or belong to certain caste and neglect their beliefs. No one is above the law as authenticated by the Hadith, narrated by Abu Hurairahﷺ that when the verse was revealed, "And warn your close relatives," the Messenger of Allahﷺ summoned his tribe. Another Hadith states that he said to his daughter Sayyeda Fatimaﷺ, "O Fatimahﷺ! Save yourself from the Hellfire because I do not have the power to save you from Allahﷻ." [Muslim : 204, Tirmidhi : 3185]

If one decides to follow a heedless, whose heart is indulged in the worldly desires, it will arouse the same in the heart of the person who would follow him. In fact, keeping the company of such heedless men is extremely detrimental, as the Beloved Prophetﷺ said, "A man's religion is like that of his close friend, so let each of you look at whom he keeps close company with" [Sunan Abi Dawud 4833].

The ignorant pretender who neither truly associated with a Shaykh nor embraced the true understanding of the discipline of *Tasawwuf*, would only mislead the innocent and lead him astray. There have been false guides and pretenders in *Tasawwuf*, as in any discipline, but this cannot undermine the discipline itself. One may not allow an imposter to look after his wealth so how can a pretender be the custodian of one's *Iman*. Imam Al Raziﷺ said, "Avoid the company of three classes of men: the heedless (*Ghaafil*), the hypocritical Qurán reader and the ignorant pretender to *Tasawwuf*."[8]

Bayazid al-Bustami؛ said, "If you see a man who has been given the ability to perform miracles, so much so that he can fly in the air, then do not be deceived by him until you see his state with regards to observance of Shariáh." Junayd al-Baghdadi؛ said, "All paths are closed on the entire creation, except that path which follows Allah's Messenger؛ in totality." [*Ta'lim al-Din, p:182*]

Another Hadith condemns the fake spiritual pretenders as the Messenger؛ said, "In the later days, people will emerge who will deceptively acquire the world in exchange for their religion. They will wear the skins of sheep and their tongues will be sweeter than sugar, while in their hearts they will be wolves. Allah؛ says, 'Are these people deluded by Me? Or are they displaying their audacity against Me? I take an oath on Myself; I will subject them to tribulation which leave even the most forbearing among them in trauma." [Tirmidhi:2404]

The Hadith clearly warns about the fake spiritual pretenders; and the tribulation to be faced, in case one deviates from the true path of Shariáh. Then, there are many pretenders out there who claim to be Shaykh and would say that they have reached a station where they do not need to perform Salah or follow other Islamic injunctions. Junayd al-Baghdadi؛ was once told about a group who claimed that they had arrived to a state in which Islamic injunctions as *Salah* or fasting no longer applied to them. Junaid؛ said, 'Indeed! They have arrived, but to Hell.'[9]

Some ignorant, so-called *Peer* proclaim that they are the disciples of the great masters and deem themselves above the Shariáh requirements and compliance as if being a disciple of a great master is the means for redemption.

Their misunderstanding is apparent from the Hadith where someone even in the service of the Beloved Prophetﷺ was retributed for the sin. If one does not follow Shariáh and the rulings of Shariáh, the association to a great Shaykh would not allow deliverance from the hellfire. The Hadith validates the futility of Bayá which does not follow practice. It is narrated that a man named Kirkirah was in charge of the Messenger's ﷺ baggage. When he died, the Beloved Prophetﷺ said, *"He has gone to the Fire."* When the Companions looked at the man's possessions, they found a cloak he had misappropriated from the spoils of war. [Bukhari 3704]

At times people believe that the Sufi masters know everything and can foretell future. The Last Prophetﷺ was given the most knowledge, yet he admitted to not knowing what was to come. Therefore, those who hold such beliefs that there are people who can foretell everything about future are in great error. The absurdity of this belief is apparent from the Hadith narrated by Jabir﷛ as part of a lengthy narration concerning the farewell Hajj, that Allah's Last Prophetﷺ said, "If I had known then what I know now, I would not have brought these animals with me for sacrifice." [Bukhari 1651, Muslim 1216]

There are those who fool innocent people telling them of their mystical exertions which are actually *'istidraj'* from Satan, Izz ibn Abd al-Salam﷛, a Shafi'i scholar and mujtahid, writes, "If one sees someone who can fly through the air, walk on water, or inform one of the unseens, but who contravenes the Sacred Law or Shariáh by committing an unlawful act without an extenuating circumstance that legally excuses it, or who neglects an obligatory act without lawful reason, one should know that such a person is a devil whom Allahﷻ has placed as a temptation to the ignorant. Nor is it far-fetched that such a person should be one of the means by which Allahﷻ chooses to lead men astray, for the Antichrist (al-Dajjal) will bring the dead to life and make the living die, all as a temptation and affliction to those who would be misled."

Mujaddid Alf Thaniﷺ reiterated, "This world is the ground for the Hereafter. His is a sad case who did not plant, but rather neglected his land, wasting away the seeds of his deeds. You should know that the land can be wasted away in two ways: Firstly, by not laying any seed at all or by sowing the wrong and rotten seeds. In comparison, this second wasting is more harmful than the first one. And, wrong and rotten seed consists in entering into bay`a (pledge) with an imperfect Peer. An imperfect peer suffers from greed and follows evil desires. He will pass these traits to his disciples. He himself is misguided and can only misguide others. In contrast, an accomplished Shaykh is like elixir, his sight is medicine and his talk is cure."[10]

Reality of the Pledge (Bayá)

In *Tasawwuf*, Bayá is an oath taken to the path of *Ihsan* with the connection of the heart to the Shaykh and the connection of the soul to the Awliya of the chain back to the Prophetﷺ. The basic principle within the Bayá is to keep the religion above the worldly affairs, consider Shariáh superior to the intellect and follow the Will of Allahﷻ. Bayá in Tasawwuf is not an ordinary pledge, it is a pledge to follow Shariáh, therefore, one must find someone who is fully adherent to Shariáh and capable of leading. Bayá is a pledge hence, spoken words are enough, however, it is a Sunnah for men to offer their hands when taking Bayá with their Shaykh.

The Beloved Prophet ﷺ took pledge from the Companions on various occasions. On the occasion of *Hudaibiya*, the pledge was taken from the Companions to be steadfast and to have fortitude in battle, Allah ﷻ approved of the pledge as;

"Indeed those who pledge allegiance to you[Muhammad ﷺ]- they are actually pledging to Allah. The hand of Allah is over their hands.

[Qurán, Surah Fath 48:10]

Some object that the pledge was only taken for the purpose of being steadfast in the war, but that is not true. There were various other occasions when the pledge was taken from the Companions for matters other than war. It is narrated that Awf bin Malik ؓ said, "We were in the company of the Messenger ﷺ nine, eight or seven of us, when Allah's Messenger ﷺ said, 'Will you not pledge your allegiance to the Allah's Messenger ﷺ?' As we had only recently pledged our allegiance to him, we said, 'We have already pledged ourselves to you, O Messenger of Allah ﷺ!' Yet again, he asked us, 'Will you not pledge yourselves to the Messenger of Allah?' So, we extended our hands and said, 'O Allah's Messenger ﷺ! To what shall we pledge?' He replied, 'That you worship Allah ﷻ and not associate anything with Him, that you perform the five daily prayers, and that you hear and obey.' Then, he whispered something to us. He said, 'And do not ask anyone for anything.' Since then, I have witnessed those men that even if they drop their whips [while mounted] would not even ask anyone to hand it up to them.' [Muslim 1043]

The above Hadith also indicates how the Companions followed the words of the Beloved Prophet ﷺ. The condition which was described in the later part of the Hadith prohibiting them from asking anyone, intended to prohibit the Companions to ask for anything that belonged to others.

Yet the Companions followed the words of the Beloved Prophetﷺ in the intended and the literal meanings and never asked for anything even if that belonged to them.

Allah's Last Prophetﷺ was Allah's vicegerent and everything he did was by the will of Allahﷻ. After him the Companions were the guiding stars and they did the same and after them the righteous men followed in their footsteps. Another Hadith verifies the importance of Bayá where the Beloved Prophetﷺ took a pledge from a group of his Companions and said, "Give me your pledge that you will not ascribe partners to Allahﷻ and that you will not steal." [Bukhari:18, Muslim:1709, Tirmidhi:1439]

The Companions took the pledge at the occasions of the battles, to testify Allahﷻ, to be righteous, to obey in everything good or not to die except firmly upon Islam. Not only are there examples of pledge for performing good deed but there are also examples of taking the pledge for forbiddance as mentioned in the Hadith. Therefore, Bayá or taking the pledge is a Sunnah. Mowlana Ashraf Ali ؒ, the great scholar explains that the type of Bayá taken by Sufis, which is a pledge to adhere to Shariáh and perform all the deeds and practices in accordance with Qurán and Sunnah is often criticized.

According to these critics, Bayá is a *Bidá* or a blameworthy innovation, not supported by Qurán or Hadith. The only Bayá the critics recognize is the one for the conversion to Islam or for Jihad, however in the above Hadith the type of Bayá is spiritual because the one who performed the Bayá were the Companions who already pledged to Islam. Therefore, this was not the Bayá for Islam, it was neither a Bayá for Jihad as obvious from the text. Rather, it was a Bayá to obey certain injunctions and to perform certain practices, therefore it is

The Guide-Shaykh

obvious that the Bayá in *Tasawwuf* does have its precedent in the Sunnah."[11]

There are also examples of pledge taken from the women as Qurán mentions;

"O Prophet ﷺ, when the believing women come to you pledging to you that they will not associate anything with Allah, nor will they steal, nor will they fornicate, nor will they kill their children, nor will they bring forth a slander they have invented between their arms and legs, nor will they disobey you in what is right-then accept their pledge and seek forgiveness for them from Allah. Indeed, Allah is Forgiving and Merciful."

[Qurán, al Mumtahinah 60:12]

Before the Beloved Prophet ﷺ migrated to Madinah, women from Madinah came to Makkah to meet the Beloved Prophet ﷺ and the Beloved Prophet ﷺ took oath from them. However, it is narrated by Sayedda Ayesha ؓ that, 'Never once in his life did Allah's Messenger ﷺ touch the hand of a woman who was not related to him. He took Bayá from them verbally. And when a woman pledged, he would then say to her, 'Go, I have accepted your pledge.' [Bukhari : 2713, Muslim : 1866]

No one is more chaste than the Beloved Prophet ﷺ and he was extremely cautious, therefore, one must follow in his footsteps. It is important that one who takes the pledge be pubescent and sane. It is narrated that a child was presented before the Prophet ﷺ so that he may take the pledge. The Prophet ﷺ patted his head and prayed for blessings for him and did not take the pledge from him.

Connection (Tálluq)

The knowledge of *Tasawwuf* has to be imparted from a living Shaykh and the connection is called '*Tálluq*', where the Shaykh not only ensures the transfer of knowledge but also the state. As a true teacher, the Shaykh helps to eliminate the blameworthy traits and helps attain the state or '*hal*' of perpetual remembrance. Often, people who learnt merely through books have the information but lack state or '*hal*' which comes with '*Tálluq*'. They may carry the burden of the blameworthy traits as pride or '*riya*' which only '*Tazkiyah*' through connection with a true Shaykh could eliminate.

It was Mowlana Rumi's meeting with the dervish Shams-e Tabrizi that completely transformed his life, from an accomplished teacher and jurist to an ascetic. It is narrated in Haji Bektash Veli's book, "Makalat", that a dervish in a black suit, covered from head to toe, named Shams Tabrizi came to the famous inn of Sugar Merchants of Konya. He was enlightened that he would find a man in Konya who could take his state or *hal*. Eventually, he found Rumi, sitting next to a large stack of books, teaching his students.

Shams Tabrizi, asked him, "What are you doing?" Rumi scoffingly replied, "Something you cannot understand, this is the knowledge of '*Qaal (Qurán and the Hadith)*'." Upon that, Shams Tabrizi threw the stack of books in a nearby pond which Rumi hastily salvaged. To his surprise the books were all dry, Rumi then asked Shams, "What is this?" To which Shams replied, "Mowlana! This is what you cannot comprehend, this is the knowledge of *hal(state)*."[1213]

Rumi requested Shaykh Sham-e Tabrizi to take him as a disciple and it was after that *Tálluq,* Rumi wrote the famous Mathnavi. As he said,

Maulvi Hargiz Na Shud Maula-e-Rum

(Maulvi could never be Maula-e-Rum)

Ta Ghulam E Shams Tabraizi Na Shud

(Had he not devoted himself to Shams-e-Tabriz)

As any other discipline of *Deen*, the way of *Tasawwuf* is to be learnt from someone who has the unbroken line of teachers extending back to the Prophet. Those who claim to be Sufis without a lineage of teachers up to the Beloved Prophet are pretenders, as *Tasawwuf* is a discipline like any other discipline of religion and the source of all religious knowledge is the Prophet. University qualifications or research may show the attainment of that person for the purpose of a degree but cannot be substituted for the purpose of *ilm* or true knowledge as it is not authenticated by the unbroken chain.

These are challenging times, as there are many who have not done the traditional studies of the religion, but merely by gathering information, claim to be scholars and misguide others. Our computers have all sorts of information but does that imply that we should take the computer as our guide. For example, someone would not perform a heart surgery upon himself or anyone else just by gathering information from the a you tube video. One would obviously seek specialist advice from a medical specialist and get treated.

It is however, quite frightening that people trust their own judgement or gather information over the internet for the matters relating to *Iman*. It is the matter of one's *Iman*, therefore, one should be very careful as the information gathered from such sources can be incorrect and unreliable, thus misguiding. As the Prophetﷺ said, 'Truly, Allah does not remove Sacred Knowledge by taking it away from people, but rather by taking back the souls of Islamic scholars(death), until, when He has not left a single scholar, the people take the ignorant as leaders, who are asked for and give Islamic legal opinion without knowledge, misguided and misguiding.' [Bukahri, 1.36:100]

The discipline of *Tasawwuf* is realised by being committed to someone who has been through the process and holds the criteria of a true guide. For the true state or *'hal'* to be acquired one needs to have been in connection (*Tálluq'*) with a living teacher for prolonged period of time, it cannot be achieved in a sitting. The state of the teacher affects the seeker in either way; if the teacher knows the taste of the Divine Love, he would be able to take the seeker through the journey otherwise, if the teacher himself has not trudged the path, his state of the heart would affect the seeker and they would both remain lost.

Same goes for the modern Sufis who claim to be authorities on *Tasawwuf* or so-called Sufism by reading books; they are those who stand at the ridge without any knowledge of the worlds beyond. The writers may write long passages, but it is the one who drinks from the fountain that knows the taste of the Divine Love. The books are the great source of information but it is when combined with *Tálluq"* that the information becomes knowledge and when this knowledge is imparted to others, it becomes worthwhile and affects the heart. The scholars say that a book written on worldly matters by someone whose heart is pure, may be more beneficial as compared to a book written on religious matters by someone whose heart is still engulfed in darkness, as the state of the writer affects the state of the reader.

Shaykh Abdul Qadir Gilaniﷺ, Shaykh Ahmad Sirhindiﷺ and many others great scholars who by the special blessings of Allahﷻ, were born 'Wali'(friend of Allahﷻ) are known for their works on Islamic Jurisprudence and Fiqh, maintained *'tálluq'* with a Shaykh. This is *tálluq* which produces scholars who are true heirs of the Prophetﷺ that their students follow them in knowledge and character and succeed to bring a change.

The Beloved Prophetﷺ said, "Allahﷻ said, 'Those may be assured of My love who love each other for My sake, who sit with each other for My sake, who visit each other for My sake and who spend on one another for My sake.'" [Muwatta Imam Malik: 1710]

The reference is made to the virtues of the company of those who meet each other for the sake of Allahﷻ as the disciple and the Shaykh or the fellow disciples. Abu Dharr﷜ once asked Allah's Prophetﷺ, "O Allah's Prophetﷺ! What about someone who really loves a certain group but is unable to do what they do?" The Beloved Prophet ﷺ replied, "O Abu Dharr﷜! You will always be with those you love." [Abu Dawood:5126, Tirmidhi:2387]

The Hadith clearly indicates the virtue of those who love their teacher, quite often, a Shaykh would initiate a person who is lesser in spiritual developments, solely for the reason that he possesses the requisite desire. The disciples vary in their level of purity and *taqwa* but the true Shaykh guides them with his own example and through classical works of the scholars of the lineage. The readiness and enthusiasm with which the seeker absorbs and practice the teachings of the Shaykh will determine his progress and that is the key to the success in the path.

Communication (Raabta)

Raabta e Shaykh is the broad term used for attending the meetings of the Shaykh and informing him of the changes either good or bad in one's self. The disciples who live in the close vicinity are encouraged to visit their Shaykh for the weekly meetings and the ones living remotely should still visit him when they can. Another way of getting the benefit from the Shaykh is to travel with him or perform *Eitikaf* with him (Ritual retreat in the Mosque during last ten days of Ramadan). The extended period during the journey or *Eitikaf* gives one an opportunity to observe the routines of the Shaykh and through his example the disciple finds it easy to follow. It is worth noting that a true Shaykh always follows in the footsteps of Rasul Allahﷺ and ensures that the disciples do the same, as connecting them to the Prophetic Sunnah is the ultimate goal. Another benefit in attending the meetings or travelling with Shaykh gives the Shaykh an opportunity to observe the disciple and help him to overcome his shortcomings.

There is no substitute to *'tarbiya'* or training, *'tarbiya'* means the spiritual training by a Shaykh and this happens best when one attends the meetings of the Shaykh or listens to his words, whilst keeping him updated with his state. At times people take the pledge but never attend the meetings of the Shaykh neither do they listen to his words or inform him of his states, *tarbiya* cannot take place in this instance. It has been the tradition that the Shaykh organises lectures based on the books written by great Awliya as *Futuh ul-Ghaib* by Abdul Qadir Gilani رحمۃ or *Maktoobat Mujjadid Alf Thani* رحمۃ. These lessons benefit the seeker when taught by his own Shaykh.

Generally, a disciple would visit the Shaykh, listen to his words, take benefit and apply it to his life and follow up with

The Guide-Shaykh

him. At times one may be bound by distance or time and cannot be in the presence of one's Shaykh hence, the question arises if that person can benefit from his Shaykh from distance. The answer is that the *nur* or light of the Shaykh's teachings would reach the disciple if he is ready to accept it, even at a distance. Therefore, one shall not be disheartened as someone who lives far from the Shaykh may be the closest to his heart.

In past, when travelling was hard and the disciples lived far from their Shaykh, letters were the common mode of communication. In this regard the letters of Mujaddid Alf Thaniﷺ written to his disciples are the perfect example. These letters show great care and attention (*tawajjuh*) towards his disciples and his focused guidance for them in all matters worldly and religious.

Letters were written to disciples who lived away from Mujaddidﷺ but they still carry the light or *'nur'* of his words to the extent that they are still read and used as a great reference to *Tasawwuf*. Nowadays, technology has made it easier to save and spread the words of the Shaykh making it accessible to the ones not living in the vicinity of the Shaykh. Though, the importance of the company of the Shaykh cannot be denied, it has its own profound benefits, but the intent can be gathered from his words, may it be heard or read.

Allah'sﷻ Divine concern or *inaya* has its own ways, the best way prescribed is still the traditional way of listening to the words of Shaykh and keeping him informed of one's *ahwal* or states. Quite often, by the Divine Blessing of Allahﷻ, the seeker may have a question in mind and would find answer in the words of his Shaykh without even posing a question. Listening to the lectures of one's own Shaykh is the most beneficial form of getting the benefit, no doubt, Jalaul Din Rumiﷺ began the Mathnavi with the word, 'Listen'.[14]

Etiquettes with the Shaykh (Adab)

Tariqa entails *'adab'* meaning respect- respect for the Word of Allahﷻ, and following it in every aspect of life, respect for Allah's Messengerﷺ and following him in every deed, respect for the Companions and the ones who followed in their footsteps. A true Shaykh is an emissary, connecting one to the Prophetﷺ and ensuring that the seeker follows the Prophetﷺ in every aspect of his life. The seeker would benefit from the Shaykh only if he has the respect for the Shaykh, it is a connection between hearts and the knowledge is absorbed by the soul(*ruh*). If the seeker's heart is doubtful, then the benefit and the flow of the knowledge can be restricted.

It is narrated that while Prophetﷺ was delivering the Friday sermon, a man came and stood at the doorway of the Masjid, when the Prophetﷺ told him to sit down, he immediately complied and sat on the spot. Of course, the Beloved Prophetﷺ intended him to come inside and listen, but the Companion out of love and respect obeyed the words. The respect and obedience is of utmost importance for anyone who hopes to benefit spiritually from a true Shaykh.

Adab means respect but in *Tasawwuf* the word *adab* has a broader meaning which encompasses all the aspects of the life of the seeker, respect for Allah's word, respect for Sunnah, respect for one's Shaykh. It is respect which initiates the seeker and takes him to know the Divine. It initiates the connection which bears the fruit on the path, a common saying in Persian is "*Ba adab ba naseeb, bay adab bay naseeb*" meaning the one who is respectful is blessed and the disrespectful is condemned. This is true in all aspects but for the disciple *adab* is crucial.

The Guide-Shaykh

Love for one's Shaykh is also part of *adab* as in the Hadith narrated by Abu Musa ؓ who stated, "Allah's Prophet ﷺ said to me, 'If only you had seen me this morning as I listened to your recitation [of the Qur'an]! Surely, you have been granted a musical instrument from among the musical instruments of the family of Dawood!' and I said, "By Allah! Had I known that you were listening to my recitation, I would have adorned it!" [Abu Ya'la in his Musnad, as quoted in Fath al-Bari: 9:114]

The Hadith above clearly indicates the approval to love the Shaykh for the sake of Allah ﷻ. To seek the pleasure of the Shaykh is like seeking the pleasure of the Almighty, reason being that the Shaykh's pleasure is actually a means to the pleasure of Allah ﷻ. The mission of the Shaykh is to connect the seeker to Allah ﷻ. The intention of the true Shaykh is that the seeker follows the Beloved Prophet and achieve the pleasure *'Rida'* of Allah ﷻ. The relevant maxim here is *'effort expended along the way is effort expended towards achieving the objective.'*

The seeker cannot reach his destination by following the path of spirituality on his own accord. It is the duty of the Shaykh to connect the seeker with Allah ﷻ, therefore, the seeker must accept the Shaykh as his teacher and guide and follow him with true integrity. Respect and honour for the Shaykh and his family is important to achieve success on the path of spirituality. The following are some of the basics that the seeker should abide by in regards to etiquettes with his Shaykh. Junaid Baghdadi ؒ said, "The one who treads this path without a true teacher will only mislead himself and others. Whosoever disrespects the spiritual Shaykh, Allah ﷻ will make him detestable amongst people." The seekers who stay connected with the Shaykh and listen to his advice, even if they lack capacity, would reach the station of Divine Love.

The seekers should try to read the book 'Adab al-Mardiyya', written by Shaykh Muhmmad al-Buzaydi ﷺ. Some of the manners include;

> Show the Shaykh respect and politeness due to him as a teacher and guide. One must stay loyal and honour the Shaykh even in his absence. It is ill-bred for disciples to discuss another Shaykh of the path in front of the Shaykh. If someone talks ill of one's Shaykh, the disciple must rebut him.
>
> Listen carefully and carry out his instructions to the best of the capability. The seeker should consult his Shaykh about major life decisions such as marriage, travel and profession. The seeker should follow the Shaykh's advice in worldly and spiritual matters. If the Shaykh's advice is against the seeker's wish, one should still follow and trust the wisdom of his Shaykh. One must not question the Shaykh about the positive or the negative aspects of the advice or present his opinion to the Shaykh. The blessings of the true Shaykh would emanate for the seeker and Allah ﷻ would still bless the seeker for his intentions. The seeker must acknowledge every word of his Shaykh as true. If the seeker is unable to comprehend the meanings, then he must consider it as his own flaw.
>
> One must attend the gatherings of the Shaykh with true integrity. It is incumbent for the seekers living in the same city to attend the gatherings regularly. Hazrat Shaykh Yousuf Aja'mi ﷺ said, "The seeker who missed his Shaykh's gathering without a valid excuse shall condemn himself in front of his brothers in oath." In case the seeker lives in another country or city, still an effort is to be made to visit the Shaykh when possible. Nowadays, recordings may be available of the Shaykh's lecture, so

one must listen to those recordings if unable to attend the gatherings due to distance. Quite Often a sincere disciple may find answers to his questions without planning. The seekers who are blessed to be in the close proximity of their Shaykh, they must not consider themselves superior. Suhaib Roomi🕊 and Salman Farsi🕊 came from far off lands and were blessed whereas, Abu Jahal and Abu Lahab, even being close to the Prophetﷺ, were profane.

The seeker must conduct at his best in the presence of the Shaykh. Abu Ali Daqaq🕊 said, "If the seeker is dissident, the pledge is broken, therefore, he must renew his pledge with the Shaykh."

One must be attentive towards his Shaykh, neither should he indulge in conversation with others nor occupy himself with any other matter during attendance with his Shaykh. The seeker must refrain from talking in the presence of his Shaykh. Even if the Shaykh is quiet, the seeker's heart still benefits from the Shaykh. The seeker must not perform Dhikr or optional prayers around his Shaykh without his prior permission. The time spent in Shaykh's company is to observe him and follow the Shaykh in all matters e.g., dressing, ibadah.

The seeker must not discuss his spiritual matters with anyone except for his own Shaykh.

The seeker shall never be jealous or apprehensive of his brother in pledge, otherwise the seeker would lose his way. Shaykh Abdur Rahman🕊 said, "The one who finds himself resentful towards his Shaykh or his brothers in oath, must know that Allahﷻ resents him."

The seeker must honour the teachers and family of the Shaykh.

Even if the Shaykh looks pleased, the seeker must not

cross his limits and remain obedient. One must know that he is being assessed.

The seeker shall never consider his obligation fulfilled, even if he is utterly devoted and spends thousands; otherwise, he will lose his path.

Just as it is inappropriate to associate other than one's own father, it is inappropriate to associate with anyone other than one's own Shaykh. The seeker must believe that the Shaykh is the source of blessing from Allahﷻ. Shaykh Abdul Qadir Gilaniﷺ said, "The one who does not believe in his Shaykh will never succeed". The seeker must appreciate the spirituality of the Shaykh and not be concerned about the physical aspects. One shall not depend on the spirituality of his forefathers, as it is not inherited; it has to be earned through constant desire and effort.

The seeker must not begrudge his Shaykh. Even if the Shaykh seems indignant, the seeker must know that the *Mashaikh* do not avert a Muslim for a moment. The Shaykh is a guide to the seeker and does everything in his best interest. If the Shaykh is angry, the seeker should apologize, even if the seeker is unaware of his wrongdoing. The seeker shall not consider his apparent *Ibadah* better than his Shaykh's *Ibadah*. He must know that one day of the Shaykh's *Ibadah* is better than a thousand days of his own *Ibadah*. One should consider Shaykh's sleep superior to his own *Ibadah*.

Hazrat Ali bin Wa'faﷺ, once said that the Shaykh is like a mirror to the seeker. Once a seeker said to Hazrat Bayazeed Bustamiﷺ, "My teacher! Last night in my dream, I saw your face as a pig." Hazrat replied, "Son! I am your mirror. Once you purify your inner self from all the characteristics of a pig and look at me, you will see your own true face."

The seeker should honor and respect Shaykh's wife as his mother, as per Qur'an, "His wives are their mothers"

If the Shaykh awards something for example, cap, gown, shoes, *siwak* etc. the seeker must not use that for commercial purposes as these gifts have the blessings from Shaykh.

If by the will of Allahﷻ, a seeker reaches the same status as of his Shaykh, he must still honor his Shaykh as it was due to his Shaykh's blessings that the seeker reached the subject status.

Syed Ali bin Wa'fa؇ said, "Beware if the Shaykh is gracious and be glad if the Shaykh is harsh". When the Shaykh is gracious it can still be a trial and when Shaykh is harsh it is for the best interest of the seeker.

The seeker shall not expect his Shaykh to come to him. Once a disciple of Syed Ali؇ assumed that his Shaykh should visit him to acknowledge his arrival from Hajj. As his wish was not granted, he begrudged his Shaykh, therefore, lost his spirituality.

Syed Ali Khawas؇ said, "One must consider his Shaykh's friends as his friends and his Shaykh's enemies as his own enemies, otherwise Satan would overcome him."

The seeker must connect his heart towards his Shaykh and associate any spirituality towards him. Even, if the blessings were received from another Shaykh, he should still associate those towards his own Shaykh; otherwise, it will be a grave mistake. If the Shaykh ordains the seeker to withhold from the company of a particular scholar, the seeker must cease, otherwise, he will be at a loss. The seeker must not visit any other scholar even if he is Shaykh's friend, without the prior permission of his Shaykh, as it can cause distraction. If the Shaykh does not respond to a visiting Shaykh, then the seeker must not respond either as it would be harmful for the seeker.

If the seeker wishes to visit the Shaykh, he must make a prior appointment. If for any reason, the seeker is unable to make it to his appointed time; he must inform the Shaykh and not keep him waiting. The seeker must leave as and when the Shaykh indicates so. At times, the Shaykh may not say it verbally, but the seeker must understand that the Shaykh has other commitments, therefore, beg leave once his intended discussion is finished. During a visit to the Shaykh, the seeker must ensure that he does not extend his visit to an unreasonable time.

While reporting the spiritual matters, the seeker must be concise. Do remember that the Shaykh has traversed the path already and fully understands your spiritual matters. The Shaykh has the appointment from Allahﷻ and his reward is due from Allahﷻ. As a seeker one cannot repay for the effort and time the Shaykh spends in his training. Therefore, the seeker must pray for his Shaykh, for his well-being, health and *Iman*. One must pray for all the *Mashaikh* of the Silsila that Allahﷻ raise their spiritual degrees.[15]

Attention (Tawajjuh)

The Beloved Prophetﷺ was in the cave of Hira when Gabrielﷺ came and asked him to recite. Allah's Messengerﷺ said, *"I cannot recite."*

Gabrielﷺ embraced the Beloved Prophetﷺ and pressed his chest against him, declaring *"Recite."*

The Beloved Prophetﷺ replied, *"I cannot."* For the third time Gabriel seized the Beloved Prophetﷺ and said, *"Recite."*

The Beloved Prophetﷺ then recited the message of Allah:

"Recite in the name of your Sustainer who created. He created the human being from an embryo. Recite! Your Lord is the most Generous. He taught by the Pen, teaching humans what they did not know."

[Qur'an, al Alaq 96:1-5]

The scholars consider that Gibrael's three embraces during the first revelation to the Beloved Prophetﷺ was a form of transmission of knowledge from Allah. According to Hadith, one day the Beloved Prophetﷺ was holding Umar's and, when Umar said to him, "O Allah's Apostleﷺ! You are dearer to me than everything except my own self." The Prophetﷺ said, "No, by Him in whose hand my soul is, [you will not have complete faith] until I am dearer to you than your own self." Then, Umar said to him, "However, now by Allah, you are dearer to me than my own self." The Prophetﷺ said, "Now, O 'Umar, [now you are a believer]." [Bukhari : 6632]

The concept of *tawajjuh* or attention can be validated through Hadith as narrated by Alja bin Ka'b, "When I was in the masjid, a man came in and started his prayers. He recited the Qur'an in a manner that appeared incorrect to me. Then, another man came in and recited Qur'an in yet another way. I went to Allah's Messengerﷺ and told him how these people had recited the Qur'an. Allah's Messengerﷺ asked both men to recite Qur'an and they did. Allah's Messengerﷺ then said that both were right. My heart was filled with evil doubt that was even stronger than that of the period of ignorance (*jahiliyya*).

The Guide-Shaykh

When the Beloved Prophetﷺ saw my state, he struck my breast with his hand. I started perspiring profusely and my state of fear and awe was such that I felt I was witnessing Allahﷻ." [Muslim: 820]

It was narrated that Ali؇ said, "Allah's Messengerﷺ sent me to Yemen. I said: 'O Allah's Messengerﷺ! you are sending me to judge between them while I am a young man, and I do not know how to judge.' He struck me on the chest with his hand and said, 'O Allah! Guide his heart and make his tongue steadfast.' And after that I never doubted in passing judgment between two people." [Sunan Ibn Majah 2310] There are many other occurrences to prove the effects of spiritual transmission, however, it is true that spiritual transmission is not the real source of the effect, the attainment of the final goal is only possible with Allah'sﷻ Grace and guidance and by following the Sunnah and the company of the pious. As mentioned in Qur'an:

> "You do not guide those whom you like, but Allah guides those whom He will." [Qur'an, al Qasas 28:56).

It has been the way of *Tasawwuf* to eschew concern with worldly affairs and critics label the Sufis as unproductive, yet Allahﷻ declares that He is the provider and Sustainer, so once the servant submits himself to Allah'sﷻ worship, Allahﷻ fills his heart with virtue and the seeker finds peace, as mentioned in Qurán:

> 'No doubt, by the remembrance of Allah the hearts find peace."
>
> [Qurán, ar Raád 13:28]

It is narrated that the Prophetﷺ recited the verse; "Whomsoever Allahﷻ wills to guide, He expands his breast for Islam.", he commented, "When light enters the breast it expands." The Companions asked, "O Allah's Messengerﷺ!

Is there a way to identify this?" Allah's Messenger ﷺ replied, "Yes, avoidance of the abode of deception [this world], attention to the abode of eternity and preparation for death before its descent." [Shuáb al Iman:10552-Bayhaqi]

The Hadith refers to the state of *Iman* and *Ihsan*, the spiritual excellence, where the worldly desires no longer cling to the heart and the seeker is focussed in the preparation of afterlife. So, the one who devotes himself in the acts of worshipping, is freed as his heart is filled with virtue and Divine Light, yet it is the heedless who would toil yet never be content with what he has. The Last Prophet ﷺ said, "Allah ﷻ says, 'O son of Adam! If you devote yourself to worshipping Me, I will fill your chest [to wealth and virtue] and I will render you free from desire. But if you do not do this, I will fill your two hands to overflow with toil, and I will not render you free from want." [Tirmidhi : 2466, Ibn e Majah: 4107]

Affinity (Nisbah)

The word *nisbah* means affinity or connection, in *Tasawwuf* it denotes the affinity between Allah ﷻ and the seeker. The essence is that the seeker should develop virtues to an extent that they should permeate through him. When those virtues become an essential part of one's being, it can be termed as spiritual affinity. The Companions and the ones who came after them used to obtain spiritual affinity through consistency and regularity in the performance of the obligatory prayers, voluntary prayers, *Dhikr*, recitation of the Qur'an, remembrance of death and the fear of the Day of Judgment. This led to the state of perpetual piety known as '*Taqwa*' and they guarded this affinity.

In Tasawwuf, it is the connection to Allah's Messenger ﷺ

and finally with Allah﷾, where every true Shaykh takes his disciples to follow in the steps of Allah's Messengerﷺ. Affinity is explained in the Hadith narrated by Anas﷛ that the Prophetﷺ stated as a part of a lengthy discourse, "No servant ever, approaches Allah﷾ in complete sincerity except that Allah﷾ makes the hearts of the believers incline towards that person with love and care; while Allah﷾ is the first to bring that person every manner of goodness."[16] [al-Haythami in Majam az zawaid 10/247]

As explained by the scholars there are two essentials for the heart to be filled with the Divine Light; constant remembrance and constant obedience. Under most conditions, this is said to be the essence of internal affinity and the above-mentioned Hadith alludes to this affinity. Another Hadith refers to the harmony between the souls as reported on the authority of Abu Hurairah﷛ that Allah's Messengerﷺ said, "The souls of humankind were [in the spirit world) as an army gathered. Then those who were acquainted with one another [in that world) will harmonise [in this world), and those who were unknown to one another they will fall into discord here." [Muslim and Abu Dawood]

In the first stage of affinity, love for Allah's Messengerﷺ is acquired and the heart is cleansed to a degree, but the connection is still weak, till the time the person stays in the company of the Shaykh, the connection is strong but upon leaving the company, the connection diminishes. The example of this connection is just like an electronic object working till the time the power is connected, this is the first stage called *Nisbat e Inekasi* or reflective affinity. Second stage is called *Nisbat e Ileqai* or inspirational affinity, where the connection is stronger than the first stage but needs to be revived to stay connected. The same example of an electronic object, but in this case the object can hold the charge for some time before it needs to be re charged. Third stage is the *Nisbat e Islahi* or reformative affinity where the connection becomes steady as a continuous flow.[17]

Fourth stage is the one which Abu Bakr﷠ had with Allah's Messengerﷺ which is called *Nisbat e Ittahadi or* associative affinity where the disciple becomes an image of his Shaykh in all aspects. It is mentioned in a Sahih Hadith in Bukhari as narrated by Abu Saíd Khudri﷠ that the Beloved Prophetﷺ addressed the people and said that Allahﷻ has given option to a slave to choose this world or what is with Him and the slave has chosen what is with Allahﷻ. Abu Bakr﷠ wept and the Companions were surprised as to what had caused him to cry as the Beloved Prophetﷺ mentioned a slave who had been offered a choice. Abu Saíd﷠ said that they later learnt (when the Beloved Prophetﷺ passed away) that the Beloved Prophetﷺ himself was the person who was given the choice and Abu Bakr﷠ cried as he understood what the Beloved Prophetﷺ meant. [Bukhari: 3654]

At the time of al-Hudaibiya, when Umar﷠ asked the question, Abu Bakr﷠ responded just as the Beloved Prophetﷺ did. [Bukhari: 2731,2732, Dawood:2765] This shows that Abu Bakr﷠ had the strongest affiliation with the Beloved Prophet ﷺ. It also proves that he was the best of the Companions, the most perfect of them and the most knowledgeable of them regarding Allahﷻ, His Messengerﷺ and His Religion and the strictest of them in conforming to it.[18]

Benefit from One's Shaykh (Tauheed e Matlab)

One has to remember that success is through one's own Shaykh and going from one Shaykh to another retards the progress of the seeker. This concept is called *Tauheed e Matlab* in *Tasawwuf*. One can visit another Shaykh only if permitted by his own Shaykh. The one who does not follow the rule of *Tauheed e Matlab* would struggle on the path. In any other discipline one has to first learn and then practice, but in *Tasawwuf*, one first practices and then gets the knowledge. Imam Al Ghazaliﷺ after spending time in the company of his Shaykh, wrote the masterpiece, *Ihya ul Uloom*.

As an example, usually there are many doctors in a town but a sick person would only consult one. It is important to honour and respect all the *Mashaikh* but for training and *Tazkiyah* (purification) one needs to follow his own Shaykh. It is a common observation that seekers may go and attend the assemblies of any Shaykh without prior permission of their own Shaykh. This leads to confusion and retards their journey. Once, a seeker in a chaotic condition came to Mowlana Maseehullahﷺ for help. Upon enquiry Mowlana Maseehullahﷺ found out that after establishing a *taálluq* with one Shaykh, he was following another. Mowlana Maseehullahﷺ told him that he had put himself in a grave situation.

The seeker who does not stay steadfast in his commitment to his own Shaykh and goes elsewhere without any justification is called '*Murtid fil Tariqa*'. There are conditions when a seeker can leave his Shaykh and perform Bayá with another. For instance, the Shaykh deviates from the path or the seeker, even though following all the instructions of the Shaykh, is not getting any improvement in his state, then the seeker may find another Shaykh. If the seeker is unable to get any *Fayd* or benefit from his own Shaykh, then he can discuss the issue with his Shaykh and with his permission find another Shaykh. In case, the

Shaykh passes away or the seeker finds out that the Shaykh does not follow Shariáh, then the seeker is to find another Shaykh.

Succession (Khilafah)

It is common for the Shaykh to nominate a successor or several successors from among the disciples to carry on the work of the order. The basis for this can be authenticated by the Hadith narrated by Jubayrﷺ who saw a woman went to the Last Prophetﷺ and spoke to him about something. When finished, the Beloved Prophetﷺ told her to come and talk to him again, to which the woman asked, 'And if I do not find you?' as if to refer to his passing away. The Prophet ﷺ replied, "If you do not find me, then go to Abu Bakrﷺ." [Bukhari 2659, Muslim 2386]

Many so-called Sufis appoint successors for the purpose of perpetuating their order, regardless of whether the appointed is worthy of the position. As is important to nominate a successor, it is equally important that the person be qualified for the role. It is quite a common that a son or a brother or a close relative is chosen. If it is because of the relation rather than the qualifications, then it jeopardises the sanctity of the order.

Women on the Path

Many a times, the question is posed, whether women can join the Tariqa and take the path of *Tasawwuf*? Allahﷻ mentions in Qurán:

"O Prophet ﷺ! When the believing women come to you, pledging to you that they will neither associate anything with Allahﷻ in worship, nor steal, nor fornicate, nor kill their children, nor falsely attribute illegitimate children to their husbands, nor disobey you in what is right, then accept their pledge, and ask Allah to forgive them. Surely Allah is All-Forgiving, Most Merciful.

[Qurán, al Mumtahanah 60:12]

The answer is simple, Báya or pledge is proven from Qurán and women have every right to take the path of *Tasawwuf* and reach the level of *'ihsan'*. However, women cannot be appointed as Shaykh. There have been many examples of great women who reached the level of excellence, for example Rabia Basriﷺ and the mother of Shaykh Abdul Qadir Gilaniﷺ. Even nowadays, there have been women who have taken the path and reached the stations of *Walaya*.

Islam encourages women to follow Shariáh and Sunnah as they are the ones who provide the foundations to the next generation of Muslims. Asmá bint Yazeedﷺ was a woman from the Ansar and an eminent Companion of the Beloved Prophetﷺ. She was distinguished for her knowledge and eloquence and known as the "Orator of all Women". Eighty-one Hadith are reported from her as a reliable narrator by Abu Dawood, Al-Tirmidhi, Al-Nassaie, Ibn Majah and other major scholars of Hadith. Asmáﷺ was also keen on *jihad*, joining Muslim armies on several occasions. She accompanied the Beloved Prophetﷺ on his expedition to the conquest of Makkah to Islam. She also participated in the great Battle of Al-Yarmook, against the Byzantines, during the reign of Umar ibn Al-Khattabﷺ. She is reported to have killed nine enemy soldiers, using the pole of her own tent.

One day, she came to the Beloved Prophetﷺ as he was sitting with a number of his Companions. Addressing him, she said: "Allah's Messengerﷺ! May both my parents be sacrificed for you (This was a traditional phrase of endearment used figuratively). I am an emissary from women to you. Allahﷻ has sent you as His Messenger to both men and women. We believe in you and your Lord. Yet we, women, are restricted, home bound. We stay in your (i.e., men's) homes, give you your pleasure and bear your children. You, men, have been favoured over us with attending Friday prayer and congregational prayers in mosques, visiting the sick, attending funerals, offering the pilgrimage repeatedly, and with what is more than that: fighting for Allah's cause.

When a man goes out intending pilgrimage or *jihad*, we take care of your property, sew your clothes and bring up your children for you. Do we have a share of your reward?"

The Beloved Prophet turned to his Companions asking them: "Have you ever heard a better statement by a woman than this one who is asking about matters of her faith?" They said: "We would not have thought that a woman would ever be able to express such meanings, as this lady." The Beloved Prophet turned to Asmá and said: "Listen woman! And inform other women who sent you that a woman who is a good wife, keen to please her husband and doing what he likes is equal to all that." As she left, she was glorifying Allah and repeating statements of His oneness. [19]

May Allah be pleased with Asmá who obtained this assurance from the Beloved Prophet that women are not lesser than men in faith or their reward. As a woman takes care of the future generation, she earns as much reward as man.

It is the practice of certain ignorant and imprudent men to hold the hands of women while taking Bayá. This is completely vunacceptable in Shariáh as it is prohibited to touch an unrelated woman. A female seeker is not supposed to perform Báya by holding the hand of the Shaykh, if the Shaykh is not her '*Mahram*' (related as per the Shariáh law). As already mentioned earlier, it is narrated by Sayedda Ayesha that, 'Never once in his life did Allah's Messenger touch the hand of a woman who was not related to him. He took Bayá from them verbally and when a woman pledged, he would then say to her, 'Go, I have accepted your pledge.' [Bukhari : 2713, Muslim : 1866]

When it comes to keeping *'Talluq'* meaning connection with the Shaykh, it has to be done according to the outlines defined by Shariáh. The female seekers can write to their Shaykh and seek guidance. In past, when travelling was hard and the disciples lived far from their Shaykh, the seekers used to get the benefit through letters. Nowadays, technology has made it easier to communicate with one's Shaykh. If women cannot attend the gatherings of the Shaykh, because there is no separate arrangement, they can still get the same benefit as men by listening to their Shaykh in their own homes. Although, for men it is important to attend the gathering of the Shaykh, however, for women the intent can be gathered from his words, whether heard or read. Those who sincerely listen to the words of their Shaykh and keep him informed of their states or *ahwal* are not deprived as Allah's ﷻ Divine concern or *inaya* has its own ways and women will not be deprived in any way.

Chapter Five

ARTICLES OF FAITH (AQAID)

The Hadith about *Iman* and *Ihsan* signifies that there are three levels in Deen: *Islam, Iman* and *Ihsan*, and every level consists of certain articles. There are six articles of faith that a person must uphold without any doubt in order to be a Muslim. He must believe in:

> Allah
> His Angels
> His Scriptures
> His Messengers
> The Day of Judgement
> Qadá and Qadr

Belief in Allah ﷻ

Allahﷻ is the proper Name, which applies to the true God Who exists necessarily by Himself, Who is named with all the excellent Divine names and qualified by all the attributes of perfection. Allahﷻ is One and Unique, He has neither a wife, nor a son, nor a partner, nor an equal. He is the sole Creator and the Lord of the Universe. Every creature has an inherent faith in His Oneness, Divinity and in the uniqueness of His attributes and names. His essence does not resemble the essences. He does not inherent in anything, nor does anything inherent in Him.

Articles of Faith (Aqaid)

"There is nothing that resembles Him." [Qurán ash Shurah 42:11]

He is the One, the Sole, and the Indivisible. He is Omnipotent and Omniscient. His knowledge comprehends everything, hidden and manifests in perfect manner. He is too great to be encompassed by the knowledge of His creatures. Nothing occurs in the visible or invisible worlds without His will, determination and decree. Whatever He wills takes place, and whatever He does not, will not take place. There is none to alter His commands or decrees. He is Merciful Whose mercy and justice encompasses everything and ensures smooth running of the Universe, in which nothing is out of order. There is none to share His domain and He stands in need of none of His creatures. He is the Lord (Rubb) of the worlds. The Beloved Prophet Muhammadﷺ said, "I am commanded to fight people until they profess that there is no true god except Allahﷻ, and Muhammadﷺ is the Messenger of Allahﷻ." [Riyad as-Salihin: 390]

The Hadith narrates that, "Every human is born with the primordial nature of acknowledging Allahﷻ as his Creator, but his parents either convert him into a Jew, a Christian or a Zoroastrian." [Bukhari 1359]

Whenever a believer is in need of Allahﷻ, or supplicates to Him, He responds to him. He is above the Seven Heavens, above His Arsh (Throne), above it in a manner which suits His grandeur and majesty. This means that all the legitimate acts of worship must be dedicated to Him alone. It also means that He is the sole Creator and maintainer of the universe and what is in it. Moreover, one must believe that He has the qualities and attributes of perfection. Imam Abu Ja'far at-Tahawi﷫ said, "We say regarding the belief in the Oneness of Allahﷻ, 'Allah is One without a partner.'" [*Al-Aqeedah at-Tahawiyah, p. 77, al-Maktab al-Islami*]

Oneness of Divinity or State *(Tawheed al-Uloohiya)* is to believe that Allah﷾ is the only God who has the right of *Uloohiyah* (Divinity) over all His creatures. There is absolutely no creature that has a Divine attribute. Allah﷾ has neither a son, nor a wife, nor a partner. He stands in need of none of His creatures. Allah﷾ says:

> "Say, the truth is that Allah is One. Allah is Besought of all, needing none, He neither begets nor was He begotten. Nor is there anyone who is comparable to Him." [Qurán, al Ikhlaas 112]

He is the only God Who deserves to be worshipped, hence, no devotional rite should be devoted to other than Allah﷾. Believing otherwise constitutes major *shirk* or polytheism.

The belief of Oneness of Allah's Lordship *(Tawheed ar-Ruboobiyah)* is the belief that Allah﷾ alone is the Rubb (Lord) of everything, that is, the Creator, the Provider, the Proprietor, the One in Whose hand is the disposal of all affairs. He has the power over all things. He gives life, causes death, grants honour, victory and defeat. The term Rubb is derived from the verb 'to rear' or 'to raise'. Since Allah﷾ is the One Who provides man with all his needs from His bounty hence, He rears his creatures and nourishes them with His favours and bounty.

In return, man should express his gratitude to Allah﷾ by worshipping Him alone, ascribing no partner to Him. *Tawheed ar-Ruboobiyah* is the central creed, yet upholding it without upholding the other two types of *Tawheed* is not enough to save one from Hell. The pagans at the time of the Prophet ﷺ, acknowledged that Allah﷾ is the Creator of the heavens and the earth, and the Provider, yet this would not benefit them or save them from Fire on the Day of Resurrection. As Allah﷾ mentions in Qurán:

Articles of Faith (Aqaid)

"If you should ask them who created Heaven and Earth, they would say: 'The Powerful, the Aware has created them'"

[Qurán, Az Zukhruf 43:9]

The belief of Oneness of Allah's Names and Attributes (*Tawheed al-Asma wus-Sifat*) is to believe that Allahﷻ enjoys unique Divine names and attributes with which Allahﷻ has named and qualified Himself, and those with which His Messengerﷺ named and qualified Him, without comparing Him with His creatures, and without suspending, distorting the meaning of His names and attributes:

"Lord of the heavens and the earth, and all that is between them, so worship Him (Alone) and be constant and patient in His worship. Do you know of any who is similar to Him?"

[Qurán, Maryam 19:65]

Tawheed ar-Ruboobiyah entails believing in *Tawheed al-Uloohiyah*, that is to believe in Allahﷻ as the Rubb, as described above and acknowledge by necessity, that no one deserves to be worshipped except Allahﷻ. Believing in the names and attributes of Allah is one of the articles of faith, i.e., believing in Allahﷻ, His *Ruboobiyah, Uloohiyah* and His names and attributes. Therefore, this article enjoys great significance in Islam. No one can worship Allahﷻ in a perfect manner until he knows the names and attributes of Allahﷻ, the Exalted and worships Him knowingly and properly. The Essence of Allahﷻ must have names and qualifications, because it is impossible for any essence to exist without attributes. That is why believing in Allah's names and attributes entails believing in Allahﷻ Himself. The attributes of Allahﷻ is a matter which belongs to the invisible world. This means that one must believe in them as they occur in the texts of the Qur'an and Hadith.

Articles of Faith (Aqaid)

The first rule is that all of the names of Allah ﷻ are absolutely fine and beautiful; for they connote the attributes of perfection and are free from every probability of defect.

Second rule is that the names of Allah ﷻ are both appellations and epithets; appellations in term of His essence, and epithets in term of the meaning and significance. As for the appellations, such as the Living, the Knower, the Hearer, the Seer, the Merciful, the Powerful, the Wise, are all names of One God, Allah ﷻ, the Exalted. While, in terms of epithets, each one of these names has a different significance than the others. That is, His name, 'the Living', has a different meaning than that of the Hearer, or the Knower.

The third rule is that the names of Allah ﷻ necessitate confirming the name as one of Allah's ﷻ; confirming the attribute that the name signifies as one of Allah's ﷻ and confirming the ruling of that name. For example, Allah ﷻ is Merciful, meaning that for sinners who repent to Him, He turns to them with mercy.

The fourth rule is that the names of Allah ﷻ are not subject to opinion. In other words, we cannot give Allah ﷻ names that He has neither named Himself with nor did His Messenger ﷺ named Him with.

The fifth rule is that the names of Allah ﷻ are not limited to a certain number. Although there is a Hadith which is related to the Beloved Prophet ﷺ mentioning that Allah ﷻ has 99 names, but this does not mean that He has no other names. Rather, there are names of Allah ﷻ that He has not mentioned in the Qurán, nor taught them to any of His creatures.

The sixth rule is that the names and attributes of Allah ﷻ

should not be suspended or distorted. This is common practice of the deviant sects where they either deny some of these names, their signification or rulings or hold them to resemble human attributes. Some even give Allahﷻ names that He has not named Himself with, as the Christians call Him 'The Father.'[1]

Belief in Angels

As a believer, one is to believe in the existence of the angels who are bodies of light and inhabit the heavens. The Beloved Prophetﷺ said: "There is no space of a hand span in the heaven but is occupied by an angel who is prostrating·" [Riyad as-Salihin:406]

Sayedda Ayeshaؓ reported that the Beloved Prophetﷺ said, "Angels were created from light, jinns were created from a smokeless flame of fire, and Adam was created from that which you have been told." [Riyad as-Salihin:1846]

Angels are honourable slaves of Allahﷻ who execute their duties perfectly without objection and celebrate His praise day and night without slackening. They are neither male nor female, nor do they eat or drink. They worship Allahﷻ continuously and celebrate His praise day and night without boredom or exhaustion. They execute certain chores and perform assigned tasks for example, registering the future of the foetus, assisting believers, recording man's deeds, death and grave duties, attending the circles of *Dhikr*, guarding Madinah and Allah knows the best. They are too many that only Allahﷻ knows their number. Allahﷻ mentions in Qurán;

> "No one knows the troops of your Rubb except He."
>
> [Qurán, al Mudhatthir 74:31]

Articles of Faith (Aqaid)

Just to give an idea, there is a place in the seventh Heaven called, *'al-Bait al- Ma'moor'* (The Continuously Occupied House) about which the Beloved Prophetﷺ said, "Seventy thousand angels enter it every day and never get the chance to re-enter it again." [Sunan ibne Majah 4077]

Belief in Scriptures

One of the fundamentals of faith is to firmly believe in the Messages with which Allahﷻ sent His Messengers and Prophets to mankind and to believe that they did convey the message to their respective nations. Allahﷻ destructed nations who accused their Prophets and Messengers of lying. Therefore, it is our duty to believe in all the Scriptures in general. Allahﷻ revealed to His Messengers as Torah which was in a written form, sent down to Musa۝ or sheets like those that were sent down to Abraham۝, verbal revelation like those which were revealed to Isma'eel۝, Is'haq۝ or Ya'qoob۝ or Qurán which was revealed in segments to Allah's Last Prophetﷺ.

It is incumbent to believe in every word that Allahﷻ revealed to His Prophets and Messengers. However, we believe that every latter Book abrogates the set of laws of the former one, partially or entirely. Based on this, the Qurán abrogates many laws that were contained in the Torah and the New Testament. Divine Scriptures are Torah which was revealed to Musa۝, *Zaboor* revealed to Dawood۝ (David), *Injeel* or the New Testament revealed to Eesa۝ and the Qurán. It is the word of Allahﷻ and His final Scripture, which He revealed to Muhammadﷺ to convey it to mankind at large and the principal source of the Islamic Shariáh law. Allahﷻ sent it down to make manifest everything and the means of guidance and mercy to both men and jinn. Since

Articles of Faith (Aqaid)

Qurán is the last Message, which Allahﷻ sent to mankind, He has promised to preserve it saying;

"Verily, it is We Who sent the Qur'an, and We will certainly be preserving it."

[Qurán, al Hijr 15:9]

Belief in the Messengers

Belief in the Messengers is the firm attestation that Allahﷻ did send a Messenger to every nation inviting them to worship Him alone. This belief entails denouncing all gods that are worshipped beside or to the exclusion of Allahﷻ. This entails believing that all Messengers were truthful and did convey the Message of Allahﷻ to their nation. Allahﷻ sent many Messengers whose number is known to Him alone. The mercy of Allah and His wisdom require sending Messengers to mankind inviting them to worship Him alone. He did not bring the creation into existence in vain, hence, believing in Allahﷻ entails believing in His Messengers, as mentioned in Qurán:

"Those who disbelieve in Allah and His Messengers and want to make distinction between Allahﷻ and His Messengers, saying, 'We believe in some and disbelieve in some,' and want to pursue a course in between. It is they who are the real infidels."

[Qurán, An Nisa 4:150-152]

It is obligatory for all Muslims to believe in all Prophets and Messengers, he who denies one of them, denies all. The first Prophet was Adam۩ and the first Messenger was Noah۩ and the last Prophet and Messenger is Muhammadﷺ. They were all humans and did not possess Divine qualities. Allahﷻ distinguished them by commissioning them as Prophets and Messengers and supported them with miracles. They had no knowledge of *al-ghaib* [the invisible world] except what was

Articles of Faith (Aqaid)

revealed to them thereof by Allahﷻ. They had no power to benefit or harm others nor did they have a share in the Dominion of Allahﷻ.

Believing in the Messengers of Allahﷻ means believing that they were trustworthy in what they conveyed to their people and that Allahﷻ protected them from what would hamper their mission. Amongst the Prophets, the most prominent and steadfast are Nuh؏, Abraham؏, Musa؏, Eesa؏ and the Last Prophet Muhammadﷺ. Every Prophet or Messenger before the Beloved Prophet Muhammadﷺ was sent to his own nation, but the Beloved Prophet Muhammadﷺ was sent to mankind at large. This implies that every human being must follow the Last Prophet Muhammadﷺ because he is sent to the whole mankind. As Allahﷻ mentions in Qurán;

"And We have not sent you but as mercy for all the worlds"

[Qurán, al Anbiya 21:107]

Allah took a covenant from all of them that they must believe in Muhammadﷺ and support him. As Allahﷻ mentions in Qurán;

"And when Allah took a covenant from the Prophets, saying, since I gave you the Book and the wisdom and then when a Messenger comes to you believing what is with you, you should believe in him and support him. Allah then said, 'Do you testify to this and accept this covenant?' They said, 'We agree and testify to it.' Then Heﷻ said to them, 'Therefore, bear witness and I do so along with you. [Qurán, Aal e Imran 3:81]

Every Messenger gave his people the glad tidings of Last Prophet'sﷺ advent as a Messenger:

"And when Eesa, son of Maryam, said, 'O Children of Israel! Surely, I am the Messenger of Allah to you, ascertaining that which is before me of the Torah, and giving glad tidings of a Messenger who will come after me, his name will be Ahmed."

[Qurán, As Saf 61:6]

Hence, whoever believed in Musaﷺ, until the advent of Eesaﷺ, it was mandatory on him to believe in Eesaﷺ and follow him. Since Muhammadﷺ is the last of the Messengers that Allahﷻ sent to mankind, it is binding on every human being to believe in him, adhere to his guidance, and love him. There is no Prophet or Messenger after him, as Allahﷻ mentions the prophethood of the Beloved Prophet Muhammadﷺ as the Seal of Prophets, meaning there would be no prophet after him;

"Muhammad is not the father of any of your men, but (he is) the Messenger of Allah, and the Seal of the Prophets: and Allah has full knowledge of all things."

[Qurán, al Ahzab 33:40]

The Beloved Prophetﷺ said, "I am Muhammadﷺ and I am Ahmadﷺ, and I am *al-Mahi* (the obliterator) by whom unbelief would be obliterated, and I am *Hashir* (the gatherer) at whose feet mankind will be gathered, and I am *'Aqib* (the last to come) after whom there will be no Prophet." [Sahih Muslim : 2354a]

In another narration the Beloved Prophetﷺ said, "My similitude in comparison with the Prophets before me is that of a man who has built a house nicely and beautifully, except for a place of one brick in a corner. People go about it and wonder at its beauty, but say: 'Would that this brick be put in its place!' So I am that brick, and I am the seal of the Prophets." (Bukhari : 3535)

The Beloved Prophetﷺ told the Ummah about the liars who would falsely claim to be prophets, "In my ummah there will be twenty-seven liars and dajjals, among whom are four women, (but) I am the seal of the Prophets, there is no prophet after me."[Musnad Ahmad ibn Hanbal:22747; at-Tabarani, Mújam al-Awsat: 5596, Mújam al-Kabir:2957; at-Tahawi, Mushkil al-Athar:2493]

None of Allah's Messengers or Prophets claimed to be god or semi-god. Allahﷻ mentions in Qurán:

> "Allah has not taken a son for Himself, nor is there a god with Him. Otherwise, each god would have taken away what he creates, and some of them would surely have nominated over the others. Allah is above all what they attribute to Him."
>
> [Qurán, al Mominun 23:91]

As Muslims we believe in all of the Prophets and Messengers of Allahﷻ and accept Eesaﷺ as a Messenger and slave of Allahﷻ. Allahﷻ describes Eesaﷺ as:

> "He is only a slave whom We have graced, and made him an example for the Children of Israel."
>
> [Qurán, al Zukhruf 43:59]

We as Muslims do not believe in Trinity or Eesaﷺ as the son of God, even though he was born of a virgin, without a father. Islam rejects any idea of Eesaﷺ being a son of God, hypothesis of God or incarnate. Allahﷻ mentions his birth in Qurán:

> "O people of the Scripture (Christians)! Do not exceed the limits in your religion, nor say of Allah aught but the truth. The Messiah 'Eesa (Jesus), son of Maryam (Mary), was (no more than) a Messenger of Allah and His Word, ("Be!" - and he was) which He bestowed on Maryam (Mary) and a spirit (Ruh) created by Him; so believe in Allah and His Messengers. Say not: "Three (trinity)!" Cease! (it is) better for you. For Allah is (the only) One Ilah (God), Glory be to Him (Far Exalted is He) above having a son. To Him belongs all that is in the heavens and all that is in the earth. And Allah is All-Sufficient as a Disposer of affairs."
>
> [Qurán, an Nisa 4:171]

Eesaﷺ did not die on the cross, instead Allahﷻ raised him up to heavens and someone else was crucified. As Qurán mentions:

"They neither killed him, nor crucified him, it appeared so to them. Rather, He took him up to Him. Allah is ever Mighty, Wise."

[Qurán, an Nisa 4:157-158]

Eesa﷩ will come down to earth at the end of time as a major sign of the Final Hour. There are many authentic Prophetic traditions and rulings in Qurán regarding Eesa's﷩ return to earth. As Allahﷻ mentions:

"And verily, he is a sign of the Final Hour."

[Qurán, az Zukhruf 43:61]

It is reported from Jabir bin Abdullah﷛ that the Beloved Prophetﷺ said, "A section of my people will not cease fighting for the Truth and will prevail till the Day of Resurrection. Jesus, son of Mary would then descend and their (Muslims') commander would invite him to come and lead them in prayer, but he would say: 'No, some amongst you are commanders over some (amongst you). This is the honour from Allah for this Ummah.'" [Sahih Muslim : 156]

Belief in the Day of Judgement

As a Muslim one should firmly believe in the truth about the events of death, questioning in the grave, resurrection, the Assembly, the Reckoning, the Bridge over Hell, the Scale, Jannah, Hell and the other events regarding the Day of Judgement. It was narrated that the Beloved Prophetﷺ used to seek refuge with Allahﷻ from the torment of the grave and the trial of the Dajjal, and he said: *"You will be tested in your graves."* [Sunan an-Nasa'i : 2065]

It is only Allahﷻ Who knows the timing of the Final Hour as Qurán mentions;

"People ask you concerning the Final Hour. Say to them, 'The information about it is kept with Allah alone. What do you know? It may be forthcoming."

[Qurán, al Ahzaab 33:63]

There are many minor and major signs of the Final Hour. The minor signs are the advent of the Beloved Prophet Muhammadﷺ, the fire which will erupt in the Hijaz Province, contraction of time, speaking of inanimate things and animals, the competing of the shepherds in erecting tall buildings, vain glory of people over building fancy mosques, prevalence of commotion, excessive murders and prevalence of fornication. The major signs include the advent of the Dajjal (Pseudo-Messiah), an impostor who would claim to be god whose followers will be mostly Jews.

This would be a time of great trial for the believers as he could bring rain and make the earth produce. Then, there would be the descent of Eesa؈ (Jesus) from the heaven who would kill Dajjal. There are other signs as indicated by the Beloved Prophetﷺ, "The Final Hour will not come to pass until you witness ten signs of which are, the rising of the sun from the West, the smoke, the emergence of the Beast from the earth, the appearance of *Yajuj Majuj*, the descending of Eesa, son of Maryam from heaven, the appearance of the Dajjal, and three earthquakes; one in the East, one in the West, and the third in the Arabian Peninsula and a fire which will erupt from underground in Aden to drive people to the Assembly Land. It will accompany them, stopping wherever they stop, day and night. [Sahih Muslim 2901a]

This world will come to an end by the first blow of the Trumpet as mentioned in Qurán;

Articles of Faith (Aqaid)

"And the Trumpet will be blown, then all those who are in the heavens and on earth will be shocked to death except those whom Allah exempts. Then it will be blown for the second time, and behold; they will be standing, witnessing the horrors of that Day. Then the earth will shine with the light of its Rubb, the records will be laid open, the Prophets and the witnesses will be brought, and humankind will be judged fairly, and they will not be wronged."
[Qurán, az Zumar 39:68-70]

Men will emerge from their graves bewildered, naked, uncircumcised and barefoot. The Day of Reckoning would be fifty-thousand years long. The Beloved Prophet Muhammadﷺ would intercede with Allahﷻ on behalf of the mankind. Allahﷻ will then begin taking accounts of the deeds. Those who will receive their records in their right hand would be prosperous and those who would receive their records in their left hand or from behind their back will be doomed.

The first one to cross the Bridge will be the Beloved Prophet Muhammadﷺ and the believers. [Sunan an Nisai:1140]

The Beloved Prophetﷺ described, "As-Sirat is a Bridge extended over the midst of Hell, on which the feet shall not be firm. It has hooks and thorns as of *as-Si'dan* tree. It is sharper than a sword and thinner than a hair. On each side of it are hooks to pull down whomever it is commanded to. Some will cross it swiftly, others slowly, and yet others will cross it sustaining scratches and cuts, while the rest will land in Hell." [Sahih Bukhari 806]

Hawdh e Kauthar is a great pool, which Allahﷻ has granted the Beloved Prophet Muhammadﷺ which his Ummah will attend on the Day of Resurrection. It is narrated from Ibn Umarﷁ that the Beloved Prophetﷺ said, "*Kauthar* is a river in Paradise whose banks are of gold and its bed is of rubies and pearls. Its

Articles of Faith (Aqaid)

soil is more fragrant than musk, its water is sweeter than honey and whiter than snow." [Sunan Ibn Majah : 4334]

The Beloved Prophetﷺ said, "I will be at my Lake-Fount (*Kauthar*) waiting for whoever will come to me. Then, some people will be taken away from me whereupon I will say, 'My followers!' It will be said, 'You do not know they turned Apostates as renegades (deserted their religion).'" [Sahih al-Bukhari : 7048]

The Scale will be set on the Day of Resurrection for weighing deeds. It is a real Scale with two actual sides, in fulfillment of Divine justice. The one whose good deeds will outweigh his bad deeds, will prosper and go to Jannah and the one whose bad deeds would outweigh his good deeds will be sent to Hell-Fire.

> *"And the weighing on that Day will be real. So, those whose good deeds are heavy in the scale will prosper. While whose good deeds are light, it is they who will have ruined themselves because they denied Our signs."*
>
> [Qurán, al A'raf 7:8-9]

Allahﷻ has different levels in Jannah, each according to the believer's rank, *Iman* and piety. Then, there is Hell, which will be the abode of the sinful and the ones who denied Allahﷻ and His Messengers;

> *"And what do you know what Hell is? It spares nothing; it leaves nothing intact; it scorches (even) the skin."*
>
> [Qurán, al Mudhathir 74:27-29]

Belief in Predestination (Qadr)

The belief in *Qadr* is that Allah ﷻ ordained everything before their occurrence, and recording them in the Preserved Tablet. Allah's Messenger ﷺ said, "Allah ordained the measures (of quality) of the creation fifty thousand years before He created the heavens and the earth, as His Throne was upon water." [Sahih Muslim : 2653b]

Belief in *Qadr* is the firm attestation to the fact that all general and particular decrees have been pre-recorded and Allah ﷻ has created everything and assigned it a proper measure. As mentioned in Qurán:

> "Verily, We have created everything by a decree."
>
> [Qurán, al Qamar 54:49]

As Muslims, we believe that Allah ﷻ is well acquainted and His knowledge encompasses everything. Qurán mentions:

> "Do you not know that Allah knows whatever is in the heavens and the earth? Surely, it is all preserved in a record, and that is easy for Allah."
>
> [Qurán, al Hajj 22:70]

Nothing takes place in the heavens or on earth without the will of Allah ﷻ:

> "Verily, His command, when He wants a thing, is only that He says to it, 'Be'! And it is."
>
> [Qurán, Ya sin 36:82]

Everything is assigned and preserved in the Tablet as Qurán mentions:

> "There is nothing, which takes place on earth, or in you, but is foreordained before We brought it into existence."
>
> [Qurán, al Hadid 57:22[

Ali﷿ reported that one day Allah's Messengerﷺ was sitting with a wood in his hand and he was scratching the ground. He raised his head and said, "There is not one amongst you who has not been allotted his seat in Paradise or Hell.' The Companions said, 'Allah's Messengerﷺ! then, why should we perform good deeds, why not depend upon our destiny?' Thereupon, he said, 'No, do perform good deeds, for everyone is facilitated in that for which he has been created; then he recited this verse: *Then, who gives to the needy and guards against evil and accepts the excellent (the truth of Islam and the path of righteousness it prescribes), We shall make easy for him the easy end...*" (Qurán al Layl 92: 5-10)." [Sahih Muslim : 2647c]

Life of the Prophetﷺ after Death (Hayat un-Nabi)

It is the belief of the *Ahle Sunnah Wal Jamaá* that the Beloved Prophetﷺ is alive in his grave, in a manner that his body is attached to the soul. He is nourished by Allahﷻ in his grave, and he engages in the performance of Salah. He also hears the *Salawat* (benediction, blessings, durood) sent to him by one who stands close to his grave. This belief is established from the Qurán, Hadith, the statements of the Companions of the Prophetﷺ, Tabayéen, Tabé Tabayéen and the pious predecessors. With respect to the evidence from the Qurán, the Scholars have highlighted the verse from Qurán:

"And do not say about those who are martyred in the path of Allah that they are dead. Nay! They are alive, but you cannot understand."

[Qurán, al Baqarah 2:154]

It is clearly stated in Qurán about those who have died in Allah'sﷻ path as being alive. Although, everyone who passes away is normally referred to 'as having died' or 'a dead person', Allahﷻ mentions about the martyrs that *'they are alive'* and *'do not call them dead'*. This statement shows that a special favour is given to them and their being alive after martyrdom is different from other people. The scholars establish *'Hayat un-Nabi'* from this verse, because if this is the honour for the martyrs who are ordinary believers, then to a greater extent it is established for the Prophets, who were the greatest martyrs.

In order to show that the life given to those honoured ones is different from others in the state of *Barzakh*, Allahﷻ explains the nature of their life by highlighting the point *'that the martyrs are alive'*. Then, the mankind is addressed by mentioning that, *'However you cannot understand'*, meaning that mankind is unable to comprehend the concept of that life after death. About this life, Qurán states;

> *'Think not of those who are killed in the way of Allah as dead. Nay, they are alive, with their lord, and they have provision'. 'They rejoice in what Allah has bestowed upon them of His bounty and rejoice for the sake of those who have not yet joined them, but are left behind (not yet martyred) that on them no fear shall come, nor shall they grieve. 'They rejoice in a Grace and a Bounty from Allah, and that Allah will not waste the reward of the believers."*
>
> [Qurán, Aal e Imran 3:169-171]

Regarding the abovementioned verse, the great scholar Imam Shawkani﷫ writes, "It is established from the text of the book of Allahﷻ that martyrs are alive, being nourished by Allahﷻ and that their lives are connected to their bodies. When this is so, then much more is established for the Prophets." [Nayl al-Awtar Vol.III pg. 211]

There are many sound and authentic narrations regarding the life of the Prophets after death, as Anas bin Malik﷜ narrated that the Beloved Prophetﷺ said, "The Prophets are alive in their graves and are engaged in praying."[2] [Musnad Abi Yala:3425]

Articles of Faith (Aqaid) 117

The Beloved Prophetﷺ said, "Among the most excellent of your days is Friday; On this day Adam علیہ السلام was created; On this day shall be the *Nafakhah*(Trumpet); on it all creation will be swoon. So, send a great dealing of blessing upon me on this day, for your blessings will be presented to me.' The Companions asked, 'Allah's Messengerﷺ! How can our blessing be submitted to you, when your body is decayed?' Heﷺ said, 'Allah has prohibited the earth from consuming the bodies of the Prophets.'" [Sunan Ibn Maja Vol.1: Hadith:1626]

The Beloved Prophetﷺ said, "I passed by Musa علیہ السلام at the red hilltop on the night of Míraj and I saw him performing Salah in his grave." [Sahih Muslim: 5858; Sunan Nisai:1630]

The Beloved Prophetﷺ said, "Certainly Allah ﷻ has made it Haram (unlawful) upon the earth (to destroy) the bodies of the Prophets." [Abu Dawood, Nasai, Ibn Majah]

The Beloved Prophetﷺ said, "If anyone of you greets me, Allah ﷻ returns my soul to me and I respond to the greeting." [Abu Dawud Book 004, Hadith Number 2036]

In the explanation of the Hadith, Imam Jalal ud-din Suyuti رحمۃ اللہ علیہ wrote, "The word "*radda*" means `ala al-dawam*," i.e., permanently, and not temporarily, in other words, Allah ﷻ does not return the *Ruh* and take it back, then return it again and then take it back again, but He returned it to the Prophetﷺ permanently, and the Prophetﷺ is alive permanently. [Al-Hawi lil Fatawi, Vol.2, p.271-272]

Allah's Messengerﷺ said, "Whoever visits my grave after my death, it is as he has visited me in my life." [Tabrani Vol.012, Hadith:406, Bayhaqi Sháb al-Iman Vol.III, Hadith:489]

In *Al-Qaulul Badee*, it is mentioned, "We believe and testify as the truth that the Prophetﷺ is alive in his grave. And upon

Articles of Faith (Aqaid) 118

this there is Ijma." Mulla Ali Qaari has written in his *Al Mirqaat* which is the commentary of *Mishkaat*, "Certainly the Prophets are alive in their graves and this is Ijma."

There are many other statements which have been written to prove the consensus by the great scholars which conform to the above-mentioned belief of the *Ahlus Sunnah Wal Jamm'ah*. Hence, all the scholars of *Ahlus Sunnah Wal Jama'ah* have recorded *'Ijma'* consensus on this belief.

Chapter six

REMEMBRANCE (DHIKR)

It is evident that the path of *Tasawwuf* is in the knowledge of *Shariáh* and following the Prophetic Sunnah. The disciple must adhere to the inner and outer aspects of Shariáh and engage in constant remembrance as the essence of this path is not to waste a breath without the remembrance of Allah. Often, the question is asked, "Where in Shariáh does it say to perform *Dhikr* and why is it necessary?" The answer is in Qurán:

"*And remember Allah often so you may be successful.*"

[Qurán, al Jumáh 62:10]

This verse is a command not a request and the name of our Lord is 'Allah'. It is the *Dhikr* of 'Allah' that is the source code of this universe as mentioned in Hadith, "The final hour shall not arise until it is no longer said on earth: 'Allah, Allah'" [Muslim:148 s]. *Dhikr* may take many forms, but the essence of all methods is the invocation or remembrance of the Divine Name, 'Allah' and through '*La ilaha illallah*' meaning 'there is no god but Allah'. Qur'an underlines the importance of invocation in words such as:

"*Remember Allah standing and sitting...*" [Qurán, Aale Imran 3:191]

and in another verse:

"*Those who believe and do good deeds, and remember Allah much...*"
[Qurán, Ash Shuára 26:227];

Remembrance (Dhikr)

And:

> *And remember your Lord within yourself in humility and in reverence, without loudness in words, in the mornings and evenings. And do not be among the heedless."*
>
> [Qurán, al Aáraaf 7:205]

And also;

> *"Surely the Remembrance of Allah is Greatest"*
>
> [Qurán, al Ankabut 29:45]

All souls are born on nature *(fitrah)* but slowly steadily they are tainted by the world and its desires. The only salvation for that soul is the remembrance of Allahﷻ until all doubts and delusions are annihilated and the soul becomes pure again. It is through the Dhikr of Allahﷻ that the heart is cleansed and state of excellence *(Ihsan)* is achieved which is as in the Prophetic phrase, "as though you see Him." The food for the soul or Ruh is the remembrance of Allahﷻ. The acts of obedience increase the light of certainty and Iman in the soul, and Dhikr is among the greatest of them.

As proven by the *sahih* Hadith that the Prophetﷺ said, "Shall I not tell you of the best of your works, the purest of them in the eyes of your Master, the highest in raising your rank, better than giving gold and silver, and better for you than to meet your enemy and smite their necks, and they smite yours?" They said, "O Allah's Messengerﷺ! What is it?" and he said, "The remembrance of Allah Mighty and Majestic." [*al-Mustadrak 'ala al-Sahihayn, 1.496*].

The world with all its attractions can easily distract the believer from the remembrance of Allahﷻ and these worldly possessions would be of no value on the Day of Judgement. All the possessions of this world cannot save one from hellfire. The

Remembrance (Dhikr)

verse in Qurán specifically addresses the believers as a command not to be distracted from the remembrance of Allah as the one who gets diverted will be at loss:

> "O, you who have believed! Let not your wealth and your children divert you from remembrance of Allah, and whoever does that, then those are the losers."
>
> [Qurán, al Munafiqun 63:9]

The question arises then, how much remembrance is enough? The answer is in the Qurán; "*Dhikran Katheera*", [Qurán 33:41-42] which means in abundance. Allah commands the believers to remember much, morning and evenings-countless and limitless.

> O you who believe! Remember Allah with much remembrance and glorify Him morning and evening."
>
> [Qurán, al Ahzaab 33:41,42]

> "Invoke the Name of your Lord in the morning and the day's end" [Qurán, ad Dahr 76:25]

The excessive *Dhikr* is validated through the Hadith as Allah's Messenger said, "Be excessive in remembrance of Allah to the extent that the hypocrites say you are showing off." [*Al Mu'jam al-Kabir: 12786 Tabarani [12;131]*

And one may ask what the reward for that remembrance is? The following verse answers that question by saying:

> 'So, remember Me and I will remember you.'
>
> [Qurán, al Baqara 2:152]

And what happens when Allah, the Creator, the Almighty, the All-Knowing remembers someone; the answer is in the Hadith.

Allah's Messenger said "Allah thus stated, I am near to the thought of my servant as he thinks about Me, and I am with him as he remembers Me. And if he remembers me in his heart, I also remember him in my Heart, and if he remembers me in an assembly, I remember him in an assembly better than his and if he draws closer by the span of a palm, I draw near him by the cubit and if he draws near me by the cubit, I draw near him by the space covered by two hands and if he walks towards me, I rush towards him." [Muslim 6805.s]

Subhan Allah, this is the reward for remembrance, the greatest reward for a lover is that the Beloved remembers him. Imagine when one remembers Allah☬ the Almighty, the Creator of All remembers him. Though, in this world it is not possible to behold Allah's vision by the eye, but by due remembrance the servant can achieve the perpetual state of *Ihsan* and behold the vision of Allah☬ through his heart. For the believers, the everlasting sweet reward would be in the hereafter- the visage;

'On that day shall faces be radiant, gazing upon their Lord'

[Qurán, al Qiyamah 75: 22-23]

In this time and era, people complain about their worries gnawing at their souls; anxiety, depression, and mental health issues are on the rise. With all the comforts of this world people take drugs for apnoea and still find it hard to have a good night's sleep. The concept of true happiness is lost in the vortex of worldly desires. If these worldly possessions could provide pleasure, then, why do we see people crumbling under the worries? Allah☬, the Creator who created mankind, gave the secret for happiness as:

"Verily, only through the remembrance of Allah do hearts find peace"

[Qurán, ar Ráad 13:28]

When the Creator has set the rule and announced that the contentment can only be found in His remembrance, then

Remembrance (Dhikr)

there is no other means to satisfaction, may it be wealth, fame or status. If pleasure was to be found in the wealth or fame then one wonders why all these people who are called celebrities, own millions of dollars and are famous, take drugs for depression or commit suicide. Qurán is not just a book of blessings as we assume, it is a manual and a code for conduct for the mankind revealed by the Creator. One can choose not to follow those rules but the repercussions have to be faced not only in the afterlife but also in this world.

Throughout the daily course of life, the only way to revive *Iman* is through *la ilaha illallah* meaning 'there is no god but Allahﷻ' as according to the Hadith, *'Revive your Iman through Lailaha'* [Ahmad]. And according to another Hadith, "The best remembrance is *'La ilaha illallah.'* [Tirmidhi 3383]

It is through *Dhikr* that the faith is strengthened, the soul is elevated and it was in this context that ʿUmar ibn al-Khattabؓ said, "If the *Iman* of Abu Bakrؓ were weighed against the *Iman* of the entire Umma, it would outweigh it." *Dhikr* cleans the mirror of the heart to reflect the Divine light. As mentioned in Hadith, the Messenger of Allahﷺ used to say, "There is a polish for everything and the polish for hearts is the remembrance of Allahﷻ." [Al Bayhaqi 2:254]

It is this Dhikr of *La ilaha* which reaches the Throne of Allahﷻ as Allah's Messengerﷺ said, "When a person sincerely says *'la ilaha illallah'*, the doors of the sky are opened, until it reaches the Throne so long as he avoids major sins." [Tirmidhi: 3590]

There is the glad tiding for intercession by Allah's Messenger ﷺ for the person who says *la ilaha* as he said, "The fortunate person who will gain my intercession will be that person who says 'La ilaha illallah' sincerely from his heart" [Bukhari: 99]. The statement *'La Ilaha Illallah'*, brings the servant to the highest levels of faith, as Allah's Messenger ﷺ said, "Faith has seventy-some odd doors, the lowest of which is removing something harmful from the road, and its highest is the statement *La Ilaha Illallah.*" [Jami` at-Tirmidhi 2614]

According to Mujaddid Alf Thani ﷺ, "The seeker is to perform the *Dhikr, la ilaha* to the point that the heart is void of everything except for Allah ﷻ."[1]

In another letter he wrote, "One is to remain engaged in the *Dhikr* of Allah ﷻ and except the "Remembered one" (Allah ﷻ) everything else should depart from his chest and there should not remain any sign and symptom of "other than Allah" (*masiwā*) in him. Anything "other than Allah" even as an illusion should not enter his heart. Even if one intentionally tries to visualize "other than Allah" (*ghair*) in his heart, then this should not be availed due to that "forgetfulness" which his heart has achieved about everything else, except the 'Remembered one'".[2]

At times, people say that they are distracted and inattentive while performing *Dhikr*, but that shall not be the reason to stop the remembrance. One may be heedless in invocation which is far better than being completely and utterly heedless. Allah ﷻ through His *inaya*, may grant the one who is invoking His Name inattentively to invocation with attention and that is not difficult for Allah ﷻ. There is the account of the person who was a disbeliever and invoked the name of his godling, *'Ya sanam'* (idol made out of stone) and while beseeching, by the slip of the tongue he uttered, *'Ya Samad'* (Allah's attribute) and Allah ﷻ replied, 'I am all Hearing, My servant'. The angels submitted to Allah ﷻ that the person called upon His name only by mistake. Allah ﷻ knew it was by mistake, but the man invoked the name

Remembrance (Dhikr)

of his false god for years and the god could never reply, but when the servant invoked His name, He is the One All Hearing and He replied to His servant. It is said that the person's heart was illuminated by the light and he accepted the truth.[3]

Remembrance increases the level of certitude, *yaqeen* and one goes through the stations of *ilm ul yaqeen* to *ain ul yaqeen* to *haq ul yaqeen*. Initially, it may be a struggle, then, it becomes effortless and finally becomes a habit, then unconsciously one performs *Dhikr* through the heart and the self is completely absorbed by *Dhikr*.

Assemblies of Dhikr (Halqah)

It is a common practice to hold gatherings where *Dhikr* is performed. The sanctity of these gatherings can be verified by the Hadith narrated by Abu Hurairah who reported Allah's Apostle as saying, "Truly Allah has angels going about the ways, looking for people of *Dhikr*, and when they find a group invoking Allah, they call to one another, "Come to what you have been looking for!"

And they circle around them with their wings up to the sky of this world. Then Allah asks them although, He knows it all; "What do My servants say?"

And, they reply, "They say, *SubhanAllah* [Exalted is Allah's perfection beyond any comparison], *Allahu Akbar* [Allah is ever Greatest], and *Alhumdulillah* [All praise be to Allah], and they extol Your Glory."

Allah says, "Have they seen Me?"

And the angels reply, "No, by Allah, they have not seen You." And Allah says, "How would it be, had they seen Me?"

And the angels say, "If they had seen You, they would have worshipped You even more, glorified You more, and exalted You even more."

Allahﷻ says, "What do they ask of me?"

The Angels say, "They ask you Paradise." Allahﷻ says, "Have they seen My Paradise?"

They say, "No, Our Lord! They have not seen it."

Allahﷻ says, "How would it be if they had seen My Paradise?"

And the angels say, "If they had seen it, they would have been more avid for it, sought it more, and been more desirous of it."

Then, Allahﷻ asks them, "From what do they seek refuge?" And they answer, "From Hell."

Allahﷻ asks them, "Have they seen it?" And the angels reply, "No, by Allah, they have not seen it."

And Allahﷻ says, "How would it be if they had seen it?" And the angels say, 'If they had seen it, they would have fled from it even more, and been more afraid of it."

Allahﷻ says, "I charge all of you to bear witness that I have Forgiven them."

Then, one of the angels say, "Our Lord, there is one amongst them such and such who happened to pass [by the assembly] and sat along with them [who had been participating in that assembly], he only came for something he needed."

Allahﷻ would say, "I also Forgive him, as they are companions through whom no one who keeps their company shall meet perdition." [Bukhari 6408. S]

The above Hadith endorses the significance of the gatherings of *Dhikr*, primarily the gatherings to invoke Allahﷻ. It is narrated by Abu Sa'id Khudri؇ that Mu'awiya؇ came to a circle in the mosque and said, "What makes you sit here?" They replied, "We are gathered here to remember Allah؇." He said, "I adjure you by Allah? (To tell me whether you are sitting here for this very purpose)"

They said, "By Allah! we are here only for this very purpose." Thereupon, he said, "I have not demanded you to take an oath, because of any allegation against you and none of my rank in the eye of Allah's Messenger؇ as I am the narrator of few Hadith. The fact is that Allah's Messenger؇ went out to the circle of his Companions and said, "What makes you sit?" They replied, "We are sitting here to remember Allah؇ and praise Him for He guided us to the path of Islam and He conferred favours upon us."

Thereupon, he adjured by Allah؇ and asked if that was the only purpose for their gathering, they said, "By Allah! we are sitting here only for this very purpose," whereupon, Allah's Messenger ؇ said, "I am not asking you to take an oath because of any allegation against you but for the fact that Gibrael؇ came to me and informed me that Allah؇ was talking to the angels about your magnificence." [Musnad Ahmad: 5416s]

It happens that when one goes to an assembly of *Dhikr*, special peace and tranquillity settles upon the heart, the phenomenon is explained by the Hadith as Allah's Prophet؇ said, "Never will a group of people gather in a house from among the houses of Allah for the recitation of Allah's Book, or to study it among themselves, except that a state of spiritual tranquillity, *sakina*, will descend upon them, and they are overcome by Divine Mercy, and they are surrounded by angels, and they are mentioned by Allah as being among those closest to Him." [Abu Dawud:1455, Sunan Ibn Majah: 3791]

Silent Dhikr

It is narrated that the Messengerﷺ said, "The silent *Dhikr* which even the angel scribes *(al kiram al katibun)* cannot hear is seventy times superior [to vocal *Dhikr*] on the day of Resurrection. Allah will gather all of His creation for accounting of their deeds and the angel scribes will bring forth whatever they had preserved, Allahﷻ will say to them, 'Is there anything else which is left?' They will reply, 'As far as we know and what we recorded, there is nothing that has been left out or unrecorded.' Allahﷻ will say [to the person], 'I have a good deed of yours which even they are unaware of, and I will reward you for it, the deed is silent *Dhikr*.'" [*Suyuti al Budur as-Safirah, Abu Yala Majam az-Zawaid 10:81*]

Those who are concerned that if the words are not uttered by the tongue, remembrance is not valid, this Hadith validates the consideration of silent *Dhikr* as even the angel scribes cannot hear it. However, verbal utterance is unanimously considered necessary in certain injunctions as recitation of Qurán, in Salah, in the contracts as marriage or divorce and many other situations. Depending on the *tariqa*, the Shaykh may teach verbal remembrance or the silent remembrance with the heart.

Chapter Seven

PURIFICATION OF THE SOUL (TAZKIYAH)

Lack of Sincerity (Riya)

Allahﷻ mentions in Qurán:
> "Indeed, sincere devotion is due only to Allah"
> [Qurán, az Zumar 39:3]

Abu Umamah؅ narrated that the Beloved Prophetﷺ said, "Allahﷻ said: The most beloved act with which my servant worships me is sincerity for my sake." [Musnad Ahmad 21687]. Sincerity is to keep Allah's pleasure as the sole object of one's worship, excluding everything else. It is also to conceal one's deeds from being observed by people as one of the soul's most sinister traits is its tendency to take delight in praise. A sign of this condition is that when praise is withheld from the person, his spiritual state reverts to indolence and ineptitude.

For many years a certain Sufi master used to pray in the front row of the mosque. One day, something prevented him from arriving early at the mosque, so he prayed in the last row. Then, he was not seen in the mosque for a while. When someone asked him about the reason for that, he answered, "I prayed in the front row for so many years. As I was performing my daily prayers, I thought that I was dedicating them to Allahﷻ only. The day I was late I was overcome with a shame of sorts because the people in the mosque saw me in the last row. That's when I came to realize that my zeal all these years had derived from my desire to be seen doing my prayers."

It is related that Abu Muhammad al-Murtaish ﷺ once said, "I used to go on the pilgrimage without any provisions or riding animal. I then realized that all my effort was tarnished by my taking pleasure in doing that. One day, my mother asked me to bring a jar of water for her. When I found that request burdensome, I suddenly realized that my eagerness to perform the pilgrimages sprang from my soul's taking pleasure in that and from a blemish that remained in it. If my soul had been annihilated by ascetic rigors, it would not have found it burdensome to do something that is prescribed by the Divine Law."

Sincerity is to realise that everything originates from Allah ﷻ and not from one's own self. As a result, the seeker frees himself from pretensions to any power and ability to act on his own at any time. The seeker then becomes protected from the evil of his soul through Allah's ﷻ assistance, for if this assistance is not extended to him, his knowledge of his self and of Allah ﷻ will be of no use to him.

In the words of Dhu al-Nun al-Misri ﷺ, "Corruption afflicts men when the desire to work for the sake of the Hereafter is weak; when body becomes hostage to the lust; when one holds high hopes for the future, while life is so short; when one strives to please creatures instead of pleasing the Creator and when one pursues his own passions, while turning the back on the Prophet's Sunnah." Al-Fudayl ﷺ said: "Abandoning good works for the sake of people is hypocrisy; doing them for the sake of people is polytheism; sincerity is that God absolves you from both."[1]

Pride

Allahﷻ absolutely does not like anyone arrogant and proud:

> 'Surely Allah does not like the one who is arrogant and boastful.'
> [Qurán, An-Nisa 4:36]

Abdullah bin Mas'ud﷛ narrated that the Beloved Prophetﷺ said, "None shall enter the Fire (of Hell) who has in his heart the weight of a mustard seed of Iman and none shall enter Paradise who has in his heart the weight of a mustard seed of pride." [Muslim:0165]

Arrogance, vanity and pride are the heritage of Satan and Pharaoh, whereas humility is the heritage of the Messengers. Satan was arrogant and became the accursed whereas Adam ﷺ was humble and accepted his wrongdoing hence, Allahﷻ forgave him. As narrated by Abu Hurayrah﷛ that the Messenger of Allahﷺ said, "Allahﷻ said, 'Pride is my cloak and greatness My robe, and he who competes with Me in respect of either of them I shall cast into Hell-fire." [Abu Dawud, Ibn Majah and Ahmad]

Islam strictly prohibits display of pride and vanity as all human beings are equal. Islam does not recognise any superiority in terms of caste, colour or creed. It is immoral to display pride over caste, status, knowledge or wealth. Pride and vanity lead to arrogance and humility is considered as the standard of closeness to Allahﷻ. When the seeker is humble, the journey becomes easier for him. Pride is only allowed when it is displayed to show power and supremacy over the enemies of Allahﷻ and Islam. Such pride is proved from the Companions of the Prophetﷺ, but pride due to arrogance is strictly prohibited.

Unnecessary Talking

Abu Sa'id al-Khudri؏ reported that the Beloved Prophetﷺ said, "When the son of Adam wakes up in the morning, all of his limbs defer to the tongue and they say: Fear Allah regarding us, for we are only a part of you. If you are upright, we are upright. If you are crooked, we are crooked." [Sunan al-Tirmidhi 2407]

The Beloved Prophetﷺ was asked about that for which people are admitted into Paradise the most, so he said: "Taqwa or piety of Allahﷻ, and good character." And he was asked about that for which people are admitted into the Fire the most, and he said: " The mouth and the private parts."[Jami at-Tirmidhi 2004]

The tongue, therefore, can take one to the dark pits of the hell through sins which at times we do not even consider. Backbiting, gossip, obscene and misleading talk, bickering, lying, mockery, derision, and falsehood, and many more faults can affect a servant's tongue. The sins of the tongue ruin the heart and cause one to lose happiness and pleasure in this life and success in hereafter. Abu Hurairah؏ narrated that the Beloved Prophetﷺ said, "He who believes in Allahﷻ and the Last Day must either speak good or remain silent." [Muslim, Riyad as-Salihin: 1511]

The clerk of Al-Mughira bin Shu`ba؏ narrated, "Muawiya؏ wrote to Al-Mughira bin Shu`ba؏: "Write to me something which you have heard from the Prophetﷺ." So, Al-Mughira؏ wrote, "I heard the Prophetﷺ saying, "Allahﷻ has hated for you three things: Vain talks, (useless talk) that you talk too much or about others, wasting of wealth (by extravagance) and asking too many questions (in disputed religious matters) or asking others for something (except in great need)." [Bukhari : 1477]

Purification of the Soul (Tazkiyah)

The Beloved Prophet ﷺ said, "Shall I not tell you how to control all that?" I said, "Yes do, O Allah's Messenger ﷺ." So, he held his tongue between his fingers, and then he said: "Restrain this." I said, "O Allah's Prophet ﷺ! Are we accountable for what we say?" The Prophet ﷺ said, "May your mother be bereft by your loss! Is there anything more than the harvest of the tongues that throws people on their faces (or he said 'on their noses') into the Fire?" [Ibn Majah 3973]

'The harvest of the tongues' is a phrase used for the punishment for saying forbidden things. A man, through his actions and words, sows the seeds of either good or evil and on the Day of Judgement, he will harvest their fruits. Those who sow the seeds of good words and deeds will harvest honour and blessing sand those who sow the seeds of evil words and deeds will reap only regret and remorse.

Narrated by Abu Hurairah ؓ, the Beloved Prophet ﷺ said, "A slave (of Allah) may utter a word which pleases Allah ﷻ without giving it much importance, and because of that Allah ﷻ will raise him to degrees (of reward): a slave (of Allah) may utter a word (carelessly) which displeases Allah ﷻ without thinking of its gravity and because of that he will be thrown into the Hell-Fire." [Bukhari 6478]

Sahl bin Sa'd ؓ reported that Allah's Messenger ﷺ said, "Whosoever gives me a guarantee to safeguard what is between his jaws and what is between his legs, I shall guarantee him Paradise." [Al-Bukhari, Riyad as-Salihin 1513]

Abu Hurayrah ؓ narrated that Allah's Messenger ﷺ said, "Part of the perfection of one's Islam is his leaving that which does not concern him." [Tirmidhi, Hadith 12; 40 Hadith an-Nawawi]

Unrestrained Glances

"Tell the believing men to lower their gaze and guard their modesty; that is more purifying for them. Surely Allah is aware of what they do."
[Qurán, An Nur 24:30]

Unrestrained glances result in fornication of the eyes as the Beloved Prophetﷺ said, "Man's share of fornication which he will inevitably commit is decreed for him. The fornication of the eyes consists in looking, of the ears in hearing, of the tongue in speech, of the hand in violence, and of the foot in walking. The heart lusts and wishes, and the private parts accord with that or reject it." [Mishkat al-Masabih 86]

It is narrated that the Beloved Prophetﷺ once said, "The glance is a poisoned arrow of Satan. Whoever lowers his gaze for Allahﷻ, He will bestow upon him a refreshing sweetness which he will find in his heart on the day that he meets Him." [al-Mustadrak, 4/314; Ahmad, al-Musnad, 5/264]

Satan uses the arrow of the glance and fuels the desire for sin. An unrestrained glance distracts the heart and makes it forget its more important concerns. There is a direct connection between the eye and the heart, if the eyes are corrupted, then the heart follows. Letting the gaze roam free darkens the heart just as lowering the gaze for Allahﷻ covers it in light. The unrestrained gaze makes the heart blind to distinguishing between truth and falsehood, between Sunnah and innovation; while lowering it for Allahﷻ, gives it a penetrating, true and distinguishing insight. Whoever lowers his gaze from what Allahﷻ has forbidden, Allahﷻ gives his inner sight and heart abundant light.[2]

Backbiting (Ghiba)

Allah﷾ mentions in Qurán:

"Do not backbite one another; would any of you like to eat the flesh of his dead brother?"

[Qurán, al Hujurat 49:12]

The Beloved Prophetﷺ said, "O community of people, who believed by their tongue, and belief did not enter their hearts, do not back-bite Muslims, and do not search for their faults, for if anyone searches for their faults, Allah﷾ will search for his fault, and if Allah﷾ searches for the fault of anyone, He disgraces him in his house." [Sunan Abi Dawood 4880]

Someone mentioned backbiting in the presence of Abdallah bin al-Mubarak﷫, he commented, "If I were ever to slander anyone in his absence, I would slander my parents, for they are more deserving of my good deeds than anybody else." Yahya bin Muadh said: "Let each believer benefit from you in the following three ways: if you cannot be of help to him, at least do not harm him; if you cannot make him happy, at least do not make him sad; if you cannot praise him, at least do not blame him."

Hudhaifah﷛ narrated that Allah's Messengerﷺ said, "A backbiter will not enter Paradise." [Bukhari 6056]

Abu Hurairah﷛ narrated that it was said, " O Allah's Messengerﷺ! What is backbiting?" Heﷺ said, " Mentioning your brother with that which he does not like." He said " What if it was true?" He said: "If what you said about him is so, then you have backbitten him, and if it is not as you said, then you have slandered him." [Jami` at-Tirmidhi 1934]

Backbiting is a sin which takes away the good deeds, it is said that the backbiter is a person who has installed a catapult and shoots his good deeds in all directions.

Envy

Allahﷻ mentions in Qurán as a supplication for protection against evil forces, with a mention of envy:

> "[I take refuge] from the evil of an envier when he envies."
>
> [Qurán al Falaq 113:5]

It is narrated by Abu Hurairah☬ that the Beloved Prophet ﷺ said, "Beware of envy, for it devours good deeds just as fire devours wood or grass." [Sunan Abi Dawud 4903]

The scholars say about the words of Allahﷻ:

> "Say, My Lord has only forbidden indecencies, those that are apparent and those that are hidden" [Qurán, al Aáraf 7:33]

Envy is manifested in one's desire for the loss of someone else's blessing from Allahﷻ. The words "those that are hidden" refer to envy. It is said: "Among the sins of the envier is that he flatters, when he is present, backbites when he is absent, and rejoices at calamity when it befalls [others]." The envier feels perplexed whenever he sees Allah'sﷻ beneficence towards others and rejoices when he sees somebody committing a fault. Imam Ghazali☬ said that if one despises that part of the self which causes envy then it is a sign that the person is not an envious person. The cure is in the *Dhikr* of Allahﷻ, detesting the *Nafs* and not following the caprice.

Anger

Allahﷻ mentions the characteristics of true Muslims in Qurán:

> "They are those who donate in prosperity and adversity, control their anger, and pardon others. And Allah loves the good-doers"
>
> [Qurán, Ale Imran 3:134]

It is narrated by Abdullah ibn Mas'ud﷠ that the Beloved Prophetﷺ said, "Whom do you consider to be a fighter amongst you?" The Companions said, "The one whom men cannot wrestle down." The Beloved Prophetﷺ said, "It is not so, rather, it is the one who controls himself when angry." [Muslim 2608]

If one desires to achieve Allah'sﷻ pleasure, then it is important to control the temper as it displeases Satan. Anger is a sign of an uncontrolled ego, once, the ego is restrained the temper is controlled. When the person stops reacting to a provocation, the negativity in the adversary fades and he is also able to see his fault. Although anger is a natural feeling, it has negative effects on those who allow it to control them. It affects one's mental health, leading to anxiety, depression, guilt, frustration, and isolation. It also affects the physical health by causing hypertension, ulcers, headaches, and many other issues.

When a person becomes angry, he intensifies hatred amongst himself and people around him, as a result, it affects the family and social structure. The person who can control his temper, stays positive and his relationships improve which helps build a positive family unit. The positive attitude creates harmony, mutual love and respect. The person reaps the benefits in this life and the hereafter as narrated by Anas ibn Malik﷠ that Allah's Messengerﷺ said, "Whoever restricts his tongue, Allahﷻ will cover his faults. Whoever restrains his anger, Allahﷻ will restrain his punishment on the Day of Resurrection. Whoever apologizes to Allahﷻ, Allahﷻ will accept his apology." [Shu'ab al-Iman 7818]

Gluttony

Abu Umamah reported that the Beloved Prophet said, "My Lord presented me with the valley of Makkah that He might turn it into gold for me. I said: No, O Lord, rather, I will be satiated some days and hungry some days. When I am hungry, I will humble myself to You and remember You. When I am satiated, I will be grateful to You and praise You." [Sunan al-Tirmidhi 2347]

Al-Miqdam ibn Ma'd narrated that the Beloved Prophet said, "The son of Adam cannot fill a vessel worse than his stomach, as it is enough for him to take a few bites to straighten his back. If he cannot do it, then he may fill it with a third of his food, a third of his drink, and a third for his breath." [Sunan al-Tirmidhi 2380]

The consumption of small amounts of food guarantees tenderness of the heart, strength of the intellect, humility of the self and better control over worldly desires. Immoderate eating brings about the opposite of these praiseworthy qualities. Whoever safeguards against the evils of overfilling his stomach prevents great evil as it is easier for Satan to control a person who has filled his stomach.

Ibrahim ibn Adham said: "Anyone who controls his stomach is in control of his *deen* and anyone who controls his hunger is in control of good behaviour. Disobedience towards Allah is nearest to a person who is satiated with a full stomach and furthest away from a person who is hungry."[3]

Bad Company

Allahﷻ mentions in Qurán:

"And keep yourself patient [by being] with those who call upon their Lord in the morning and the evening, seeking His countenance. And let not your eyes pass beyond them, desiring adornments of the worldly life, and do not obey one whose heart We have made heedless of Our remembrance and who follows his desire and whose affair is ever [in] neglect."

[Qur'an, al Kahf 18:28]

Abu Hurairah﷜ narrated that the Beloved Prophetﷺ said, "A man is upon the religion of his best friend, so let one of you look at whom he befriends." [Sunan al-Tirmidhi 2378]

It is a fact that a man is known by the company he keeps. The blessings and virtues of good company have been discussed. At times, one understands the evil of bad company but finds it hard to disassociate with them for many social reasons. The best way to get rid of the bad company is to find the company of those who adhere to the truth and are strong believers. This would help the seeker to refrain from sins and misdeeds. Changing the environment is hard, but slowly steadily, the heedless friends would lose interest in the person and leave him alone.

When one engages with someone who does not care about the evils of the tongue as backbiting, gossip then, inadvertently he will get dragged in the situation and do the same. These are the habits that need to be broken and one can only do so by staying away from the company of those who engage in such hideous activities. Once, the habit of minor sins is broken, the heart finds peace in the acts of worship and one finds it easier to be obedient to Allahﷻ. If a sin occurs, the best is to accept responsibility and repent. The friends with whom one commits sin and the companions of worldly benefits will be the first to abandon their friend on the Day of Resurrection as Allahﷻ mentions in Qurán:

> "Close friends, that Day, will be enemies to each other, except for the righteous." [Qurán, al Jathiya 45:67]

When a person mingles with the wicked, he is counted as one of those, even if he does not approve of their conduct. It is important to stay away from those who are heedless and engage in bad behaviour. One should try to acquire the companionship of a person better than him so he can see his own faults and be concerned with one's own moral and spiritual reformation. On the other hand, when one chooses the company of a man worse than himself, then the *Nafs* would regard itself to be pious and self-conceit '*ujub*' will take over. The seeker will certainly gain the impression that he is better and be discerned towards his own deficiencies.

The friendship of the worldly is mostly unreliable as when they discover each other's faults, they sever the relationship. The Creator maintains His relationship with His servants despite being aware of their innumerable deficiencies. Only He is the true Companion, for He is firm in His Friendship even while having the knowledge of the faults of His servants. The friends of Allahﷻ *'Wali'* who have cultivated in themselves Divine Attributes also maintain their relationship with a person even after discovering their defects and will conceal the greatest sins. Thus, a man should establish his relationship with Allahﷻ or with those who are linked to Allahﷻ.[4]

Stinginess

Allahﷻ mentions in Qur'an:

"Those who are miserly and enjoin miserliness on other men and hide what Allah has bestowed upon them of His Bounties. And We have prepared for the disbelievers a disgraceful torment."

[Qurán, Al Nisa 4:37]

Stinginess or *'bukhl'* is described as a trait applied for shortcoming in giving financial rights. Abu Hurairah⌘ narrated that the Beloved Prophetﷺ said, "The parable of the miser and the spender is that of two men clad in armour from their chests to their collars. As for the spender, he does not spend but that it extends or broadens over his skin until it covers the tips of his hands and feet. As for the miser, he does not want to spend anything but that every ring contracts in its place; he tries to loosen it, but it will not." [Bukhari : 1375, Muslim : 102]

Abu Hurairah⌘ reported that Allah's Messengerﷺ said, "The dust in the way of Allahﷻ and the smoke of Hell can never be combined on the face of a man. Greed and faith can never be combined in the heart." [Sunan al-Nasai : 3111]

The origin of this disease is love of the ephemeral world. The one who holds the worldly possessions close to heart finds it hard to give them away. The person who is possessed by the thoughts that he will not be left with enough whereas Allah's Messengerﷺ said, "Allahﷻ said: 'O son of Adam! Spend in charity, and I will spend on you.'" [Bukhari 5352, Sahih Muslim : 993]

The one who withholds for the fear of future and relies on his resources is even worse as Allahﷻ promises that He is the one who provides sustenance and be relied upon. However, the miser relies on his possessions and resources, which is 'shirk' in itself.

Sayedda Asmah﷐ narrated that Allah's Messengerﷺ said, "Spend in charity and do not count it, lest Allahﷻ counts it against you. Do not hoard it, lest Allahﷻ withhold from you." [Bukhari : 2451, Muslim : 1029]

Chapter Eight

JOURNEY OF THE SEEKER

A true Sufi's attention towards creation is not disruptive in his cognizance of Allahﷻ. The service to creation is by the Command of Allahﷻ and the purpose of his duty towards the creation is to carry out the order of Allahﷻ and to achieve His pleasure. Thus, his attention towards creation is solely for the sake of Allahﷻ. His attention towards creation, rather being disruptive becomes an aide to his cognizance with Allahﷻ. As mentioned in Quran:

"*Indeed, you have plenty of work during the day,*"

[Qurán, al Muzammil 73:7]

and after mentioning the rights of creation, it is stated:

"*Always remember the Name of your Lord, and devote yourself to Him wholeheartedly.*" [Qurán, al Muzammil 73:8]

The indication is towards keeping constant vigil as the reminder is given at the beginning and the end.[1]

It is narrated that Umar؇ met a group of people who were sitting idle. He asked them who they were. "We are of those who put their affairs in the hands of Allahﷻ, and we trust in Him," they replied. "Indeed, you do not!" he angrily responded. "You are nothing but freeloaders, parasites upon other people's efforts! For someone who truly trusts in Allahﷻ first plants the seed in this earth, then hopes and expects and puts his affairs in the hand of the Sustainer!"[2]

Some Shaykhs assert that work in the professions, crafts, and businesses is a condition of faith as according to Hadith, the truthful and trustworthy businessman will be in the company of Prophets, saints and martyrs on the Day of Judgment. [Darimi, Tirmidhi]

The certainty of faith is defined by carrying out the religious obligations and lawful earning as mentioned in Qurán:

> *"But when the prayer is ended, disperse abroad in the land and seek of Allah's grace, and remember Allah much that you may be successful."*
>
> *[Qurán, Jum'ah 62:10]*

Allah's Messengerﷺ has given a comprehensive definition of a believer, as he said, "Have I not informed you? The believer is the one who is trusted with the lives and wealth of people. The Muslim is the one from whose tongue and hand, people are safe. The one striving in *jihad* in the way of Allahﷻ is the one who wages *jihad* against himself in obedience to Allah. The emigrant is one who emigrates away from sins and evil deeds." [Musnad Ahmad: 23958]

Sayeedina Husayn ibn Ali؇, the dear grandson of the Beloved Prophetﷺ narrated, "I asked my father about what the Messenger of Allahﷺ used to do when he entered his house. He replied: 'When he went to his house, he would divide his time in three: one part for Allahﷻ [e.g., engaging in optional acts of worship], one part for his family [speaking and conversing with them], and one part for himself [personal relaxation]. He would then divide his personal time between necessary work and work for the benefit of the people. [In other words, some time for his own work and some time for the people]. This portion [which he set aside for the people] was spent by conveying to his close associates [who would then convey this] to the masses. He would not withhold anything from them. As for the portion which he set aside for the ummah [outside his house], it was his habit to give preference to the people of virtue." [*Tirmidhi has recorded this in his ash-Shama'il in the 'Chapter of what has been reported about the Humility of the Noble Messenger ﷺ*]

It is important to spend every breath with the cognizance of Allah ﷻ. Every duty which Allah ﷻ has assigned to a Muslim is a form of worship, even the resting time. In another Hadith, it is narrated that Allah's Messenger ﷺ once saw a rope stretched between two supports in the Masjid, "What is this?" he asked. The Companions replied, "This is Zaynab's ؓ rope, when she is tired at worship, she props herself up with it." The Messenger of Allah ﷺ said, "Take it down. You should only worship for as long as you are fresh. When you are tired, you should rest." [Bukhari: 1150, Muslim: 784]

Three Essentials

It is said that the seeker cannot reach the station of proximity unless he abides by the three essentials; Seeking Allah's ﷻ forgiveness meaning *'istighfar'*, Sending blessings upon the Beloved Prophet ﷺ *'Salwat'* and performing the night vigil prayers, *'Tahajjud'*.

Seeking forgiveness erases the misdeeds and the believers are commanded to do so in Qurán:

> "And seek forgiveness from Allah; surely, Allah is Forgiving, compassionate."
>
> [Qurán, al Muzammil 73:20]

And, Allah ﷻ mentions in Qurán that He forgives those who seek forgiveness:

"And whoever does evil or wrongs his own soul, but afterwards seek Allah's forgiveness, will find Allah is Forgiving, Compassionate."

[Qurán, an Nisa 4:110]

Seeking forgiveness means repenting and seeking Allah's mercy through the tongue. The Beloved Prophet ﷺ said, "I swear by Allah ﷻ that I supplicate for Allah's forgiveness and turn to Him more than seventy times a day." [Bukhari]

Seeking forgiveness is a form of supplication in recognition of the wrongdoings and sins. At times, a person may think that he cannot abstain from a particular sin, but the scholars advise that even when one finds it hard to abstain from a sin, he should still seek Allah's forgiveness. Allah ﷻ by His Mercy will help the person to abstain from that sin or if the person dies during that time, at least he would have sought forgiveness from Allah ﷻ.

Anas ؓ narrated that Allah's Messenger ﷺ said, "Allah ﷻ has said: 'O son of Adam! I shall go on forgiving you so long as you pray to Me and aspire for My forgiveness whatever may be your sins. O son of Adam! I do not care even if your sins should pile up to the sky and should you beg pardon of Me, I would forgive you. O son of Adam! If you come to Me with an earth full of sins and meet Me, not associating anything with Me in worship, I will certainly grant you as much pardon as will fill the earth.'" [Tirmidhi, Riyad as-Salihin 1878]

The second essential is sending blessings upon the Beloved Prophet ﷺ. Allah ﷻ commands the believers:

"Verily, Allah sends blessing upon the Prophet and His angels do as well. O you who believe, send blessing upon him and ask for peace."

[Qurán, Al-Ahzab 33:56]

Sending blessings upon the Beloved Prophet ﷺ is the Sunnah of Allah ﷻ Himself as mentioned in the above verse. When the servant of Allah ﷻ sends the blessings upon Allah's Beloved Prophet ﷺ, Allah ﷻ sends blessings upon his servants as the Beloved Prophet ﷺ said, "Whoever sends blessings upon me once will have Allah ﷻ send blessings upon him ten times." [Muslim 408]

اَللّٰهُمَّ صَلِّ عَلَى مُحَمَّدٍ وَعَلَى اٰلِ مُحَمَّدٍ كَمَا صَلَّيْتَ عَلَى اِبْرَاهِيْمَ وَعَلَى اٰلِ اِبْرَاهِيْمَ اِنَّكَ حَمِيْدٌ مَجِيْدٌ.

اَللّٰهُمَّ بَارِكْ عَلَى مُحَمَّدٍ وَعَلَى اٰلِ مُحَمَّدٍ كَمَا بَارَكْتَ عَلَى اِبْرَاهِيْمَ وَعَلَى اٰلِ اِبْرَاهِيْمَ اِنَّكَ حَمِيْدٌ مَجِيْدٌ.

The people who would be the closest to the Beloved Prophet ﷺ would be those who invoked blessings for him the most, as narrated by Ibn Mas'ud ؓ. [Tirmidhi 484]

How much blessings should one invoke? The answer is in the Hadith as narrated by Ubay ibn Káab ؓ, "'I said: 'O Allah's Messenger ﷺ, I frequently invoke Allah to elevate your rank. How much of my supplications should I devote to you?' The Beloved Prophet ﷺ said, 'You may devote as much as you wish.' When I suggested a quarter, he said, 'Do whatever you wish, but if you increase it, it will be better for you.' I suggested half, and he said, 'Do whatever you wish, but if you increase, it will be better for you.' I suggested two-thirds, and he said, 'Do whatever you wish but if you increase, it will be better for you.' I said, 'Shall I devote all my supplications invoking Allah to elevate your rank?' He said, 'Then you will be freed from your worries and your sins will be forgiven.'" [Tirmidhi]

The third essential is the night vigil prayers, *Tahajjud*, as Allahﷻ mentions in Qurán:

> "And they who pass the night prostrating themselves before their Lord and standing." [Qurán Al-Furqan 25:64]

The Beloved Prophetﷺ said, "The best prayer after the obligatory prayers is the night prayer." [Muslim]

Salman Al-Farsi ؓ narrated that the Beloved Prophetﷺ said, "Observe the night vigil Prayer; it was the practice of the righteous before you and it brings you closer to your Lord and it is penance for evil deeds and erases the sins and repels disease from the body." [At-Tabarani]

A man once asked a righteous man that he was unable to perform the *Tahajjud* prayers and asked for a solution. The righteous advised him, "Do not disobey Allahﷻ during the day and He will keep you up in His Mercy at night."

Abu Hurairah ؓ narrated that Allah's Messengerﷺ said, "Our Lord, the Blessed, the Superior, comes every night down on the nearest Heaven to us when the last third of the night remains, saying: "Is there anyone to invoke Me, so that I may respond to invocation? Is there anyone to ask Me, so that I may grant him his request? Is there anyone seeking My forgiveness, so that I may forgive him?" [Bukhari 1145]

Love of Allah

Allahﷻ mentions in Qurán:

> "O believers, whosoever of you turns from their religion, Allah will assuredly bring forth a people [instead of you] whom He loves, and who love Him"
>
> [Qurán, al Maidah 5:54]

Allah's Messenger ﷺ said, "He who loves to meet Allah ﷻ, Allah ﷻ also loves to meet him, and who dislikes to meet Allah ﷻ, Allah ﷻ abhors to meet him. There is death before (one is able to) meet Allah ﷻ. (Sahih Muslim 2684c)

Sayeddina Abu Bakr ؓ said, "He who tastes the pleasure of Allah's ﷻ love will never want to seek the world and will be disinclined towards people."

For a believer, the three sources, love of Allah ﷻ, fear of Allah ﷻ and hope in Allah ﷻ have to be combined together. Ibn Rajab ؒ explained, "It is known that worship is built from only three sources: fear, hope, and love. Each one is an intrinsic duty, and combining the three is an obligatory injunction. Because of this, the Forebears censured whoever devoted oneself to one while neglecting the other two.

The innovation of the *Khawarij* and those resembling them came about from emphasizing fear while avoiding love and hope; the innovation of the *Murji'a* [those who believe that man guarantees the unrepentant safety from punishment for grave sins] came about from clinging to hope alone while avoiding fear; and the innovation of *ibahiya* (advocates of freethinking) and Divine indwelling (hulul) who ascribe themselves to devotion came about from singling out love while avoiding fear and hope."[3]

The Beloved Prophet ﷺ said, "There are three things which if a person finds them, he has found the sweetness of faith: when Allah ﷻ and His Messenger ﷺ are dearer to him than all else; when he loves a person for no other reason than for the sake of Allah ﷻ; and when he hates to return to *kufr* (disbelief) after Allah ﷻ has saved him from it as he would hate to be thrown into fire," [Bukhari].

When one loves someone, the desire arises in the heart to be loved by the beloved. The way to love Allahﷻ and to gain His love is to follow the Beloved Prophetﷺ. As Allahﷻ gave the believers the way to His Divine Love:

> "Say, [O Muhammad], "If you should love Allah, then follow me, [so] Allah will love you and forgive you your sins. And Allah is Forgiving and Merciful."
>
> [Qur'an, Aal e Imran 3:31]

Jabir﷛ narrated, "Sáad ibn Mu'ad﷛ was wounded by an arrow on the Day of the Hosts, during the Battle of the Trench, so that the medial vein in his arm was severed. Therefore, Allah's Messengerﷺ attempted to cauterize it. However, when he did, the arm began to swell, and after a short while the blood started flowing again. Again, an attempt was made to cauterize the wound, and again the arm was swollen. When Sáad﷛ saw what had happened, he said, "O Lord! Don't take my life until my eyes have been soothed by the sight of Bani Qurayza."

The blood ceased to flow from his wound, and not a single drop of blood seeped from it until [finally, after having been brought to their knees by the Muslim blockade of their quarter] Bani Qurayza agreed to submit to whatever Saad﷛ decided concerning them. Then, Sa'ad﷛ decided that their men must be put to death, and that their women [and children] be allowed to live. Allah's Messengerﷺ said, 'You have decided their fate in conformance with the decision of Allahﷻ. The number of their men was four hundred, when [the sentence had been carried out] the men of Qurayza had been executed, Saa'd's﷛ wound began to flow as before. And shortly, he died of it." [Tirmidhi:1582]

Saád﷠ desired to live, so he could see the end of the enemy of Allahﷻ and once the men of Qurayza were executed, his wound reopened. This Hadith shows the love of the Companions for Allahﷻ, as they wished to live for Allahﷻ and desired death for Allahﷻ. From the prayer of Saa'd﷠, the rationale behind living for Allahﷻ and dying for Allahﷻ is clearly expressed. Thus, the love of life springs from love of involvement in the practices of worship and devotion as Saád ﷠ said, "Then let me live so that I may fight for You against them." And desire for death was based on no more than his wish to preserve the religion and be united with Allahﷻ.

It is narrated by Jabir﷠, that soon after Saád bin Muad﷠ passed away, the Beloved Prophetﷺ said, "The Throne was shaken." and in another version, he said, "The Throne of the Merciful was shaken ... at the death of Saa'd ibn Mu'ad." [Bukhari: 3802, Muslim: 2466, Tirmidhi: 3848, Ibn Majah: 158]

Fear of Allah (Taqwa)

Fear of Allahﷻ means that one fears His punishment either in this life or in the Hereafter. Fearing Allahﷻ is a quality attributed to the believers;

> "They fear their Lord above them."
>
> [Qurán, an Nahl 16:50]

Fear has three stages as explained by Abu Ali al-Daqqaq ﷫; Fear, dread, and awe. Fear is a precondition and demands true faith as Allahﷻ commanded:

> "Fear Me, if you are believers."
>
> [Qurán, Aal e Imran 3:175]

Dread is a precondition of religious knowledge, as Allah ﷻ mentions;

> "His servants dread Allah ﷻ, if they have knowledge.'
>
> [Qurán, al Fatir 35:28]

As for awe, it is a precondition of Divine gnosis, as Allah ﷻ mentions:

> "So, stand in awe of Me"
>
> [Qurán, An Nahl 16:51]

When one is afraid of something, he runs away from it, whereas the one who fears Allah ﷻ runs toward Him. The true fear is to abstain from sins inwardly and outwardly. Fear brings the servant to a continuous state of self-scrutiny, which burns out the carnal desires and banishes the soul. Hatim al-Asam ؓ said, "Everything has its adornment; the adornment of worship is fear; and one of the signs of fear is cutting short one's hope for this world." [4]

Allah ﷻ mentions in Qurán:

> "Surely the noblest among you in the sight of Allah is the most Godfearing of you."
>
> [Qurán, al Hujurat 49:13]

It was narrated from Jabir bin 'Abdullah that Allah's Messenger ﷺ said, "O people, fear Allah ﷻ and be moderate in seeking a living, for no soul will die until it has received all its provision, even if it is slow in coming. So, fear Allah ﷻ and be moderate in seeking provision; take that which is permissible and leave that which is forbidden. "[Sunan Ibn Majah: 2144]

Fear of Allahﷻ is the quintessence of all good things. The True Reality of *Taqwa* or piety consists of protecting oneself from Allah'sﷻ punishment through obedience to Him. The root of fear of Allahﷻ is to protect oneself from associating anything or anyone with Allahﷻ, protecting oneself from acts of disobedience and doubtful things. Allah's Messengerﷺ said, "And if you were to know you would have wept more and laughed less." [Muslim 2359a]

Abu Dharr﷛ narrated that "Allah's Messengerﷺ said to him, "Have *Taqwa* of Allahﷻ wherever you are, and follow an evil deed with a good one to wipe it out, and treat the people with good behaviour." [Jami` at-Tirmidhi 1987]

Umar﷛ said, "The nobility of the Momin is his *Taqwa*, his deen is his noble descent, his manliness is his good character..." [Muwatta Malik, kitab al Jihad, Book 21:966]

When one fears Allahﷻ, Allahﷻ makes turning away from this world easy for him. It is said that a man's fear of Allah is evident in three things; complete trust in Allahﷻ with respect to what has not been granted to him, satisfaction with what has been granted to him and patience with respect to what has eluded him. Abu Hurairah﷛ narrated that the Messenger of Allahﷺ said: "The fear of Allahﷻ and good morals are the two major characteristics which lead to Paradise." [At-Tirmidhi and Al-Hakim, Bulugh al-Maram Book 16, Hadith 1576]

Hope in Allah

Allahﷻ mentions in Qurán:

"Whosoever hopes to meet with Allah, Allah's term is coming."

[Qurán, al Ankabut 29:5]

Allah's Messengerﷺ said, "Whoever said "None has the right to be worshipped but Allahﷻ and has in his heart good (faith) equal to the weight of a barley grain will be taken out of Hell. And whoever said: "None has the right to be worshipped but Allahﷻ and has in his heart good (faith) equal to the weight of a wheat grain will be taken out of Hell. And whoever said, "None has the right to be worshipped but Allahﷻ and has in his heart good (faith) equal to the weight of an atom will be taken out of Hell." (Bukhari 44)

Just as fear occurs in regard to something that may take place in the future, so does hope occur in regard to something that is anticipated in the future. Hope is different to longing as the person who is hopeful takes action whereas the one who longs does not take action; hence it is of no benefit. Hope is the sustenance and freedom of the heart; it means following the commands of Allahﷻ and hoping for His mercy. Ali al-Rudhbari said: "Fear and hope are like two wings of a bird. When they are balanced, the bird's flight is straight and balanced, whereas if one of them is deficient, the flight becomes deficient, too. And when both are missing, the bird enters the precinct of death."

Reliance on Allah (Tawakkul)

Allahﷻ mentions in Qurán:

"And whosoever puts his trust in Allah, He shall suffice him."
[Qurán, at Talaq 65:3]

It is reported on the authority of Imranؓ that Allah's Messengerﷺ said, "Seventy thousand people of my Ummah would be admitted into Paradise without rendering any account. The Companions said, "Who would be those (fortunate persons)? The Beloved Prophetﷺ said, "Those who do not cauterise and practise charm, but repose trust in their Lord." 'Ukkashaؓ then stood up and said: "Supplicate (before) Allahﷻ that He should make me one among them." The Beloved Prophetﷺ said, "You are one among them." Imranؓ narrated, "Another man stood up and said, 'Allah's Messengerﷺ, supplicate (before) Allahﷻ that He should make me one among them.'" The Prophetﷺ said, "'Ukkasha has preceded you (in this matter).'" [Sahih Muslim 218a]

It is important to understand that the place of trust is in the heart. Once, the servant has ascertained that determination comes from Allahﷻ, he realises that any hardship is pre-determined by Allahﷻ and any success is also facilitated by Him. According to the great Sufis, the one who puts his trust in Allahﷻ goes through three stages: trust in Allahﷻ, surrender to Allahﷻ, and relegating one's affairs to Allahﷻ. The one who practices trust in Allahﷻ relies on His promise of sustenance. The one who surrenders himself is content with his knowledge of Allahﷻ and the one who relegates his affairs is satisfied with His Decree.

However, there are rules that need to be followed, as reported by Anas ibn Malikؓ that a man asked the Beloved

Prophet ﷺ, "O Allah's Messenger ﷺ! should I tie my camel and trust in Allah ﷻ, or should I leave her untied and trust in Allah ﷻ?" The Prophet ﷺ said, "Tie her and trust in Allah ﷻ." [Sunan al-Tirmidhi 2517]

Another Hadith proves the importance of taking measures. It was at the time when Jinn came to accept Islam and Allah's Beloved Prophet ﷺ drew a circle of protection called Hisar around Ibne Masud ؓ and gave him specific instructions. As narrated by Ibn Mas'ud ؓ, "Allah's Prophet ﷺ performed his evening prayers and when he finished, he took my hand and went out to the rocky flood plain of Makkah where he sat me down. Then he drew a circle around me and said, "Do not cross beyond your line. Many people will come to you. Do not speak to them, and they will not speak to you." [Bukhari: 7281, Tirmidhi: 2861]

Love of the Beloved Prophet ﷺ

As humans we need role models and Qurán clearly defines that Allah's Messenger ﷺ is the best example:

"Indeed, in the Messenger of Allah you have an excellent example, for whoever has hope in Allah and the Last Day, and remembers Allah often."

[Qurán, Al-Ahzab, 33:21]

The love for the Beloved Prophet ﷺ is a condition for every believer. The belief is incomplete without the love for the Beloved Prophet ﷺ as the Beloved Prophet ﷺ said, "None of you have faith until I am more beloved to him than his children, his father, and all of the people." [Bukhari:15, Muslim 44]

The way to love the Prophet ﷺ is to follow his Sunnah, as the Beloved Prophet ﷺ said, "Whoever actively observes my Sunnah, then he has loved me. And whoever loves me, shall be with me in Paradise. [Tirmidhi]

As a believer, we are to follow the Prophetic sunnah including morals and ethics as this was the part of the Prophetic mission. The Beloved Prophet ﷺ said, "I was sent to perfect good character." [Bukhari]

However, moral values cannot be isolated from the physical aspects of the Prophetic Sunnah as they are an integral part of the same. Anas bin Malik ؓ reported a Hadith where three men came to the Prophet's wives inquiring of the Prophet's acts of worship. When they were informed of it, they realised that they could do much more. The first of them said: "As for me, I will stand awake the whole night and pray throughout". The second said: "I will fast for a year and will not break my fast". The third then said: "I will isolate myself from women and will never go into marriage". When the Beloved Prophet ﷺ came and heard their comments, he said, "As for me, I am the most fearful of Allah ﷻ and the most God-conscious among you. Yet, I fast and break my fast. I pray and I rest. I even get married. Whoever deviates from my Sunnah, is not with me." [Bukhari]

Love tends to transcend reason; therefore, it is equally important to build our innate feelings of love based on sound knowledge rather than arbitrary emotions that may delude us or falter away. For that reason, it is important that we learn about the life of the Beloved Prophet ﷺ and walk in his footsteps as that is the only way to Allah ﷻ. Narrated Ibn 'Abbas that Allah's Messenger ﷺ said, "Love Allah ﷻ for what He nourishes you from His Blessings, love me due to the love of Allah ﷻ, and love the people of my house due to love of me." [Jami` at-Tirmidhi 3789]

Anas narrated, "A man asked the Prophet about the Hour (Day of Judgment) saying, "When will the Hour be?" The Beloved Prophet said, "What have you prepared for it?" The man said, "Nothing, except that I love Allah and His Apostle ." The Beloved Prophet said, "You will be with those whom you love." We had never been so glad as we were on hearing that saying of the Prophet ("You will be with those whom you love.") Therefore, I love the Prophet, Abu Bakr and 'Umar and I hope that I will be with them because of my love for them, though my deeds are not similar to theirs." [Bukhari: 037]

Narrated Abu Musa that Allah's Messenger said, "A man may love some people but he cannot catch up with their good deeds." "Everyone will be with those whom he loves." [Bukhari 6170]

The faith of a Muslim is incomplete till he loves the Prophet more than his family and his own life, as narrated by Abdullah ibn Hishaam, "We were with the Prophet, when he was holding the hand of 'Umar ibn al-Khattaab. Umar said to him: "O Messenger, you are dearer to me than everything except my own self." The Prophet said: "No, by the One in Whose hand is my soul, not until I am dearer to you than your own self." 'Umar said to him: "Now, by Allah, you are dearer to me than my own self." The Prophet said: "Now (you are a true believer), O 'Umar." [Bukhari Vol: 008, Book 078, Hadith: 628]

During the Battle of Uhud, an Ansari woman's father, brother and husband were killed in the fighting for Allah's Messenger. She asked, "What has happened to Allah's Messenger, may Allah bless him and grant him peace?" They said, "He is as well as you would like, praise be to Allah !" She said, "Show him to me so I can look at him." When she saw him, she said, "Every affliction is nothing now that you are safe." [Bayhaqi Volume 003, Pg 302]

One night 'Umar ؓ went out to observe the people. He saw an old woman tending wool in the lamp light and reciting a quatrain. Listening to the quatrain, Umar ؓ sat down in tears. [al-Zuhd pg. 362-363]

> *"The prayer of the good be upon Muhammad ﷺ,*
> *May the blessed bless him!*
> *I was standing in tears before dawn, if only I knew, when death gives us different forms,*
> *Whether the abode will join me to my beloved!"* (Prophet ﷺ)

It is narrated that Allah's Messenger ﷺ used to deliver sermon reclining on the trunk of a palm tree. The Companions made a pulpit for him and he delivered a sermon from it. Upon that the trunk wept like the weeping of a she-camel. So, he descended and stroked it and it stopped crying. [Jami Tirmidhi:3647, Bukhari:783]

Once the Beloved Prophet ﷺ said, "I wish I could meet my brothers." The Companions said, "Are we not your brothers?" The Beloved Prophet ﷺ said, "You are my Companions, but my brothers are those who believe in me although they never saw me." [Imam Ahmad]

Abu Huraira ؓ narrated that Allah's Messenger ﷺ said, "By Him in Whose Hand is the life of Muhammad ﷺ, a day would come to you when you would not be able to see me, and the glimpse of my face would be dearer to one than one's own family, one's property and in fact everything." [Muslim:5833]

Uways al-Qarni ؓ had never seen the Beloved Prophet ﷺ therefore, he remained a Tabaée, yet his love for the Beloved Prophet ﷺ is legendary. It is narrated by Umar ؓ that the Beloved Prophet ﷺ told him, "There will come to you one Uways ibn 'Amir'" In the same Hadith, he said, "If you can ask him to seek forgiveness for you, then do so." [Muslim: 2542]

Allahﷻ specifically mentioned the respect for the Beloved Prophetﷺ:

"O believers! Do not raise your voices above the voice of the Prophet, nor speak loudly to him as you do to one another, or your deeds will become void while you are unaware.

[Qurán, Al Hujurat 49:2]

On the day of Judgement, we do not have any deeds which would take us to Jannah, the Beloved Prophetﷺ would be the one to intercede on our behalf. Anasؓ narrated that the Beloved Prophetﷺ said, "The believers will gather on the Day of Resurrection and will say: 'Should we not ask [someone] to intercede for us with our Lord?' So, they will come to Adamؑ and will say: 'You are the Father of mankind; Allahﷻ created you with His hand, made His angels bow to you and He taught you the names of everything, so intercede for us with you Lord so that He may give us relief form this place where we are.'

And, Adamؑ will say: 'I am not in a position [to do that] and he will mention his wrongdoing and will feel ashamed and will say: Go to Noahؑ, for he is the first Messenger that Allahﷻ sent to the inhabitants of the earth'. So, they will come to him and he will say: 'I am not in a position [to do that] and he will mention his having requested something of his Lord about which he had no [proper] knowledge (Qurán,11: 45-46), and he will feel ashamed and will say: Go to the Friend of the Merciful-Abrahamؑ.'

So, they will go to him and Abrahamؑ will say: 'I am not in a position [to do that]. Go to Mosesؑ, a servant to whom Allahﷻ spoke and to whom He gave the Torah.'

So, they will go to him and he will say: 'I am not in a position [to do that] - and he will mention the taking of a life, (Qurán

28:15-16), and he will be ashamed in the sight of his Lord and will say: Go to Jesus ﷺ, Allah's servant and Messenger, Allah's word and spirit.'

So, they will go to him and he will say: 'I am not in a position [to do that]. Go to Muhammad ﷺ, a servant to whom Allah ﷻ has forgiven all his wrongdoing, past and future.'

So, they will come to me and I shall set forth to ask permission to come to my Lord, and permission will be given and when I shall see my Lord, I shall prostrate myself. He will leave me thus for such time as it pleases Him and then it will be said [to me]: 'Raise your head, ask and it will be granted, speak and it will be heard, intercede and your intercession will be accepted'.

So, I shall raise my head and praise Him with a form of praise that He will teach me. Then, I shall intercede and He will set me a limit [as to the number of people], so I shall admit them into Paradise. Then, I shall return to Him, and when I shall see my Lord [I shall bow down] as before. Then, I shall intercede and He will set me a limit [as to the number of people]. So, I shall admit them into Paradise.

Then, I shall return for a third time, then a fourth, and I shall say: 'There remains in Hellfire only those whom the Qurán has confined and who must be there for eternity. There shall come out of Hellfire, who has said: There is no god but Allah and who has in his heart goodness weighing a barleycorn; then those shall come out of Hellfire, who has said: There is no god but Allah and who has in his heart goodness weighing a grain of wheat; then, there shall come out of Hellfire, he who has said: There is no god but Allah and who has in his heart goodness weighing an atom." [Bukhari, Muslim, Tirmidhi, Ibn Majah]

Virtuous Character (Ikhlaq)

The word *Ikhlaq* appears in Qurán in the verse that says of the Prophet ﷺ:

> *"Indeed, you are of lofty character"*
>
> [Quran, al Qalam 68:4]

Allah's Messenger ﷺ said, "I was sent to perfect good character." [Muwatta Malik, 47:8]. *Ikhlaq* is mentioned in numerous Hadith affirming its necessity and importance in Islam. As the Beloved Prophet ﷺ said, 'The best of you in Islam is the best of you in character when they possess understanding (of the deen)."[Al-Albani Book 14:273]

The Beloved Prophet ﷺ also said, "Nothing is placed on the Scale that is heavier than good character. Indeed, the person with good character will have attained the rank of the person of fasting and prayer." [Jami` at-Tirmidhi 2003]

In his book *al Ihya ul Uloom*, al-Ghazali ﷺ defined good character or *Ikhlaq* as, "Character is a term for a firmly entrenched form in the soul from which actions emanate with ease and facility, without need for reflection or deliberation. As this form in the soul produces beautiful and praiseworthy actions by the measures of reason and the Shariáh, it is called a good character; and in as much as it produces repugnant actions, it is called a bad character. We have specified that it should be firmly entrenched, for he who spends his wealth rarely, and for a specific need of his, cannot be called generous unless this quality is firmly established within him. And we have further stipulated those actions proceed from him with ease and without deliberation because he who spends his wealth or remains silent during anger only after some effort and deliberation, it cannot be said of him that he possesses a generous or patient character."

There are four conditions for *Ikhlaq*; a beautiful or repugnant action, the ability to perform the action, knowledge and an entity in the soul which inclines a person to either excellence or repugnance. *Ikhlaq* is not limited to actions, for example a person may be generous but cannot spend either due to lack of money or some other hindrance, or alternatively a person may be a miser, and though he may spend but just to show off.

According to Ibn e Arabi, "A seeker, needs to have high morals, good character, proper behaviour and identify bad traits. The relationships of the seeker with others must be based on the best of conduct and whoever neglects his duties is considered to have bad character."[5]

Repentance (Tawba)

Repentance is the characteristic of the believers, as Qurán mentions:

"And turn all together to God [in repentance], O you believers."

[Qurán, an Nur 24:31]

Repentance has its causes, sequence and divisions. At first, the heart awakens from the slumber of heedlessness and the servant becomes aware of his evil condition through Allah's help. As narrated by An-Nu'man bin Bashir, the Beloved Prophet said, "Beware! There is a piece of flesh in the body if it becomes good (reformed) the whole body becomes good but if it gets spoilt the whole body gets spoilt and that is the heart. [Bukhari 52]

Allah's Messenger said, "When a servant acknowledges his sin and repents, Allah forgives him." [Bukhari, Muslim, Mishkat al-Masabih:2330]

Repentance is the first stage of the wayfarers and the first station of the seeker. In Arabic language, the true meaning of repentance is to 'return'. Repentance thus, is to return from what is blameworthy according to the Divine Law, to what is praiseworthy. Allahﷻ mentions in Qurán:

> "Truly, God loves those who repent, and He loves those who cleanse themselves."
>
> [Qurán, al Baqarah 2:222]

There are three essentials for repentance to be valid; remorse for acts contradicting the Divine Law, immediate abandonment of the sin and resolve never to commit similar acts of disobedience. Some of those who have attained true realisation assert that remorse is sufficient to achieve repentance, because it entails the two other conditions, since it is inconceivable that one persists in doing something one regrets or that one regrets something one has resolved to commit in the future.[6]

When the servant considers the evil deed, he has committed, he will repent and abstain from it in future then, Allahﷻ helps him to strengthen his resolve. Firstly, one is to part company with sinful friends; those who try to entice the seeker into rejecting his goal and undermine his resolve. This can only be accomplished through perseverance in contemplation, which will increase the desire for repentance and increase fear of Allahﷻ and hope for His mercy.

At this stage, the knot of persistence in sin is loosened and one can refrain from sin. At this stage the seeker is able to abandon the sin and make a resolve. Once, the seeker proceeds to live in accordance with his goal and act in accordance with his resolve, he would be in his undertaking. However, if he violates the demands of repentance once or twice, his determination would require renewal. This may happen many times but one should not despair of repentance.

When the servant abandons acts of disobedience, resolves not to commit any sin, feels remorseful and regrets his behaviour, this makes his repentance complete. The strive then becomes sincere, he substitutes solitude for the company of evil friends and spends his time in lamenting his former evil ways. The rain of his tears erases the traces of his stumbling and the beauty of his repentance treats the wounds of his failings. Repentance consists of feeling remorseful for an act of disobedience to Allahﷻ, out of fear of His retribution and love. It is to make an affirmed resolve not to repeat the sin.

The seeker must try to rectify the damage he has done to others. Either, he should meet their claims if he has enough resources or firmly resolve to fulfill their claims, as soon as he gets the opportunity. He should ask Allahﷻ with sincere prayers and supplications on their behalf. Abu Ali al-Daqqaq﷫ said, "Repentance consists of three parts, its beginning is *tawba* [repentance], its middle part is *inaba* [turning to Allahﷻ], and its end is *awba* [return to Allahﷻ]." Thus, he placed repentance at the beginning, return to Allahﷻ at the end and turning to Allahﷻ in the middle. Whoever repents out of fear of Divine punishment acquires repentance. Whoever repents out of desire of Divine reward acquires turning to Allahﷻ. And whoever repents out of compliance with Divine command not out of desire of reward, nor out of fear of punishment, acquires return to Allahﷻ.

As for turning to Allahﷻ, this is the characteristic of Allah's friends and those brought close, for Allahﷻ says:

> *"[Whosoever] ... turns with a penitent heart."*

> [Qurán, Qaf 50:33]

Dhu un-Nun Misri ﷺ said, "To ask for forgiveness without abandoning the sin is the repentance of liars." A man asked Rabia al-Basri ﷺ, "I have committed many sins and acts of disobedience, if I decide to turn to Allah ﷻ, would He turn to me?" She answered, "Only when He turns to you, then you are able to turn to Him."

In order for the sinner to reach the stage at which he will discover signs of Allah's ﷻ love toward him, he must travel a great distance. Therefore, it is incumbent upon everyone who knows that he has committed a sin to renounce all his faults and ask for Allah's ﷻ forgiveness. It is narrated that the Beloved Prophet ﷺ said, "One who makes *istighfar* is not considered persistent in sin, even if this occurs seventy times in a day" [Tirmidhi].

Imam Ghazali ﷺ explains the concept as "Just as you have taken returning to sins as a habit, then also take repentance as a habit, because through repentance you expiate your past sins, and it is very possible that you may have the fortune to die while in a state of repentance, *tawba*".[7]

Striving (Mujahida)

"And those who strive for Our sake, surely We shall guide them in Our ways; Allah is with the good-doers."

[Qurán al Ankabut 29:69]

Allah's Messenger ﷺ described striving or *Mujahida* as, "The one who strives in *jihad* is the one who strives against his lower-self." [Sunan al-Tirmidhi:1621]

The purpose of striving is to wean one's *Nafs* from its habits and to accustom it to resist its passions. *Nafs* has two traits that prevent it from doing good; pursuits of worldly desires and refusal to perform acts of obedience. When the *Nafs* tries to break loose in pursuit of its passion, it must be curbed with the reins of piety. When it becomes refractory in complying with Allah's ﷻ will, it should be directed towards opposing its desires. When the *Nafs* rebels and flies into rage, anger is to be conquered by good moral character and gentleness. When the *Nafs* discovers the sweet wine of relaxation and finds comfort in displaying, then it is necessary to break the habit.

The strictures of hunger and night vigils are easy as compared to improvement of a man's morals and cleansing of *Nafs*. Anyone who does not strive for Allah's sake will find no trace of the path. One should remember the small worth, lowly origin and the immorality of self. The common folk strive to protect their actions from sin, while the elect endeavour to purify their internal states. Abu Ali al-Daqqaq ﷺ said, "If someone adorns his externals with striving, Allah ﷻ will embellish his internal self with the vision of Him." [8]

Gratitude (*Shukr*)

Allah ﷻ mentions in Qurán:
"*If you are grateful, surely I will increase you*"
[Qurán, Ibrahim 14:7]

The Beloved Prophet ﷺ used to offer night prayers till his feet became swollen. Sayedda Ayesha narrated, "The Prophet ﷺ used to offer prayer at night (for such a long time) that his feet used to swell. I said, O Allah's Messenger ﷺ! Why do you do it since Allah ﷻ has forgiven you, your faults of the past and those to follow? He ﷺ said, 'Shouldn't I love to be a thankful slave (of Allah ﷻ)?'" [Bukhari 4837]

Gratitude is to give credit humbly for the beneficence to the true Benefactor. True Reality of gratitude is to praise the Benefactor by mentioning His beneficence. As for the servant's beneficence, it consists of obeying Allahﷻ and Allah'sﷻ beneficence consists of His bestowal upon the servant of the ability to express his gratitude to Him. The gratitude of the servant in its true sense is when he acknowledges his Lord's beneficence by his tongue, while at the same time confirming it by his heart. Thus, gratitude falls into the following categories: the gratitude of the tongue when the servant humbly acknowledges Allah'sﷻ beneficence, the gratitude of the body characterized by service and the gratitude of the heart when the servant exerts himself.

The grateful person is always in the presence of increase, because he constantly bears witness to Allah'sﷻ blessings. The learned express their gratitude by their words, the worshipers by their deeds and the Sufis by their rectitude in all of their states. Al-Junaydﷺ said, "Gratitude is to consider yourself to be undeserving of beneficence."

An ordinary grateful person thanks Allahﷻ at a time of abundance, whereas the truly grateful one thanks Allahﷻ at a time of deprivation. Al-Junaydﷺ was a seven-year-old boy, when his uncle al-Sari Saqtiﷺ had visitors and the discussion started about gratitude. Sari Saqtiﷺ asked Junaydﷺ, "My boy! what is gratitude?" Junaydﷺ replied, "That you do not disobey Allahﷻ with all the beneficence He has bestowed upon you." Upon that Sari Saqtiﷺ said, 'Soon Allah'sﷻ special blessing for you will be your tongue!" Al-Junaydﷺ used to say, "I cannot help but cry, when I remember those words uttered by al-Sariﷺ."

It is narrated that Dawud ﷺ asked Allah ﷻ as how to show gratitude when gratitude is a beneficence that comes from Him. Allah ﷻ revealed to him, "Now, you have really thanked Me!"

Musa ﷺ said in his conversations, "My Lord! You created Adam ﷺ with Your hand and did this and did that ... How can I thank You?" Allah ﷻ answered: "He knows that all this comes from Me, so his knowledge of this is his best gratitude to Me!"

Mujaddid Alf Thani ﷺ explained gratitude as; "Gratification means that the slave should consume outer and inner powers, bodily parts and its segments only for the purposes for which Allah ﷻ created them. If the same is not practiced, then the gratification cannot be achieved. Only Allah ﷻ is a giver of help to do so."[9]

It is narrated that one of the Prophets ﷺ passed by a small stone, from which water was gushing forth. When he wondered at that, Allah ﷻ made the stone speak and it said, "Since the moment I heard Allah ﷻ say: *'A [hell] fire, whose fuel is men and stones'* [Qurán 66:6] I cannot help weeping out of fear!"

The Prophet ﷺ then prayed to Allah ﷻ to protect that stone, whereupon Allah ﷻ revealed to him, "I have already protected it from the hellfire." The Prophet ﷺ went on, upon his return he found that water continued to gush from the stone. When he wondered about that, Allah ﷻ gave the stone the gift of speech. The Prophet ﷺ asked the stone, "Why do you keep weeping, after Allah ﷻ has forgiven you?" The stone answered: "That weeping was out of fear. Now I am weeping out of gratitude and joy!"[10]

Patience (Sabr)

The one who is patient is with Allahﷻ because he finds himself in the presence of the One Who puts him to test as Qurán mentions:

> "Verily, Allah is with those who are patient."
>
> [Qurán, al Baqarah 2:153]

Narrated by Anas؅, the Beloved Prophetﷺ said, "The real patience is at the first stroke of a calamity." [Bukhari 1302]

Mujaddid Alf Thani؅ said, "Without any distinction, in each situation, all praises are for Allahﷻ; in the times of happiness, sorrows, leisure, hardships, blessings, pain, troubles, comfort and in favours. The most perfect benediction and most perfect peace be on that Prophetﷺ who was given sufferings as none of the other Prophets, none has ever gone through the trials as he did, hence he is mercy for all worlds and the leader of all.

Respectable Sons! although time of calamity is rough and painful but it is an opportunity which is a privilege. During this difficult time, an opportunity is given to you, do praise Allahﷻ and stay focussed to your purpose. Do not consider any moment of this opportunity for yourself and remain busy in one of these; recitation of Qurán Karim, performing Salah with long recitation and repetition of the sacred verse, '*La Ilaha Ill Allah*'."[11]

Shaykh Madani؅ wrote, "Hardships of the world are also Allah'sﷻ mercy and it is through hardship that He brings His servant closer to Him, otherwise this person would become Pharaoh and Haman declaring '*ana rabbukum al-a'la*' [I am your great Lord] Thus, this world is a trial in which we are tested in different ways. We should make every effort to overcome these trials and should not enamour ourselves with anything but our Everlasting True Master. Make the correct intention for anything you do and it will become an act of worship. As the Hadith says, *'Verily all actions are based on intentions.'* Even your sleeping, eating, drinking, and the necessities of life can be converted into acts of worship. Any medium that leads to an act of worship is also an act of worship."[12]

Abstinence (Tabattul)

Tabattul means the knowledge of everything else and love for others should be overwhelmed by love and knowledge of Allahﷻ. It is to choose the pleasure of Allahﷻ and abandon what is against His will. It does not mean to forget the responsibilities towards others, however, if anything contradicts the command of Allahﷻ, then the seeker is to give preference to Allah'sﷻ Command and forget the rest.[13]

Generosity (Sakha)

Allahﷻ mentions in Qurán:

> "Say (O Prophet ﷺ): "Indeed, my Lord extends provision for whom He wills of His servants and restricts [it] for him. But whatever thing you spend [in His cause] – He will compensate it; and He is the best of providers."
>
> [Qurán, Saba 34:39]

And in another verse:

> "The example of those who spend their wealth in the way of Allah is like a seed [of grain] which grows seven spikes; in each spike is a hundred grains. And Allah multiplies [His reward] for whom He wills. And Allah is all-Encompassing and Knowing."
>
> [Qura'n, al Baqarah 2:262]

Abu Hurayra reported that Allah's Messenger said, "The believer is guileless and generous while the corrupt is a swindler and miserly." [Al-Adab Al-Mufrad:418]

The true essence of generosity is that one has no difficulty giving to others. Generosity is followed by munificence (*Jud*) and finally, preferring others to oneself (*ithar*). The one who gives away a portion and saves a portion for himself is generous, the one who gives away more and saves little for himself is munificent and the one who suffers from shortage, yet gives away his bare minimum to someone else, is the one who gives preference to others over himself *(ithar)*. Allah mentions in Qurán:

"And whoever withholds only withholds [benefit] from himself; and Allah is the free of need, while you are the needy. And if you turn away [i.e., refuse], He will replace you with another people; then they will not be the likes of you."

[Qurán, Muhammad 47:38]

The one who is miser has to realise the meaning of Allah's words:

"Destroy their riches and harden their hearts."

[Qurán, Yunus 10:88]

The ones who are cursed with parsimony must understand that the Beloved Prophet said, "Generosity is close to Allah, close to Paradise, close to the people and far from the Fire. Stinginess is far from Allah, far from Paradise, far from people and close to the Fire. The ignorant generous person, is more beloved to Allah than the worshiping stingy person." [Jami` at-Tirmidhi : 1961]

Ibn Arabi said that the one who gives from his sustenance attracts more than the miser. A miser, in addition to his sin of miserliness, accuses Allah and prefers and trusts his miserable goods over the generosity of his Lord. This is the unforgivable sin of attributing partners to Allah and may cause one to be rejected from Allah's mercy and lose his faith.[14]

According to the Hadith narrated by Abu Hurairah, a man came and asked the Beloved Prophet: "O Allah's Messenger! What kind of charity is the best?"

The Beloved Prophet replied: "To give *sadaqah* (charity) when you are healthy and greedy hoping to be wealthy and afraid of becoming poor. Don't delay giving in charity till the time when you are on the death bed when you say, "Give so much to so-and-so and so much to so-and so", as at that time the property is not yours but it belongs to so-and-so (inheritors)." [Bukhari:4.11]

Chastity

Chastity is to be cautious, to try to abstain from all that is unclean and sinful. It is to abstain from all that is doubtful and suspicious in and around you. As the Beloved Prophet said, "Leave that which is doubtful and reach for that which is sure." [Sunan an-Nisa'i:5398]

The Beloved Prophet spoke of the necessity of abandoning things that are rendered doubtful and hesitant and create uncertainty in the heart. The seeker must turn towards things that he renders secure and peaceful. It falls upon the seeker to examine each act, each word, each act of worship, each relation with others such as friendship or marriage. One must find whether each thing is good or bad, clean or unclean, right or wrong, lawful or unlawful. When it is clear, then the right must be chosen. In cases it is doubtful, then it should be abandoned in accordance with the advice of the Prophet.

Chastity is when one feels the need of something which is doubtful or unable to get a substitute and leaves it for the sake of Allah. Allah will reward the chaste with better than the doubtful thing that was abandoned, but one should not expect the reward immediately. Chastity is the foundation of religion and the path to truth. If one is chaste, all the deeds will be pure, sincere and in harmony with the Divine order. If one turns his back to chastity and piety, the Absolute Judge will place him in a shameful state in the hands of his ego. Such a person becomes a toy for the devil, who will find no resistance in temptation.[15]

Preach (Tableegh)

Tableegh means to reach out, to preach, make known or to let people be informed. According to scholars, *Tableegh* is *fardh*, however, the ways of *Tableegh* fluctuate with the circumstances. It is a great favour of Allah that the books are compiled and schools to learn Deen are established. The need for the current system of Islamic education, in these times, is *Tableegh*.

The illustrious Companions and the Tábayeen were not in need of the contemporary educational methods as they were devout and their memories were exceptional. In these critical times, the system in place is necessary due to weak retentive abilities and the ease with which one may be misled by the disinformation created through media. Without the compilation of books, the statements of the pious predecessors would not have reached us. Teaching and learning the Islamic knowledge are an august branch of *Tableegh*. Thus, in view of the necessity of these avenues it is established that this is not a *Bidá*, in fact it is a Sunnah.

Tableegh can be sub-divided into three divisions; *Tableegh* of the fundamentals and tenets of Islam to the disbelievers, *Tableegh* of the particulars of Islam to the general Muslim public and thirdly to prepare a group to competently perform *Tableegh*. Since, there are sub divisions of Tableegh, every person does not have to involve in all three, rather it is important to allocate in proportion to ability and competency. Responsibility should be allocated as Qurán mentions:

> "It is not appropriate for all the Momineen to go out (in Jihaad). Why not a group from every region go out..."
>
> [Qurán, al Anfaal, 122]

Since *Tableegh* has different categories, some should attend to one category whilst others should look after another. Teaching, physical help, writing, financial support are all avenues of *Tableegh*; as is established by the principles of Shariáh that the preliminaries are incorporated to the principal objective. Thus, Qurán states:

> "Aid and assist each other in righteousness and faithfulness."
> [Qurán, al Maaidah, 2]

Supporting and assisting the cause of Deen in any way or form is part of righteousness. Therefore, the responsibilities should be assigned according to competencies and abilities, otherwise a person who is unfit for the purpose may bring harm to the cause of *Tableegh*.[16]

Humility (Tawadu)

Allah mentions in Qurán:

> "The true servants of the Most Compassionate are those who walk on the earth humbly"
> [Qurán, al Furqan 25:63]

Allah's Messenger ﷺ said, "One will not enter Paradise with the weight of a seed of arrogance in his heart." [al-Mu'jam al-Kabir 21130]

Anas b. Malik ؓ reported: "Allah's Messenger ﷺ used to visit the sick, accompany funeral processions, ride a donkey and accept invitations from slaves. On the day [the Jewish tribes] of Qurayza and al-Nadir were conquered, he rode a donkey bridled with a rope of palm fibre and saddled with a saddle of palm fibre."

Humility means submission to the will of Allah ﷻ and abandoning resistance to His decree. It is said that one of the signs of humility in the servant of Allah ﷻ is that when he is prompted to anger, contradicted or rejected, he accepts all that with equanimity. Al-Hasan al-Basri ؒ said: "Humility is when fear settles in your heart permanently." Someone asked al-Junayd ؒ about humility, he answered, "It is the abasement of your heart before the One Who knows what is hidden."

Al-Hasan al-Basri ؒ said, "Do you know what is humility? Humility is that you leave your house and you do not meet any Muslim but that you view him as better than yourself." [al-Tawadu' wal-Khumul 116]

Ummul Momineen Ayesha ؓ said, "Verily, you are neglecting the best act of worship: humility." [al-*Zuhd* wal-Raqa'iq 391]

In short, humility is abasing one's innermost self in the presence of Allah ﷻ in accordance with the rules of proper behaviour. It is a feeling that enters the heart when one contemplates one's Lord and becomes humble before the power of the True Reality. Humility is a prelude to the onset of the conquering powers of awe, when the True Reality unveils itself.

Abu Said al-Khudriﷺ narrated that the Beloved Prophetﷺ used to feed [his] camel, sweep [his] house, mend [his] sandals, patch [his] clothes, milk [his] sheep, eat with [his] servant and help him grind, when he [the servant] got tired. He was not embarrassed to carry his goods from the market to his family. He would shake hands with both the rich and the poor; he was the first to greet people; he would not scorn any meal of which he was invited to partake, even if this was unripe and dry dates. He made do with free supplies [of provision], he was gentle of character, generous of nature, pleasant of company; his face was cheerful, he smiled much, without laughing and showed [his] sadness without frowning; he was humble without being self-effacing, generous without being extravagant; his heart was gentle, he was compassionate to every Muslim; he would never eat his fill and he would never stretch his hand to a thing that he desired."

Contentment (Qaná)

Allahﷻ mentions in Qurán:

"And whosoever does a righteous deed, be it male or female, and is a believer, we shall assuredly give him a fair life to live."

[Qurán, an Nahl 16:97]

Abu Dharrﷺ reported that the Beloved Prophetﷺ said, "O Abu Dharrﷺ, do you say an abundance of possessions is wealth?" I said, 'yes.' The Prophetﷺ said, "Do you say a lack of possessions is poverty?" I said, 'yes.' The Prophetﷺ repeated this three times, then he said, "Wealth is in the heart and poverty is in the heart. Whoever is wealthy in his heart will not be harmed, no matter what happens in the world. Whoever is impoverished in his heart will not be satisfied no matter how much he has in the world. Verily, he will only be harmed by the greed of his own soul." [al-Mu'jam al-Kabīr 1643]

According to scholars, the verse, *"Surely the pious shall be in bliss"* (Qurán 82:13) refer to contentment with one's portion in this life, whereas the verse, *"And the wicked are in fire"* (Qurán 82:14) refer to desire for the delights of this life. Bishr al-Hafi said: "Contentment is an angel who dwells only in the believing heart."

Someone asked Abu Yazid al-Bistami as to how he had achieved the Divine Love. He answered, "I gathered all the good things of this world, tied them together with the rope of contentment, placed them in the catapult of sincere striving, casted them in the sea of despair and then I rested."

It was during the days of the pilgrimage season al-Junayd Baghdadi was surrounded by a large group of Persians and Arabs who were born in foreign lands. A man came with five hundred gold coins and put them in front of him saying: 'Distribute them among these poor people.' Junayd asked: 'Do you have more?' The man answered: 'Yes, I have plenty of these.' 'Do you want to have more?' asked Junayd. He answered: 'Yes.' Junayd told him: 'Then take them back, for you are more in need of them than we are!' And he did not accept them."[17]

Lawful Sustenance

On the authority of Abu Hurairah, it is narrated that Allah's Messenger said, "Allah is good and accepts only that which is good. Allah has commanded the Faithful to do that which He commanded the Messengers, and Allah said: *"O you Messengers! Eat of the good things, and do right."* [Qurán, 23:51] And Allah has said, *"O, you who believe! Eat of the good things wherewith We have provided you..."* (Qurán, 2:172).

Then, he mentioned [the case of] a man who, having journeyed far, is dishevelled and dusty and who spreads out his hands to the sky [saying]: O Lord! O Lord! while his food is unlawful, his drink is unlawful, his clothing unlawful, and he is nourished unlawfully, so how can he be answered!" [Muslim:10, 40 Hadith an-Nawawi]

Abu Hurairah﷠ narrated that Allah's Messengerﷺ said, "A time will come when one will not care how one gains one's money, legally or illegally." [Bukhari 2059]

One of greatest needs, is to be sure that the food we eat is lawful sustenance as the lawfulness of all one enjoys in this world, is the foundation of our faith. It is upon this foundation that the religion can be built. To advance in the path of Tasawwuf, is to walk in the footsteps of the Prophetﷺ by following his Sunnah. One must not accept goods and favours for one's own self or anyone else from those whose hearts are dead, submerged in heedlessness. Lawful sustenance is obtained by working harder than is demanded of you. It is reported by Jabir﷠ that Allah's Messengerﷺ said, "O people, fear Allahﷻ and be graceful in seeking provision, for a soul will never die until it finishes its provision. If it is slow coming, fear Allahﷻ and be graceful in seeking provision. Take what is lawful and leave what is unlawful." [Sunan Ibn Majah 2135]

A clear sign of the lawfulness of one's gain is that it will not permit you to be either miser or an improvident. Allahﷻ has blessed us with intellect, knowledge, profession, health and all Grace and power are due to Him. The seeker should use these to gather his sustenance. Ahmad al-Sabti﷫, a prince, the son of the Abbasid caliph Harun al-Rashid﷫ used to work exceedingly hard as a manual labourer on Saturday. With what he earned in one day he was able to live a whole week. He dedicated the remaining six days of the week to working for Allahﷻ and worshipping Him. A morsel which is doubtful takes away the spirituality without any warning. Nowadays, with packaged foods, it is important to check the ingredients. If a chocolate or a packet of soup is being sold in a Muslim country, it does not make it Halal. One must thoroughly check where it is made and check the ingredients list as there are many such ingredients which are Haram. It is the responsibility of the consumer to check for those ingredients and avoid consuming any products which are doubtful.

Same goes for takeaway foods or eating at restaurants. One may have earned the money by halal sources, but if anything, doubtful goes in the body, it does affect the journey towards Allahﷻ. For the seekers who are following the path, it is suggested to be very cautious and not to eat takeaway foods or eat at a restaurant, unless in dire need. Not only the ingredients are unknown, but the food may have been cooked by someone who is in an impure state or heedless. Such doubtful food impacts the body which in turn affects the soul.

Time Management

It is important to value time and live in the present moment. The one who lives in imagination or following social media wastes himself. Allahﷻ has prescribed a duty, an act, a worship for every moment, therefore, know what it is and do it. One must perform the actions Allahﷻ has given us as obligations and follow the Sunnah of the Prophetﷺ. When one follows the Sunnah of the Beloved Prophetﷺ, time would be managed appropriately. As in his blessed life, we can see how he was as a father, a husband, a teacher and a guide. When one follows his ways, time is accorded for each and every aspect of life as a human.

When man becomes involved in social media, there is no end to its ramifications. It is indolence to postpone righteous deeds, moral reformation and spiritual upliftment for the future under the notion of obtaining a time devoid of worldly affairs. The one who gets involved with such wasteful activities destroys his present time. Eventually, life comes to an end without giving an opportunity to optimise the usage of time and death makes a sudden appearance. Unnecessary use of social media commonly known as web surfing is extremely detrimental for the journey of the seeker. Not only one would waste time but also forget the true purpose of life. If the worldly affairs are permissible activities, the seeker shall continue with *Dhikr* as it is said, *'Haath ba kar, dil bayaar'*, hands busy with work and heart busy with the Divine.

It does not matter to what extent man is involved in worldly affairs and in the execution of his family duties, he is obliged to turn to Allahﷻ at all times. There are four perpetual states which occur to the servant; bounty *(Ni'ma)*, calamity *(Museebah)*, obedience *(Atát)* and sin *(Ma'siyat)*. The rights of these states are termed as the Rights of Time or *Huqooq-e-Auqaat*. The right of the state of bounty is gratitude, right for calamity is patience, right for obedience is perception of Allah's Grace *(Mushahada)* and the right of sin is repentance. There is no separate fixed time set out for these rights since these are the rights of time itself and the existence of time is perpetual. If these rights are not honoured, compensation is not possible as the time does not stop and state keeps on changing.

Chapter Nine

DIVINE LAW AND THE REALITY

The Concept of Ihsan

Countless Hadiths and Qur'anic verses prove the importance of virtues as contentment, humility, sincerity, patience, love for Allahﷻ, gratitude and so forth. Muslims are encouraged to acquire these and avoid the opposites as greed, pride, hypocrisy, rancour, lust, jealousy and so forth. There is no doubt as to the prohibition of these blameworthy traits. The act of devotion is only accepted with certain conditions, some of those are external as laid down by the Islamic jurisprudence and some are internal. The concept of *Ihsan* as you see Allahﷻ is central to *Tasawwuf*. It is to be noted that no eye can behold His vision in this world. The only person who beheld the Divine vision is our Beloved Prophetﷺ, but other than him none of Allah'sﷻ creations, neither celestial or terrestrial can behold His vision.

The acts of devotion with the level of sincerity are best explained in the Hadith of Muslim, that 'Umar ibn al-Khattabؓ said:

"As we sat one day with Allah's Messengerﷺ, a man in pure white clothing and jet-black hair came to us, without a trace of travelling upon him, though none of us knew him.

He sat down before the Prophetﷺ bracing his knees against his, resting his hands on his legs, and said: "Muhammadﷺ, tell me about Islam." The Messenger of Allahﷺ said: "Islam is to testify that there is no god but Allah and that Muhammadﷺ is

Divine Law and the Reality

the Messenger of Allah, and to perform the prayer, give alms, fast in Ramadan, and perform the pilgrimage to the House if you can find a way."

He said: "You have spoken the truth," and we were surprised that he asked and then confirmed the answer. Then, he said: "Tell me about true faith (Iman)," and the Prophetﷺ answered: "It is to believe in Allah, His angels, His inspired Books, His messengers, the Last Day, and in destiny, its good and evil."

"You have spoken the truth," he said, "Now tell me about the perfection of faith (Ihsan)," and the Prophetﷺ answered: "It is to worship Allahﷻ as if you see Him, and if you do not see Him, He nevertheless sees you."

The Hadith continues to where 'Umar said:

"Then the visitor left. I waited a long while, and the Prophetﷺ said to me, "Do you know, 'Umar, who was the questioner?" and I replied, "Allah and His messengerﷺ know best." He said,

"It was Gibrael, who came to you to teach you your religion" [Sahih Muslim, 1.37: Hadith 8]

This is a *sahih* Hadith which explains the three fundamentals of our religion; *Islam*, or external compliance with what Allahﷻ asks of us; *Iman*, or the belief in the unseen that the Prophets have informed us of; and *Ihsan*, or to worship Allahﷻ as though one sees Him. The term *Ihsan* is described as beneficence, performance of good deeds, but in the religious sense it implies performing the good deeds over and above what is just and fair. It is indicative of the intense devotion of the servant to his Creator and Master and his enthusiasm for virtue and piety. What is implied by the term *Tasawwuf* in Islam is nothing but *Ihsan*. The aim of *Ihsan* is to create a sense of inner piety and a state where the heart is fully absorbed in the Divine Love.

Divine Law and the Reality

As the man is composed of body, mind and soul- where body is perishable while soul is everlasting and worship is to be done by all three. Mind worships by accepting the truth which is *Iman*, body worships by following the injunctions of Islam and soul follows the worship through *Ihsan*.

It is mentioned in Qur'an that the deeds will be weighed not counted:

"..So, as for those whose scale (of good deeds) will be heavy, they will be the successful (by entering Paradise)"

[Qurán, al-Aáraf 7:8]

And in another verse:

"And those whose scales (of good deeds) are light, those are the ones who have lost their souls, in Hell will they abide"

[Qurán, al-Múminun 23:103]

The question then arises as to what brings the weight to the deeds. The answer is that the rewards for the acts of obedience are only bestowed if the acts are purely for Allah, not even for a reward in the afterlife. The deeds are to be performed selflessly without any interest in this world or the next. When the heart is purified of *riya*, Allah discloses the reality and the servant is able to perform the acts of obedience in the true spirit.

The Beloved Prophet said, "None of your works shall enter any of you to paradise." The companion asked, "Not even you, O Allah's Messenger?" and the Beloved Prophet said, "Not even me, unless Allah overspreads me with mercy from Him; but do what is right." [Muslim: 2816 s]

As explained by the scholars, the Hadith confirms that no one deserves paradise for his acts of obedience. As for the verse of Qurán:

"That is paradise, bequeathed to you for that you used to do"
[Qurán, al Aáraf 7:43]

Divine Law and the Reality

This verse does not contradict the Hadith, rather the Hadith explains that one would enter the paradise through the acts of obedience, the sincerity in those acts and acceptance by Allahﷻ through His Divine mercy. Therefore, not only the deeds of obedience are needed but also the sincerity and ultimately the Divine mercy of Allahﷻ to accept those deeds which would allow the servant to enter paradise. When the act of obedience is done purely to draw closer to Allahﷻ, no matter how small the act is, it becomes significant, as the Beloved Prophetﷺ said, "If one of you were to spend the weight of mount *Uhud* in gold, it would still not be equal to one of their [Companions' alms] bushel-weights or even half of that." [Muslim 2540]

When the act of obedience is done purely with the intention to draw closer to Allahﷻ, the Almighty not only accepts those but also accepts the rest even if deficient, as in Qurán:

> *"Whoever works righteous, man or woman, while believing, We shall certainly bestow them a life wondrous fair, and shall truly requite them their wage as if each deed were the best they ever did."* [Qurán, an Nahl 16:97]

Tasawwuf is the way of *Taqwa* (God-fearing), while Shariáh is the way of *Fatwa* (permissibility). *Taqwa* is central to *Tasawwuf* which is a clear distinction, if one falls from the way of *Taqwa* he would still be within the permissible, however, if one falls from the way of *Fatwa* he might find himself in haram or the unlawful. This state of extreme caution and fear was observed amongst the Companions of the Beloved Prophetﷺ. The Companions of Badr (those who participated in the first battle of Islam known as the Battle of Badr) had great status amongst other Companions of the Prophetﷺ, yet it is narrated by Abu Mulaykah﷜ that he met thirty Companions of the Beloved Prophetﷺ who participated in the Battle of Badr. All of them feared hypocrisy and were afraid of any changes to their spiritual states. [Bukhari 6939]

Divine Law and The Reality (Shariáh and Haqiqa)

The difference between knowledge and information is to be distinguished to understand the concept of *Tasawwuf*; information is defined as knowledge gained by investigation or study and knowledge is defined as the fact or condition of knowing something with familiarity gained through experience or association. The key difference being information is gained by investigation or study and knowledge is gained through experience or association. The knowledge of religion (Shariáh) has three pillars; The Qurán, the Sunnah and the *Ijma*, Consensus. These are not mere information and should be learnt and practiced in association with someone who has attained that knowledge. Knowledge of the Truth (*Haqiqa*) has also three essentials;

> Knowledge of the Essence of Allahﷻ; the recognition that Allahﷻ exists externally by His Essence, He is infinite, not bound by space, He has neither wife nor children and He is the creator and Sustainer.
> Knowledge of the Attributes of Allahﷻ; the Knowledge of the Divine attributes requires that Allahﷻ has attributes existing in Himself.
> Knowledge of the Actions and Wisdom of Allahﷻ; the knowledge that Allahﷻ is the Creator of mankind and that He brought the non-existent Universe into being. Knowledge of the law involves your knowing that Allahﷻ has sent Messengers and that Our Last Messenger Muhammadﷺ is a true Messenger and the Last one and what he told us of the seen and the unseen is true.

The external division of the primary knowledge comprising of the tenets or *Aqaid* makes the beliefs and the internal knowledge attains the true cognition. Then, the external

Divine Law and the Reality

knowledge consists of practising devotion and the internal assists in rendering that knowledge. Therefore, the external knowledge cannot be separated from internal as the external aspect without the internal is hypocrisy and the internal without the external knowledge is sacrilege. One shall not get confused by the terms as *Suluk* and *Haqiqa* are often used interchangeably. Suluk is the path and *Haqiqa* the fruit of the path- the objective being the attainment of the state *ihsan*.

The knowledge of the Islamic religion, *ilm e Deen* and the knowledge of *Tasawwuf* are not only transferred through words but also through heart and the state called '*hal*'. The state of the teacher is considered a key factor in transmission of the knowledge as it determines the state of the disciple. If the teacher follows the inward and outward aspects of Sunnah, the disciple would follow him inadvertently and that is the pinnacle of the path. The path of *Tasawwuf* is neither in the mystical exertions as is the common belief nor in wearing a 'Suffa'. The *hal* or the state of the teacher who follows the Prophetic Sunnah inwardly and outwardly is the most effective means of transmission of knowledge, hence it is required to be taken from a succession of true masters back to the Prophet ﷺ.

Inward Sunnah is the state of the heart which is not quantifiable, yet holds utmost importance, referring back to the concept that on the Day of Judgement 'the deeds will be weighed, not counted' and 'the one who brings a sound heart.' And that the Prophet ﷺ said, "Verily, Allah does not look at your appearance or wealth, but rather He looks at your hearts and actions." [Muslim: 2564]"[1]

In the words of al-Qushayri ﷺ, the Law is Allah's ﷻ command and the True Reality is the contemplation of Divine Lordship. Any law that is not supported by the True Reality is not accepted by Allah ﷻ. Likewise, any True Reality that is

Divine Law and the Reality

not bound by the Law is not accepted either. The Law brings the servant's obligations toward Allah﷾, while the True Reality brings news of Allah's disposition of world affairs. The Law exists so that you would worship Him, while the True Reality exists so that you would see Him. The Law is the fulfillment of what He has commanded, while the True Reality is that which He has executed and predetermined, hidden and manifested.

Abu Ali al-Daqqaq﵎ further explained that the verse '*You we worship*'(Qurán 1:4) means the observance of the Law, and '*To You alone we ask for help*'(Qurán 1:4) means the affirmation of the True Reality."

The relationship between Divine Law and True Reality is explained by Imam Qushayri﵎ as, "Divine Law is servitude to Allah﷾, whereas Divine Reality is observation of the Lordship of Allah﷾. Shari'ah is to worship Him while Divine Reality is to see Him, Divine Law is to implement His order whereas Divine Reality is to observe His Decree."[2]

Thanvi﵎ further elaborated the concept as he said once the heart is purified and illuminated [through *Dhikr* of Allah], certain realities of the corporeal and non- corporeal are made evident to the seeker; more specifically, the reality of good and bad deeds, the reality of Allah﷾ in His attributes and His actions, especially those between Him and His servants. For example, one may have the information about an apple but the reality of that information would be in seeing and tasting. Likewise, when the heart is purified, the realities regarding this world and the Hereafter as explained in the Qurán and Sunnah become evident.[3]

In the words of Mujaddid Alf Thani﵎, "Shariáh guarantees all worldly and Heavenly happiness, Path (*Tariqa*) and Divine

Divine Law and the Reality

Reality (*Haqiqa*) are the subsidiaries of Shariáh. Shariáh is composed of three parts: knowledge, actions and sincerity. Only when Shariáh materialises, the pleasure of Allahﷻ will be earned, which is loftier and above all worldly and heavenly happiness – "*And the pleasure of Allah is the greatest*" (*Qur'an 9:72*). The Shariáh is therefore, the guarantor of true happiness in both worlds. There now remains no purpose that one would be in need of something other than the Shariáh.

Path (*Tariqa*) and Reality (*Haqiqa*); the qualities with which the Sufis are distinguished, are both subservient to Shariáh and serve to complete the attribute of sincerity. Hence, the purpose of acquiring them is for perfection of following the Shariáh and nothing more. Shariáh to become the first nature is the objective of the true seeker. The *hal* (spiritual states), *wajd* (ecstasy), knowledge and gnosis (*maárafa*) that the Sufis experience during their journey are not the purpose. Their status is, rather, that of those thoughts with which the beginners of path are developed. One should move beyond all these and reach the station (*maqam*) of *rida* (Allah's pleasure). This is the station in which the stations of ecstasy and *suluk* end, as the purpose of the stations of Tariqa and Haqiqa is nothing except the acquisition of sincerity. And sincerity is a requirement for the pleasure of the Creator Most High.

From among thousands, there are few who pass the gnostic and visions to reach the wealth of sincerity and the station of pleasure (*rida*). The short-sighted consider states and ecstasy and visions as their goal. It is on account of this that they remain captive in the prison of delusion and fantasy and deprived of the perfections of Shariáh. It is true that the acquisition of the station of sincerity and the status of *rida* is connected to the materialisation of those states, hence, those states are preludes to the purpose and not the [actual] purpose."[4]

Maárfa

The word *Maárfa* means, full knowledge and perception of something via contemplation and complete understanding of its signs. Though the Islamic knowledge forms the foundation, the gaining of knowledge in Tariqa is through the illumination of the heart which Allahﷻ bestows upon the heart of the seeker through rigor and *Dhikr* under the guidance of a Shaykh. It is the realisation of the transient experience until it becomes a permanent attribute, then the servant may be engaged in the daily activities of ordinary life but the heart is characterised by the remembrance of the Lord as a perpetual state. One needs to remember that *Maárfa* is not achieved due to one's own rigor or *Dhikr* or acts of obedience, rather it is the Divine favour of Allahﷻ, which He bestows upon His Servants who follow the way of the Prophetﷺ. Each of Allah's servant has a unique relationship as unique to each of His creation.

According to a *sahih* Hadith; Allahﷻ says: "He who is hostile to a friend of Mine I declare war against. My slave approaches Me with nothing more beloved to Me than what I have made obligatory upon him, and My slave keeps drawing nearer to Me with voluntary works until I love him. And when I love him, I am his hearing with which he hears, his sight with which he sees, his hand with which he seizes, and his foot with which he walks. If he asks me, I will surely give to him, and if he seeks refuge in Me, I will surely protect him." [Fath al-Bari: Hadith 6502]

This Hadith discloses the reality of *Tasawwuf* by clarifying the concept; as the slave approaches Allahﷻ with what He had made obligatory upon him, as in Qurán and Sunnah and then keeps drawing closer to Allahﷻ with voluntary works until Allahﷻ loves him. It is therefore, extremely important to learn Islamic Jurisprudence and learning is not enough, one needs to practice and implement it in all aspects of life. Scholars have divided knowledge in three classes- from Allah, with Allah and of Allah. Knowledge of Allahﷻ is *Ilm e Maárfa*, whereby He is known to His Prophets and Awliya (friends), this knowledge cannot be acquired by ordinary means as it is the result of Divine guidance. Knowledge from Allahﷻ is the knowledge of Shariáh the Science of Islamic Jurisprudence, which He has commanded and made obligatory on us. Knowledge with Allahﷻ is the discipline of *Tasawwuf*, which is unsound without the acceptance of Shariáh. [5]

According to scholars, the most unique feature distinguishing human beings from the rest of the creation, which renders them capable of undertaking the Divine exalted charge is their potential to know Allahﷻ, while the rest of the creation were afraid of the responsibility. This is the state of self-annihilation in one's own self and other creations, that the Divine Love becomes the focal point and transforms into Allah's will. The angels are maintained in the purity of their will and the prophets are maintained in the freedom from the desires of their carnal self, so they are innocent. Whereas, the friends of Allah like other humans have the responsibility of moral behaviour and not free from evil, however, in the event of forgetfulness, Allah'sﷻ mercy reminds them and they seek protection in Allahﷻ, therefore, they are safeguarded.[6]

The Beloved Prophetﷺ said: Allahﷻ said, "I am as My servant thinks I am, I am with him when he makes mention of Me. If he makes mention of Me to himself, I make mention of him to Myself. And if he makes mention of Me in an assembly, I make mention of him in an assemble better than it. And if he draws near to Me an arm's length, I draw near to him a fathom's length. And if he comes to Me walking, I go to him at speed." [Muslim, Tirmidhi]

According to another Hadith, "Whoever loves and wants to reach Allahﷻ, Allah loves to reach him, in return. On the contrary, whoever sees reaching Allahﷻ as terrible, then Allahﷻ does not love and want to reach him, as well. [Bukhari, Riqaq, 41; Muslim, Dhikr, 14-17]

Imam an Nawawi☼ wrote in his *Sharh Sahih Muslim*, "As far as Fiqh (Jurisprudence) and *Hikma* (wisdom) are concerned, Fiqh means to have a deep understanding of religion, whilst the later (*hikma*) refers to having conscious acknowledgment of Allahﷻ (*Maárfa*), coupled with self-reformation, good character and abstaining from following one's desires and falsehood." [*Nawawi, al-Minhaj Sharh Sahih Muslim, P: 158-159*]

Uthman al-Makki☼ in his '*Book of Love*' wrote, "Allahﷻ created the souls seven thousand years before the bodies and kept them in the station of proximity (*Qurb*), that He created spirits seven thousand years before the souls and kept them in the station of intimacy (*Uns*), that He created the hearts seven thousand years before the spirits and kept them in the degree of unison (Wasl) and revealed the epiphany of His Beauty to the heart three hundred and sixty times every day and bestowed on it three hundred and sixty glances of Grace. He caused the spirits to hear the word of love and manifested three hundred and sixty exquisite favours of intimacy to the soul, so that they all surveyed the phenomenal universe and saw nothing more precious than themselves and were filled with pride and vanity. Therefore, Allahﷻ subjected them to probation; He imprisoned the heart in the spirit and the spirit in the soul and then soul in the body. He then mingled reason (*Aqal*) with them and sent Prophets and gave commands, finally each one of them began to seek its original station. Allahﷻ ordered them to pray; the soul attained to love, the spirit arrived at the proximity to Allah and the heart found rest in unison with Him. The explanation of love is not love, because love is a feeling (*hal*) and feelings cannot be expressed by words (*Qaal*). If the whole world wished to attract love, they could not and if they made the utmost effort to repel it, they cannot. Love is a Divine Gift."⁷

The Beloved Prophetﷺ said, "When Allah loves a servant, He proclaims to Gibrael۩: 'Verily Allah loves so- and- so, so love him," and Gibrael۩ loves him. Then Gibrael۩ calls unto the celestials (Ahl al sama'): "Verily Allah loves so-and -so, so all of you love him," and the celestials love him. And then acceptance is put for him among terrestrials." [Bukhari: 6040]

The Hadith demonstrates the love of Allahﷻ for His servant which the servant attains through obedience. The Hadith states that a believer who is loved by Allahﷻ is also loved by Gibrael۩, all the other angels, the celestials and the terrestrials. Allahﷻ favours the servant by keeping him under His special protection and enables him to perform good deeds and safeguard him from evil. For the servant, the obligatory worship together with the supererogatory worship makes the way to Maárfa.

Shaykh Abdul Qadir Gilani﷫ explains Maárfa as; "The meaning of unison with Allahﷻ is your going out of the creation, desire and purpose and becoming established in His actions and purpose; without there being any movement in you or through you, in His creation unless it be with His order, action and command. But, union with Allahﷻ is not like union with anything in his creation, in an understandable and appointed manner. The Creator is above being similar to His creations or bearing any resemblance to anything He created. Thus, union with him is only known to those who have experienced this union, because of their realisation. Each one has a different experience which is peculiar to him and not shared by any other person."⁸

Level of Certitude

As mentioned in Qurán:

'Nor did I create jinn and mankind except to adore Me'
[Qurán adh Dhariyat 51:56]

Allahﷻ mentions in Qurán that He created Man to worship him, the scholars suggest that the word 'worship' in this verse suggests to recognise Allahﷻ. Ibne Abbas ؓ the Companion of the Beloved Prophetﷺ explained the phrase 'to adore' is used, as 'to know' (Tafsir-al-Baghawi[10], 5.230). It is not forbidden to enjoy the blessings which Allahﷻ has bestowed upon one, it is when the self gets absorbed in acquiring and fulfilling the worldly desires that the man forgets the main objective for his creation whereas, Allahﷻ commands the believers:

'O Believers, believe in Allah and His Messenger and His Book'
[Qurán, An Nisa 4:136]

This verse is addressed to the believers where Allahﷻ orders the 'believers to believe'; in this context the scholars explain that Allahﷻ commands the believers to believe as it should be. The guiding stars who reached that epitome are the Companions of the Apostleﷺ and the benchmark for the believers to believe was set by them. In another verse, the believers are ordered;

"Worship your Lord until what is certain (al-yaqeen) comes to you"
[Qurán, al Hijr 15 :99]

'*Yaqeen*' means to be certain and have firm conviction, it is the degree of knowledge which is more than just knowing. There are three levels of certitude as mentioned in Qurán:

Ilm ul Yaqeen: certitude based on information, where

Divine Law and the Reality

the certainty is the result of knowledge,
Ayn al Yaqeen: certitude based on seeing, where certainty is the consequence of contemplation and vision,
Haq ul Yaqeen', certitude based on experience, meaning the level of certainty is gained through personal experience which is supreme.

For example, seeing smoke signifies fire although one may have not seen the fire, this is *ilm ul yaqeen* as one knows that smoke signifies fire. When one actually sees the fire, he knows that the fire is burning, it is called *ayn al yaqeen*. When one can feel the warmth and burning of the fire and fully convinced of it, that is *haq ul Yaqeen*. Qurán is not just a book of information; it is a practical guide which commands the believers to follow the direction as indicated and reach the objective for which Allah created Mankind- recognise and love Allah. It is rather a command not a request by Allah for the believers to reach from *Ilm ul yaqeen* to *Haq ul yaqeen*; a journey from knowing to believing. All Muslims believe in Allah, and that He is unique in His attributes and beyond the comprehension of our intellect which is very limited and restricted. Allah in His own words describes:

"There is nothing whatsoever like unto Him"

[Qur'an, ash Shuára 42:11]

When Gibrael asked the Beloved Prophet about *Ihsan* after asking him about Islam and *Iman*, he answered, "It is to adore Allah as if you see Him, and if you see Him not, He nevertheless sees you." If there is nothing whatsoever like unto him, yet according to the Hadith, we are to "worship Allah as though you see Him,". We can deduce that it is neither through the physical eye that we can see Him nor through the mind that we can comprehend, it is only through the level of certitude, *'Haq ul Yaqeen'*, that we can know Him.

The Beloved Prophet'sﷺ state was from his own experience and this state of certitude was also attained by the Companions through their purity of heart and ultimate love for Allah and His Last Prophetﷺ. *Haq ul yaqeen* was the stage where even before Allah's Last Prophetﷺ uttered the words, the Companions were eager to follow his command and believed in every word without a hint of doubt. As Ali؆ said that his belief would not alter even if the Hell or Paradise is presented before him as his certitude was strong enough without witnessing it and that is the pinnacle of faith.

In Qurán, more than thirty verses mention Allah's special favours and closeness to the *Muhsinin*, meaning those of the state of *Ihsan*. *Ihsan* is the core of *Tasawwuf*, it is the perfection of *yaqeen* and excellence in deeds. Allahﷻ mentions in Qurán,

"And truly Allah is wholly on the side of those who excel in goodness"

[Qurán, al Ankabut 29:69]

After the prophets, Abu Bakr؆ was the one who reached the station of excellence. The Beloved Prophetﷺ said, "Whenever I invited anyone to accept Islam, he argued with me and rejected my words initially, except for the son of Abu Qauhafa (Abu Bakr؆) who accepted it immediately and remained steadfast. [*Suyuti- Tarikhul Khulafa pg. 35*]

At the time of the Battle of Tabuk, donations were required, Umar؆ resolved to surpass Abu Bakr؆ at least once and accordingly brought half of his wealth. Shortly, Abu Bakr؆ appeared with his money and goods. The Beloved Prophetﷺ enquired what had he left for his family, to which Abu Bakr ؆ replied, "Allahﷻ and His Prophetﷺ are enough." [Abu Dawood, Tirmizi]

Divine Law and the Reality

There was no one dearer to the Beloved Prophet ﷺ amongst men than Abu Bakr ؓ and there was no one dearer to Abu Bakr ؓ than the Beloved Prophet ﷺ. When the tragic news was received about the demise of Allah's Messenger ﷺ the Companions were besides themselves, even Umar ؓ was bewildered, in that instance Abu Bakr's ؓ faith was the strongest and he said, "O People! Verily, whosoever worshipped Muhammad ﷺ, let him know that Muhammad ﷺ has passed away; but those of you who worship Allah ﷻ, let him know that Allah ﷻ lives and never dies" He then, recited the verse of the Qurán:

"and Muhammad ﷺ is no more than an apostle; many apostles have already passed away before him...." [Ibn Saád-Tabaqai, pg 81]

Walaya

Allah mentions in Qurán:

> "And I am closer to him than his jugular vein"
> [Qurán, Qaaf 50:16]

And:

> "And He is with you wherever you are"
> [Qurán, Hadeed 57:4]

This is the general closeness with everyone and then Allahﷻ bestows His special closeness on the ones who seek Him as the Beloved Prophetﷺ said, "Allahﷻ says: "Whoever is hostile to a friend (*Wali*) of mine I declare war against him. My slave approaches me with nothing more beloved to me than what I have made obligatory upon him, and My slave keeps drawing nearer to Me with voluntary works until I love him. And when I love him, I am his hearing with which he hears, his sight with which he sees, his hands with which he seizes, and his foot with which he walks. If he asks Me, I will surely give it to him, and when he seeks refuge in Me, I will protect him. I do not hesitate from anything I shall do more than hesitation at taking the soul of the believer who dislikes death; for I dislike displeasing him." [Bukhari 6502 S]

According to the following verses of Qurán, the degree of faith and piety defines the degree of *Walaya*:

> "Behold! verily on the friends of Allah there is no fear nor shall they grieve. Those who believe and (constantly) guard against evil. For them is good news in this worldly life and the Hereafter. There is no change in the promise of Allah. That is truly the ultimate triumph."
> [Quran, Yunus 10:62-64]

Being righteous demands practicing the good and avoiding the prohibited:

"Indeed, the most noble of you in the sight of Allah is the most righteous of you" [Qurán, Al Hujarat 49:13]

The word '*Walí*' means friend and has two meanings, the first meaning implies passivity, as Allahﷻ mentions in Qurán;

"He [Allah] manages the affairs of the righteous."

[Qurán, al Aáraaf 7:196)

That is, Allahﷻ Himself is in charge of the affairs of His servant. The second meaning implies an intensity of action on the part of person who is thoroughly engaged in worshiping and obeying Allahﷻ to such an extent that his virtuous acts follow one upon the other without being interrupted by any disobedience. Both meanings must apply in order for the friend of Allahﷻ to be a genuine friend. He must fulfill his obligations toward Allahﷻ meticulously and exhaustively, while Allahﷻ, in turn, protects him from disobedience. One of the conditions of being a friend of Allahﷻ is to enjoy His protection (*mahfuz*), in the same way as one of the conditions of being a prophet is to be infallible (*másum*).

Allah's Beloved Prophetﷺ said, "How many people are there with disheveled hair and covered in dust, who possess no more than the clothes on their back so that no one takes notice of them; yet if they swear something by Allahﷻ, the Almighty bring it to pass." [Tirmidhi 3854]

The Hadith points to Allah'sﷻ acceptance of those who dedicate their lives to Allah'sﷻ pleasure. The description dusty, disheveled hair should not be considered conditional, rather the Hadith emphasizes that the appearance is of no importance in spiritual excellence. One can strive to be like those who have devoted themselves, emulating the early Muslims and inclined towards the minimum. At least try to be in their company, respect and love them and Allahﷻ by His special inaya may bless us with their attributes. Once someone said to the Prophetﷺ, "A man loves a group of people, yet cannot catch up with them," he replied, *"A man shall be with whomever he loves"* [Bukhari: 6170]

The enigma of *Walaya* is defined by Ibn Ata Sikandari؛ as "The affirmation of sanctity does not entail a negation of being human. Electhood is merely like the rise of the Sun; it appears on the horizon without being part of it. Sometimes, the suns of His attributes rise upon the night of your being. And sometimes, He takes that from you and returns you to your bounds."⁹

It is said that Ibrahim bin Adham؛ once asked a man, "If you would like to be a friend of Allahﷻ, then do not desire anything of this world and the Hereafter. Dedicate yourself to Allahﷻ and turn your face toward Him, so that He would turn His face to you and make you a friend of His."

Yahya bin Muadh؛ described the friends of Allahﷻ as those of His servants who have been clothed with intimacy with Him after suffering for His sake (*mukabada*). They have been granted rest after striving for His sake through arriving at the station of friendship (with Allah).¹⁰

Seekers differ in their abilities and capacities to attain the state, the one who acquires the knowledge and practices more would be great in spiritual attainment and would pass from the transitory experience (*Ahwal*) to permanent realisation (*Tahqiq*). Whereas, the one who knows less and practices less would be less in his attainments. The sun of Allah'sﷻ *Maárfa* shines upon each of His servant in as many infinite ways as His attributes. *Maárfa* is a qualitative relationship between Allahﷻ and the servant. However, for the purpose of appointments, the Awliya are divided in twelve groups.

Divine Law and the Reality

Ali ؓ reported that Allah's Messenger ﷺ said, "The Abdals are in Shaam(Syria), they are forty men. Whenever any of them die, Allah ﷻ replaces him with another...' [Musnad Ahmad:896]

'Awf ibn Malik ؓ narrated that the Beloved Prophet ﷺ said, "Among them [the people of Sham] are the *Abdal*..." [*Tarikh Ibn 'Asakir, vol.1 pg.290*]

The general acceptance of the term *Abdal* and their existence is further substantiated by the fact that many illustrious scholars were labelled as such or thought to have been *Abdal*. Imam Sakhawi ؓ has stated that Imam Shafi'i ؓ and Imam Bukhari ؓ have labelled certain people as *Abdal*. [Al-Maqsidul Hasanah, Hadith: 8]

These are the devout and sincere believers elected by Allah ﷻ. In their hierarchy, they have one imam or leader who is called, *'Qutb'*. Imam Sakhawi ؓ has labelled Imam Nawawi ؓ as *'Qutb'* in his biography entitled, *'Al-Manhalul Adhbir Rawiy, fi Tarjamatil Qutb An-Nawawi.'*

Mujaddid alf Thani ؓ has elaborated upon the hierarchy of the groups of *Awliya*. There is *Qutb al-alam* or *Qutb al-Aqtaab*, who is the senior most of all *Qutb*, he is the one who appoints *Abdal*. He has two advisors, the one on the right is senior and takes over the position at the demise of the *Qutb*. The other *Qutb* perform their duties under *Qutb al-alam*.

Ghaus is appointed to help people in need, he also supports Qutb *al-Aqtaab* in carrying out the assignments. Then, there are four *Awtaad*, in each direction of the world under the command of a *Qutb*. As mentioned earlier, there are forty *Abdal* and few hundred *'Akhyar'*. *Akhyar* are travellers and keep roaming. There are also three hundred *Naqabah* who take command from a *Qutb*. There are forty or seventy *Najabah*, who spend their lives helping others.[11]

True Knowledge (Ilm e Haqeeqi)

It is narrated on the authority of Abu Darda﷠ that he heard the Allah's Messengerﷺ say, "*Verily, the learned are the heirs of the prophets.*" *[Abu Dawud and Tirmidhi]* In this Hadith, the word "learned" refers particularly to those who have attained knowledge. A true scholar is a person who knows the Commandments of Allahﷻ, and practises upon his knowledge. A person who does not practise his knowledge cannot be deemed as a true scholar. To be a true scholar one needs to possess the knowledge of Deen, be pious and possess the praiseworthy traits.

Ali﷠ narrated that the Messenger of Allahﷺ said [among other things in a lengthy Hadith], "... and the learned will never have their fill of it; and even though it be read and re read, over and over again, it will never seem old, and its wonders will never cease." [Tirmidhi: 2906]

Thanvi﷫ elaborates the concept of true knowledge as, "The scholar who has acquired the knowledge of Deen and adheres to Sunnah is qualified to be taken as a guide in Deen. A man does not become a scholar by reading few religious books or by virtue of expertise in the Arabic language or being an orator or writer. For one to become a true scholar, knowledge of Deen is a preliminary requisite whilst fear for Allahﷻ is a vital condition.

Divine fear cannot be acquired without knowledge, however, it does not follow that fear for Allahﷻ is a consequence of knowledge. For fear of Allahﷻ there is the need for a separate effort, which is to practise upon the knowledge one has gained. One cannot claim to be a guide just by being eloquent and studying few religious books. Some scholars are ignorant, in fact, one should rather say that some ignorant are scholars."[12]

Divine Law and the Reality

Through constant remembrance and disciplines, the darkness and impurities of the *Nafs* are dispelled, Allahﷻ bestows true knowledge upon the heart of the servant. The spiritual knowledge gives depth to the attained knowledge as in the case of Rumi﷫ and the servant becomes a true scholar.

Bestowed Knowledge (Ilm al-Ladunni)

Ilm al-Ladunni is referred as knowledge bestowed directly by Allahﷻ, upon whomever He wills of His believing servants with the condition that it does not contradict the Divine Revelations [the Qurán and Sunnah]. Ibn Taymiyyah﷫ wrote, "As for llm al-Ladunni, it is true that Allahﷻ reveals to His *Awliya* and pious servants, whose hearts are pure from whatever He disapproves and pursue what He approves, the like of which He bestows upon no one else. This is supported by Qurán

> *"And then We would have given them from Us a great reward. And guided them to a straight path."*
>
> [Quran, an Nisa 4:67-68]

Ilm al-Ladunni, is only considered as knowledge within the bounds of Qurán and Sunnah. Anyone who claims to have knowledge outside the bounds of Shariáh has lost his path. Whoever does what he is commanded is guided to the right path and Allahﷻ increase them in guidance and righteousness:

> *"And those who are guided - He increases them in guidance and gives them their righteousness.*
>
> [Quran, Muhammad 47:14]

Ibn Al-Qayyim﷫ elaborated Shaykh Taymiyyah's words as he wrote, "Shaykh Ibn Taymiyyah﷫ said, 'Many who speak out of their ignorance and imagination rely on their inner thoughts and premonitions rather than the Qurán and the

Sunnah and say, 'My heart informed me on the authority of my Lord. We follow the guidance of Allahﷻ, The Ever-Living, and you follow mere mediators; we follow truths and you follow (written) symbols...' and similar statements that constitute disbelief and blasphemy. The only excuse for such a person is ignorance. When such people are told, 'Why do you not go and learn the Hadith at the hands of Abd ar-Razzaaq (Hadith scholar), they would say, 'Why would one need to learn at the hands of a Hadith scholar while he can learn at the hands of His Lord directly...!' Whoever thinks that he can dispose of the Divine revelation imparted to the Prophetﷺ and rely only on the inner thoughts and conceptions within his heart, has committed the gravest act of disbelief. The same applies to the person who believes that he can rely only on his own inner thoughts and conceptions at times and at others rely on the Divine revelation. Verily, one's inner thoughts and conceptions have no weight or authority unless judged against the Divine revelation communicated by the Prophetﷺ and proven to conform to it. In case of contradiction, such inner thoughts and conceptions are declared worthless and part of the work of Satan and sinful urges of the evil-enjoining soul.'"[13]

Fana fil~Shaykh, Fana fir~Rasool and Fana Fillah

In *Tasawwuf*, *Fana* means self-annihilation, self-effacement or dissolution from self. When the seeker is annihilated from himself, the 'limited existence' of the seeker is overpowered by the 'absolute existence' of Allahﷻ and the seeker becomes unaware of his own self and creation. When travelling, the seeker passes through different levels of *fana'*, each bringing him closer to ultimate goal. Every time a blameworthy trait is removed, it is replaced by the knowledge of the Divine. Therefore, for a true seeker, each moment brings him close to *fana'*. There are infinite levels which the seeker experiences throughout the journey, however annihilation is categorised in three types: Annihilation in the Shaykh, annihilation in the Messenger ﷺ and annihilation in Allahﷻ.

The seeker requires a Shaykh or a guide, who is a pure receptacle for the Divine Outpouring which emanates from the Beloved Prophet Muhammad ﷺ. Annihilation in the Shaykh occurs when the teachings of Qurán and Sunnah, passed on by the Shaykh, become firmly established in the heart of the seeker. The seeker becomes absorbed by the teaching, through constant meditation and contemplation of Allahﷻ. *Fana fil-Shaykh* (Annihilation in Shaykh) is not just respect or being obedient to the Shaykh, in fact it is a powerful affinity resulting in higher stages of awareness. The seeker develops a bond which is beyond physical and may experience that his own self is dissolved or annihilated in his Shaykh.

After achieving the state and firmly established in annihilation in Shaykh, the seeker moves towards the next level which is annihilation in Allah's Messenger ﷺ, *Fana fir-Rasul* which is the integral part of the journey. At this stage, the seeker is pervaded by an overwhelming love for the Beloved Prophet Muhammad ﷺ and the Prophet ﷺ becomes dearer to him than life itself.

The journey from *Fana fir Rasul* takes the seeker to *Fana Fillah*. It is when the power of the True Reality takes possession and the seeker no longer notices the essence, effects, traces or vestiges of anything other than Allah. They say of such a person: "He has been annihilated from Allah's creatures and now subsists in Allah. Once, Mowlana Rashid Ahmad Gangohi was in an ecstatic mood and the concept of *Fana fil Shaykh, Fana fir-Rasul and Fana Fillah* was being discussed. He said, "For three complete years, the face of Haji Imdad Allah (his Shaykh) remained in my heart and I did not do anything without asking him."

Then, he became more fervent and said, "For so many years (the narrator did not remember the exact number of years) the Prophet was in my heart and I did not do anything in that time without asking him." Then, he became even more ardent and said: "Shall I say more?" The audience urged, however, he remained silent and upon insistence, said: "Let it be." The next day, after much pleading, he said, "After that was the state of *Ihsan*." [14]

Ali Hujwiri described the state as, "When a man escapes from the captivity of stations and impurities of states, liberated from the abode of change and decay, becomes endowed with praiseworthy qualities, disjoined from all qualities, frees himself from self-conceit, his time is exempt from influence of thoughts, his presence with the Divine has no end and his existence has no cause, gold and dirt are the same for him and the ordinances which others find hard become easy for him. When he arrives at this degree, he becomes annihilated in Allah."[15]

Divine Law and the Reality

The concept of Fana Fillah is the level of certitude as discussed in Haq ul Yaqeen. Once the Beloved Prophet ﷺ asked Harith ibn Malik ؓ, "How are you this morning?"

He replied, "I am a true believer this morning"

The Beloved Prophet ﷺ said: 'Every claim has a reality (proof), so what is the reality (proof) of your claim?'

Harith ؓ replied, "Since this morning, I have distanced myself from the world, I spent my night awake in worship and my day fasting. [Such is my conviction, that] I can almost see the throne of my Lord being brought for accountability [on the day of Judgement]. [Such is my conviction, that] I can almost see the inhabitants in Paradise visiting one another therein, and I can almost hear the screams of the inhabitants of Hell."

The Beloved Prophet ﷺ said to him, "[You are] a slave whose heart has been illuminated with Iman (belief). Remain steadfast on this perception of yours." [Musannaf ibn Abi Shaybah: 31064]

Journey towards Allah
(Sair I'lallah and Sair Fillah)

This journey consists of two fundamental aspects, purification of the *Nafs* from blameworthy traits and adoring the self with praiseworthy traits. Once, this is achieved and the seeker is established in his stations then he reaches the stage of *Sair I'lallah*. At this stage, the Shaykh may confer on him succession and grant him permission to initiate others to the Path.

After the stage of *Sair I'llalalh*, the heart is truly engrossed with Allahﷻ and the seeker may find himself disassociated from all things other than Allahﷻ. In this high stage of spiritual development, matters pertaining to Divine Being (*Dhaat*), Divine Attributes (*Sifáat*), Divine Actions (*Af'aal*) and Divine Reality (*Haqiqa*) become manifest. This stage is *Sair Fi'llah* which is boundless and limitless; progress is proportional and continuous in relation to one's ability to cast aside all motives. When one has attained this rank, one attributes nothing to his own self.

Chapter Ten

MYSTICAL STATES AND STATIONS
(HAL AND MUQAM)

According to the Sufis, the mystical state is something that descends upon the heart of the seeker regardless of his intentions, attempts or desire. This can be the state of joy, grief, expansion, contraction, passionate longing, vexation, awe or need. States are Divine gifts, whereas stations are earnings. States come without asking, whereas stations are acquired by the sweat of one's brow. The possessor of a station is firmly established in it, whereas the possessor of a state can be taken out of his state at any moment.

It is narrated that Hanzalah﷠ said, "I passed by Abu Bakr﷠ who asked me how I was. In reply, I said, 'Hanzalah has become a hypocrite.' Abu Bakr﷠ was surprised and said, 'Glory be to Allahﷻ! Why would you say so?' I replied, 'When we are with Allah's Messengerﷺ and he reminds us of the Fire and the Gardens of paradise, at that moment it is as we are witnessing those with our eyes. But when we leave his company, we get so busy with our wives, our children and our livelihood that we forget everything else.' Abu Bakr﷠ replied, 'By Allahﷻ! I feel the same with me.' So, the two of us went to Allah's Messengerﷺ and told him what we had admitted to each other. Allah's Messengerﷺ said to us, 'By the One Who holds my life in His hands! If you were to remain in the states you attain while you are in my company, the angels would shake hands with you on the streets and your beds, but O Hanzalaﷺ, there is a time for this and a time for that.' [Tirmidhi 2514.s]

It is evident from the Hadith that Hanzalahﷺ, in recognition of his changing spiritual states, called himself a hypocrite. The term was not used in its strict legal sense of inwardly denying the truth of Allah'sﷻ message and the veracity of His Messengerﷺ. Rather, he used the term on the basis of the difference in his states as one state obliterated the other. Furthermore, the answer given by Allah's Messengerﷺ was not in refutation of the use of figurative language, but rather of the false premise that one state was necessarily any better than the other.

The intensified spiritual witnessing as mentioned by Hanzalahﷺ when he said, "It is as if we are seeing those things with our own eyes" is called *Mushahadah*. It does not mean that he could see the Fire and the Garden, but the imagination was so intense that it possessed him. Many ignorant Sufis suppose spiritual witnessing to be direct vision, but they are clearly mistaken when they attempt to apply a dictionary meaning to a spiritual state.

The seeker may experience certain mystical states in the company of the Shaykh, but the effects of these experiences may not last long as per Hanzalahﷺ complaint. No one should suppose that the reason for the change in Hanzalah'sﷺ state was due to his involvement in worldly affairs, rather it was due to his parting company with Allah's Messengerﷺ. Certain mystical states follow one's ascetic exertions or in the company of one's Shaykh, but the effects of such states reduce upon leaving the Shaykh's company, as complained by Hanzalahﷺ.

Mystical States and Stations

At times, seekers complain that they have lost a particular state or the former intensity of a particular state. The seekers get worried that they have suffered spiritual decline and become disheartened. This is especially true among neophytes who are far more susceptible to changes in their condition than more experienced travellers. It is established that the dominance of spiritual states is best when impermanent. This phenomenon of impermanence is referred to as *talwin* or variegation and is something which occurs in varying degrees to even the most experienced seeker. In the above Hadith, Allah's Messenger'sﷺ words, *"There is a time for this and a time for that"* is a reference to the fact. This phenomenon is an inevitable part of the way and should not become a cause for concern.

Someone asked Dhu ul-Nun al-Misri؅ about the states, his answer was, "It was here [a moment ago], but left." One Sufi master said: "States are like [flashes of] lightning. If they persist, they are but self-deception. States are like their name—that is, they alight upon the heart only to leave it instantaneously."

Abu Ali al-Daqqaq؅ commented on the words of the Beloved Prophetﷺ: "My heart was covered with a veil until I began to ask Allah's؅ pardon seventy times a day." Abu Ali؅ said that the Beloved Prophetﷺ was constantly advancing in his states. Whenever, he advanced from one state to another loftier state, he would take notice of the one he had just left behind and considered that state to be a veil in relation to the existing state. It is narrated on the authority of Ibn' Abbas؅ concerning the verse of Qurán, *"Surely you will traverse, stage after stage" (Qurán 84:19)* that, "This means, state after state. And the person to whom this was addressed was the Prophetﷺ." [Bukhari 4940)]

The verse stage after stage refers to an unending journey. This journey is not done on the basis of effort and deeds. The seeker makes every gain by the special blessings (*fadhl*) of Allahﷻ. The seeker who keeps the focus on Allah's blessings (*inaya*) and does not depend on his effort, reaches the destination and the one who believes in the strength of his own rigor is lost. The seeker shall not be concerned about the states as they are not the ultimate goal, the true objective of the path is to attain Allah's love by following the way of the Messengerﷺ. In the writings and discourses, it is often noted that there is no end to the progress made by the seeker. A seeker may go through many spiritual states where he may experience spiritual illuminations or witness otherworldly beings, but if he is attracted to any of these states, his journey will be endangered.

The favours that Allahﷻ has predetermined for His creations are infinite, therefore, the servant of Allahﷻ has to be constantly advancing in his states. Since, the True Reality of Allahﷻ is Supreme, therefore, one can never truly attain Him, it is in this sense that one should understand the Sufi saying: "*The good deeds of the righteous are the evil deeds of the ones who are brought close to Allahﷻ.*" When someone asked Junayd Baghdadi﷭ about this phrase, he said, "Flashes of light, when they appear, reveal the secret and announce the unification [with the Divine]."

However, seeker may experience states from *Nafs* and Satan. There have been those who considered these states as their goal and lost sight of the ultimate objective. It is important to keep the Shaykh informed and seek guidance as there are many who lost their way in the maze of these illuminations.

Mystical States and Stations

Shaykh Madaniﷺ wrote to one of his disciples, "The different spiritual states you mentioned are good but dedication is better than miracles. Dreams, illuminations, or Divine inspirations are only to encourage the seeker and keep him resolute, like a toy that is given to a child. The famous saying of the elders is: 'States are toys by which the children of the path are raised.' We are only required to worship, engage in perpetual *Dhikr* of Allahﷻ, adhere to the Sunnah of the Beloved Prophetﷺ and follow the Divine Law. The completion of faith is based on commitment to these requirements and attaining the level of *ihsan*. Fear and hope of Allahﷻ are two signs of the completion of faith."[1]

As for the word *Muqam,* it means the act of "being placed". According to Imam al-Qashayriﷺ, the station is the good manners which the servant of Allahﷻ realizes after he attains that station. The seeker can arrive at a station through concerted effort and self-imposed strictures in worshiping Allahﷻ. A precondition of the station is that one cannot advance from one station to the next unless the requirements for the former station are met. For instance, if one has not mastered the station of contentment (*qanâ*), one cannot achieve the station of trust in Allahﷻ (*tawakkul*); if the seeker has not mastered trust in Allahﷻ, then he cannot earn the station of true submission to Divine Will. Likewise, the one who has not mastered the station of repentance (*tawba*) cannot obtain the station of turning to Allahﷻ in repentance (*inaba*); one who has not mastered the station of scrupulous discernment between the licit and the illicit] (*waraâ*) is not ready for the station of renunciation of this world. The progress from station to station requires the wayfarer's personal effort and Allah'sﷻ continual blessings, otherwise, the goal cannot be achieved.[2]

Contraction and Elation (Qabd and Bast)

Contraction and elation are the two states which a seeker experiences throughout the journey. The moment of the person in the state of contraction or elation is determined by the experience that dominates him in his immediate present. The characteristics of contraction and elation differ from one seeker to another. Once a seeker entered the house of Abu Bakr al-Qahtabi☺ and saw his son engaged in unseemly pastimes that were common among the youth of his age. The visitor felt a great pity for al-Qahtabi☺ and said: 'O poor master! What a terrible affliction this son must be for him!' When the visitor entered al-Qahtabi's☺ room he saw him behave as if he was not aware of his son's unseemly entertainment. He was surprised by this and said, "May I be the ransom of him who cannot be moved even by the steadfast mountains!" Al-Qahtabi☺ replied, "We have been liberated from the bondage of the things of this world since pre-eternity!"

Contraction is caused by an experience that descends upon one's heart, as a result, contraction enters the heart and it contracts. It may imply censure or indicate that one is liable for rebuke. However, when an experience is caused by closeness or by Allah's☺ turning to the servant with gentleness, then the heart feels the elation. In general, one's contraction corresponds to one's elation and one's expansion to one's contraction. There may be a contraction whose cause and motive elude the person who experiences it.

Most seekers complain that a particular state has lost its intensity or disappeared and become confused and disheartened. It is common among beginners who are more susceptible to change than the experienced traveller. During Bast or elation the seeker finds it easier to pray or perform *Dhikr* and feels attracted towards the remembrance of Allah, whereas, during Qabd or contraction, the seeker finds it hard to concentrate and lacks passion

The masters of the Tariqa have established that the states are impermanent and occur in varying degrees to even the most experienced, therefore, this phenomenon shall not be a cause for concern. A seeker may feel contraction in his heart, yet he may not know its cause, in that case the seeker should surrender to his state. If the seeker contrives to expel it or tries to anticipate its attack beforehand on his own accord, his contraction will only become worse. If, on the other hand, he surrenders himself completely to the rule of time, contraction will soon go away.

Allahﷻ mentions in Qurán;

> *"The Lord of the east and the west; there is no god except He; so, take Him to yourself for an Ever-Trusted Trustee"*
>
> *[Qurán, al Muzammil 73:9]*

It is proven that in most cases of spiritual contraction, the heart and soul are thoroughly purified, thus, one should trust in Allahﷻ and avoid being dejected. The mention of east and west is so appropriate for spiritual contraction and elation; where east resembles elation in which lofty spiritual states settle over a person as the rising of the Sun in the east and west resembles contraction in view of the setting sun. Thus, the portrait of the east and west is to be found in the spiritual path, just as the sun becomes hidden in the west, one's spiritual excellence is concealed in contraction and with elation it reappears. It is narrated from Junayd Baghdadi﷫, "My fear of Allahﷻ contracts me; my hope [for His mercy] expands me." [3]

During contraction or Qabd, the seeker benefits more as there are less chances of mistakes. During elation one has to be cautious as it is a state which conforms to the desires of *Nafs*, hence arrogance or pride can creep in. On the contrary, contraction is a state in conflict with the *Nafs*, the attributes of humility and servitude prevail and the seeker perceives himself overwhelmed by Divine Wrath and Power. During elation or Bast, the seeker should try to remain quiet and observe the rules of proper behaviour as he is exposed to a grave danger.⁴ When the door of elation is opened, there are many who slip and veiled from their station. It is a common saying which suggests to stand on the outstretched carpets of *Maárfa*, while being wary of familiarity. These two states do not occur to the ones who have achieved the state of perfection (*kaamil*); they experience a state of equilibrium and true cognizance of Allah.

Awe and Intimacy (Hayba and Uns)

Awe and intimacy are the states superior to contraction and elation. Each awestruck person is absent from himself. The awestruck vary in their awe to the extent that they vary in their absence. Intimacy requires true sobriety, for each intimate friend is sober and they also differ from one another according to their personal share. This is why they say: "In the state of intimacy, when you throw someone into a blazing fire, this does not perturb him." Junayd said that he heard Sari Saqti say that the seeker reaches a point where even if he is struck on the face with the sword, he would not take any notice. The two states entail a change in the servant of Allah, therefore those who have achieved the state of perfection consider these as a deficiency. The spiritual states of the accomplished (*Kaamil*) are above such change as they are completely effaced by their encounter with the Divine Essence, therefore, they do not experience awe or intimacy.⁵

Ecstatic Behaviour, Rapture and Ecstatic Finding
(Tawajud, Wajd and Wujud)

Ecstatic behaviour is an attempt to deliberately stimulate ecstatic rapture. The person in this state does not experience a complete ecstasy, for if he did, he would be an ecstatic in the full meaning of this word. It is said that ecstatic behaviour or *Tawajud* is inappropriate for the one who seeks to bring it about, because it involves a deliberate effort and thus distances him from true realization.

Ecstasy may encounter the heart of the seeker and descend without any intention or effort. Abu Ali al-Daqqaqﷺ said, "Divine visitations (*waridat*) come from prayers (*awrad*). If one does not engage in the external acts of worship, one will have no Divine visitations inside. Every ecstasy that retains some part of the one who experiences it, is not a true ecstasy. Just as outward pious acts bestow sweetness of obedience upon the seeker, his inward experiences bestow ecstatic moments upon him. Therefore, sweetness is the fruit of pious acts, and ecstatic moments are the products of internal experiences."⁶

As for the ecstatic finding (*wujud*), it comes after one has raised oneself above ecstasy. The finding of the True Reality can happen only after one's human nature is completely extinguished, for there is no place for it in the presence of the Divine Reality. Al-Junayd'sﷺ words point to the same meaning: "The knowledge of Allah's ﷻ Oneness is different from finding Him and finding Him is different from knowing Him." Thus, ecstatic behaviour (*Tawajud*) is the beginning, finding (*Wujud*) is the end, and ecstasy (*Wajd*) is between the beginning and the end.

Abu Ali al-Daqqaq ﷺ explained the concept as, "Ecstatic behaviour engrosses the servant, ecstasy consumes him and finding annihilates him. It is as if one first watches the sea, then plunges into it and then drowns in that sea. Here is the sequence of this state: aspiration, arrival, witnessing, finding, and extinction. One's extinction is commensurate with [one's] finding. The person who experiences finding may have two states: sobriety and annihilation. In the state of sobriety, he subsists in Allah ﷻ whereas, in the state of annihilation he perishes in Allah ﷻ. These two states always follow one other in the mystical experience. Abu Ali al-Maghazili ﷺ asked al-Shibli ﷺ: "From time to time, a verse from the Book of Allah ﷻ reaches my ears that urges me to abandon [mundane] affairs and to turn away from this world. However, after a while, I return to my original state and to people." Al-Shibli ﷺ responded: "That which draws you to Him is His sympathy and kindness for you from Him, while that which returns you to yourself is His pity for you from Him, because it is not appropriate for you to divest yourself of all ability and power, when you turn to Him."

As for the person in whom the state of annihilation prevails, he has neither intellect, nor understanding nor sensation or consciousness. The wife of Abu Abdullah al-Tarwaghandi ﷺ narrated that during famine, al-Tarwaghandi ﷺ entered his house and saw two sacks of wheat. He screamed in anguish at the sight of that wheat as people were starving, while he had wheat in the house. As a result, he lost his mind and did not

Mystical States and Stations

come to his senses except during the times of the prayer. He would pray the obligatory prayers and then return to his disorderly mental state. He remained in this state until his death. This narration shows that regardless of his being under the ecstasy, he adhered to Shariáh. The reason for his absence from mental discernment was his compassion for fellow Muslims, which was the sign that he had achieved perfection in his mystical state yet requirements of the Divine Law were preserved for this man.⁷

Once Junayd went to visit al-Sari al-Saqati and found a man lying unconscious. He was told that the man heard a verse from Qurán. Junayd said that the same verse be recited to him again. This was done and the man came back to senses. Al-Sari asked him as to where did he learn that, Junayd said, 'The eyesight of Jacob was gone because of Joseph's shirt, but it also returned to him due to it.' Al-Sari approved his answer.

It is narrated that Sahl bin al-Tustari always stayed composed and collected during sessions of *Dhikr* and recitation of Qurán. This continued for many years, however, at the end of his life, when he heard the recitation of Qurán, he would turn pale and tremble. One day, when he returned to his original state of sobriety (*sahw*), and someone asked him about this, he answered, "I have grown weak!" This is a feature of the outstanding masters, whenever a Divine Visitation (*warid*) descends on them, no matter how powerful it may be, they prove to be stronger.

Unification and Separation (Jam and Farq)

The expressions "unification" and "separation" are often mentioned in *Tasawwuf*. Whatever the servant of Allahﷻ acquires by means of fulfilling the requirements of his servitude and by means of his status as a human being is separation. Unification is everything that comes from the Real, such as the bringing forth of new entities and the bestowal of grace and favour upon the servant. When Allahﷻ allows a person to continue to take notice of his acts of obedience and disobedience, this person finds himself in a state of separation. However, when Allahﷻ allows a person to see His own deeds, this person acquires the attribute of unification. Thus, the assertion of the created world belongs to separation, whereas the assertion of the Real is an attribute of unification. There is no escape for the servant of Allah ﷻ from both unification and separation, for he who does not have separation cannot achieve perfect servitude and he who does not have unification has no knowledge. The following verse of Qurán indicates separation;

"It is You we worship" [Qurán 1:4]

And unification;

"And You, we ask for help" [Qurán 1:4]

When the servant of Allahﷻ addresses Him in his intimate conversation as a supplicant, an adherent believer, a gratified servant, a renouncer of evil deeds or a humble beseecher; he places himself in the position of separation. And when he listens to his inner self and hears in his heart what Allahﷻ imparts to him by calling upon him, admonishing him or instructing him he finds himself under the sign of unification. Someone recited before Abu Sahl al-Sulukiﷺ; 'I have made my vision of You my [greatest] pleasure!'

Abu Sahl said that 'Made' should be read in the second person, while, Abu al-Qasim al-Nasrabadhi debated the concept. Abu Sahl persuaded him by saying that the essence of unification is more comprehensive and preferable. When the seeker says "made" in the first person, it implies that this action comes from him. As for the one who says that "made" should be in the second person, he absolves himself from any deliberate action and says to his Lord: "It is You Who have distinguished me with this quality, and I have not earned it by means of my own deliberate action." The first interpretation contains the danger of an egoistic claim, whereas the second denies one's own power and declares Allah's beneficence and generosity. There is a great difference between the one who says: "I worship You through my own effort" and the one who says: "I witness You through Your beneficence and kindness."[8]

Unification of Unification (jam al-jamá)

Seekers differ in their spiritual states and their ranks of spiritual attainment. Unification is when someone affirms both himself and the created world, yet acknowledges everything in this world as being dependent on Allah. When the seeker, under the domination of the Divine Reality, is rendered incapable of contemplating the created world and barred from one's own self, this state is unification of unification. Thus, unification is seeing everything through Allah, whereas, unification of unification is complete annihilation in Allah and the loss of perception of anything other than Him.

The next state is called, "second separation" (*farq thani*), where the seeker returns to sobriety whenever it is time to perform any of his religious obligations. In this state, the seeker may see himself being driven by Allah's will and considers Allah's power as the ultimate source of his essence and his self. The seeker acknowledges Allah's ﷻ will as the true performer of his actions and the originator of his spiritual states.

Annihilation and Subsistence (Faná and Baqá)

In *Tasawwuf*, the term 'annihilation' refers to the disappearance of blameworthy traits, whereas 'subsistence' refers to the persistence of praiseworthy qualities. The seeker on the path of *Tasawwuf* is characterized by deeds, morals and spiritual states. Deeds are undertaken through his own free will and morals are his inherent predispositions, which can be changed through rigor. However, their subsequent purity is determined by the intention of his actions. Allah ﷻ allows the person whose heart preoccupies itself with morals through its own concerted effort to improve his morality. Likewise, Allah ﷻ will allow the person who strives to purify his deeds of his own accord to protect his spiritual states.

When one is dominated by blameworthy traits, he will be deprived of praiseworthy qualities. Likewise, when the blameworthy traits of the seeker are annihilated, the praiseworthy traits are dominated. When someone abandons the evil deeds denounced by the Divine Law, it is said that he is annihilated from his worldly passions. Once, the seeker is annihilated from his passions, he subsists in the service of Allah ﷻ through his determination and sincerity. When someone renounces this world, it is said that he is annihilated from his desire of it and when he is annihilated from the desire, he subsists in the sincerity of his repentance. When someone has refined his morals by cleansing his heart of envy, malice, avarice, greed, anger, and pride, as well as any other impurities that adhere to the soul, it is said: "He has been

Mystical States and Stations

annihilated from the base character traits." And, when the seeker is annihilated from bad morals, he subsists in chivalry and truthfulness.

When the seeker observes the workings of Divine Decrees, it is said that he has been annihilated from seeing events as emanating from creatures. And when one is annihilated from perceiving events as products of secondary causes, one subsists in the attributes of the Real. The seeker is annihilated from his blameworthy traits when he avoids them and he is annihilated from his self and other creatures when he ceases to perceive both.

Once, the seeker is annihilated from himself and others (*ghair*) then, he has no knowledge or perception of those. In this state, his self exists and the creatures continue to exist objectively, however, he is oblivious of them and is capable of perceiving neither his self nor the creatures. For example, if a person enters the presence of a mighty ruler, he would be self-effaced in his reverence and become completely oblivious of his surroundings. Just as, when the women of Egypt saw Yousufﷺ, they were so awed by his reverence and beauty, that they cut their hands and did not even take notice of their pain. As mentioned in Qurán:

> "And, when they saw him [Yousufﷺ], they so admired him that they cut their hands."
>
> [Qurán, Surah Yusuf 12:31]

When a seeker is annihilated from his ignorance, he subsists in his knowledge and when he is annihilated from his passions, he subsists in his repentance. When he is annihilated from his desire of this world, he persists in its renunciation. When he is annihilated from his passionate drive, he subsists in his longing for Allahﷻ. After the seeker is annihilated from his characteristics, he advances from this stage to the next one at which he loses sight of his annihilation. The first annihilation is from one's self and one's attributes through subsistence in the attributes of Allahﷻ. Then, comes the annihilation from the attributes of Allahﷻ in the contemplation of Allahﷻ. Then, one is annihilated from the vision of his own annihilation by being subsumed in the existence of Allahﷻ Himself.

Absence and Presence (Ghayba and Hudur)

When the heart is absent from knowing the circumstances of creatures due to complete absorption of the senses by what has transpired to the heart from Allahﷻ is the state of 'absence'. One may also become absent from oneself and others through remembering Allah'sﷻ promise of reward and thinking of the punishment. It is said that Rabi bin Khuthaym﷫ used to visit Ibn Masud﷠, as he was passing by a blacksmith's shop, he saw a red-hot iron in the forge and fainted until the next morning. When he was asked, he answered: "I remembered how the people of Hell will sojourn in the fire!" This was an absence that went beyond its limit and turned into unconsciousness. It is recounted of Imam Zayn ul Abideen﷫ that he was performing Salah when suddenly his house caught fire, but he did not interrupt his prayer. When asked about that, he said: "The Greatest Fire made me oblivious of that fire."

Occasionally, a seeker can be rendered absent from his perception by something that Allahﷻ reveals to him. Abu Hafs al-Haddad﷫ was a blacksmith, while forging metal, he heard someone reciting a verse from the Qurán. At that moment, he had an experience that made him oblivious of his senses and he picked the hot iron in his hand. Upon that, his apprentice screamed and Abu Hafs﷫ realized what had just happened.

As for presence, the seeker is absent from creatures and is present with Allahﷻ, due to the fact that the recollection of Allahﷻ takes full possession of his heart. When a seeker is present, this means that his heart is in constant remembrance of Allahﷻ, without being neglectful or forgetful. In this state Allahﷻ unveils things that He has prepared for his servant only. Sometimes, the seeker returns to self-awareness and to awareness of other creatures after he was present with Allahﷻ. The states in absence may vary, for some, it may not last long while for others the absence may last for a while.

It is said that Dhu al-Nun al-Misri؇ sent one of his companions to Abu Yazid al-Bistami؇, so that he could get some description of Abu Yazid؇. The companion reached the city of Bistam, went to Abu Yazid Bistami's؇ house and knocked on the door. Abu Yazid asked him what he wanted and the man told him that he was looking for Abu Yazid Bistami؇. Abu Yazid Bistami؇ answered, "Who is Abu Yazid? Where is Abu Yazid? I am also in search of Abu Yazid." The man left saying, "This is a madman!" He returned to Dhu al-Nun Misri؇ and told him about his encounter. On hearing this, Dhu al-Nun Misri؇ wept and said: "My brother Abu Yazid has joined those who travel to Allahﷻ."

Tasting and Drinking (Dhawq and Shurb)

These terms are used to describe the results of unveiling experienced by the seeker. The first of these is tasting, then comes drinking and, finally, the quenching of thirst. The seeker attains the state of tasting through the purity of his pious deeds and then attains the state of drinking. He quenches his thirst through fulfilling the requirements of the spiritual stations. The seeker in the state of tasting behaves like a drunk and the seeker who has quenched his thirst becomes sober. When someone's love for Allahﷻ is strong, his state of drinking becomes permanent and then, he becomes sober and oblivious of all his mundane concerns. When the heart is pure, one's drinking becomes nourishment, then the seeker can neither abstain from it nor survive without it. One must remember that these states are only bestowed by Allahﷻ upon those whose hearts are emancipated and whose spirits are free from attachment of the worldly desires.

It is narrated that Yahya b. Mu'adhؓ wrote to Abu Yazid al-Bistamiؓ, "Here's the one who has drunk from the cup of love and will never feel thirsty." Abu Yazidؓ responded to him: "I am surprised at the weakness of your [spiritual] state! Here's a man who has gulped down all the seas of existence, yet his mouth is agape, wanting more." [9]

Sobriety and drunkenness (Sahw and Sukr)

Sobriety and drunkenness come after tasting and drinking. Sobriety is returning to self-consciousness after absence, whereas drunkenness is absence from one's self through a strong experience of Divine Light. In a sense, drunkenness is a complement to absence in that the drunken person may be relaxed as long as he is not fully immersed in his drunken state. On the other hand, in this state, any perception of outward things may completely disappear from his heart. This is the state of one who behaves like a drunk, because his drunkenness has not yet taken full control of him and he is still capable of perceiving outward things.

When the drunkenness of a drunk becomes really strong, his absence may surpass the absence experienced by someone

Mystical States and Stations

in the state of absence. At the same time, the absence of someone in the state of absence may be more complete than the absence of a drunk, especially when he behaves like a drunk without actually having achieved the state of drunkenness. The state of absence may visit seekers whose hearts have become preoccupied by the influence of passionate longing, awe, fear and hope.

On the contrary, drunkenness is experienced when the attributes of beauty *(jamal)* are revealed to a seeker: his spirit rejoices and his heart becomes intoxicated. One's sobriety corresponds to one's drunkenness and the one who experiences true drunkenness, enjoys true sobriety. When the seeker becomes witness to the Power of the Real, he loses his personal attributes and becomes fully consumed by the state. Allahﷻ mentioned in Qurán:

> "And when his Lord revealed Himself to the mountain, He made it crumble to dust." [Qurán, al Aáraf 7:139]

Mosesﷺ lost consciousness, despite being a Resolute Prophet, while the mountain "crumbled to dust" in spite of its mass and strength. In his state of drunkenness, the seeker finds himself under the mark of a mystical state, whereas in his state of sobriety he is under the mark of knowledge. In his state of drunkenness, he is protected by Allahﷻ without applying his own effort, while in his state of sobriety he protects himself from error through his own actions. [10]

Erasure and Affirmation (Mahw and Ithbat)

Erasure is the removal of habitual attributes and affirmation is the fulfillment of the commands of servanthood. When the blameworthy traits are replaced by praiseworthy actions, the seeker becomes a man of erasure and affirmation. It is narrated from Abu Ali al-Daqqaq that the mystical moment is both erasure and affirmation, one who has neither erasure nor affirmation is idle and abandoned. The state of erasure can be elimination of faults from one's external, removal of heedlessness from *Nafs* or removal of deficiency from one's innermost heart.

The erasure of faults is the affirmation of good deeds, the erasure of forgetfulness is the affirmation of spiritual stations and the erasure of deficiency is the affirmation of cognizance with Allah. This is erasure and affirmation in the meaning of servitude. As regards to the true erasure and affirmation, they come from Allah's mercy; erasure is what Allah conceals and denies, whereas affirmation is what He shows and makes manifest. Erasure and affirmation are determined by the Divine Will as Allah said:

"Allah eliminates what He wills or affirms it, and with Him is the Master Book." [Qurán ar-Rád 13:39]

It is said that Allah erases from the hearts of the true seekers any thought of other than Himself and He affirms the remembrance of Himself on His servants' tongues. Allah erases and affirms for each one in accordance with his internal state; self-perception is erased and He affirms the seeker through His own True Self. When He erases someone's affirmation through His True Self, He returns him to the vision of other things and settles him in the plains of differentiation. Someone asked Shibli as to why he always seemed restless. Shibli replied that when he was with Allah, he was erased in Him.

Obliteration is above erasure, because erasure leaves a trace, while obliteration leaves no trace. The ultimate goal of the seeker is when Allah obliterates their self-perception completely, never to return them to themselves.

Concealment and Manifestation (Satr and Tajalli)

If someone experiences concealment, his self-perception is determined by it, while a person in the state of manifestation is always characterized by submission. Concealment is a punishment for the common folk and a blessing for the elect. If Allahﷻ does not conceal what He unveils to them, they would be completely annihilated by the power of the True Reality. According to Hadith, the Beloved Prophetﷺ said, *"Should Allahﷻ unveil His face, the splendour of His countenance would burn everything within the range of His sight."* [Muslim 179]

Allahﷻ distracted Moses۝ with something that pleased him to reduce the impact of Divine unveiling, when Allahﷻ spoke to him. Allahﷻ asked Moses۝:

"What is that, Moses, that you have in your right hand?"

[Qurán, Tá Ha 20:117]

Allahﷻ manifests to the true seekers while concealing Himself from them. A novice may experience happiness at Divine manifestations and suffer upon concealment, however, the experienced wayfarer feels happy upon concealment.[11]

Presence, Unveiling and Witnessing
(Muhadara, Mukashafa and Mushahada)

Presence is the attendance of the heart with Allahﷻ which is achieved through continuous manifestation of the Divine proof. During presence, the seeker finds himself in Allah'sﷻ presence through the power of remembrance of Allahﷻ. This state is followed by unveiling, which is presence through clear evidence. In this state the seeker does not need the proof for Divine Reality and all doubts are erased. Unveiling is followed by witnessing, which means to be in the presence of the Absolute Truth. When the sky of the innermost heart is free from the clouds of veiling, the sun of witnessing begins to shine.

The True Reality of witnessing was captured by Junayd al-Baghdadi﷫ as he said: "Allah'sﷻ existence appears when you lose yours." The seeker in the state of presence is bound by its signs whereas, the seeker in the state of unveiling rejoices in its attributes. As for the seeker in the state of witnessing, his self is erased by his knowledge of Allahﷻ. No one has expressed the essence of witnessing better than al-Makki﷫, as he said, "The splendour of Allah'sﷻ self-manifestation appears to the heart clearly and without interruption, like an uninterrupted sequence of lightning in the middle of a dark night, turning it into day."

Proximity and Distance (Qurb and Buád)

The first degree of proximity is the proximity to obedience towards Allahﷻ and the state of being always engaged in His worship. As for the 'distance', the seeker is far removed from any boundaries, dimensions, limits or measure. Thus, the proximity is the knowledge which Allahﷻ bestows upon the seeker through His Divine Mercy. As the Beloved Prophetﷺ said, "Allahﷻ says: "My slave approaches me with nothing more beloved to me than what I have made obligatory upon him, and My slave keeps drawing nearer to Me with voluntary works until I love him. And when I love him, I am his hearing with which he hears, his sight with which he sees, his hands with which he seizes, and his foot with which he walks. If he asks Me, I will surely give it to him, and when he seeks refuge in Me, I will protect him." [Bukhari 6502]

Mystical States and Stations

The proximity of the servant of Allahﷻ begins with his proximity to faith and the attestation of His veracity. This is followed by the proximity to good deeds and the realization of the Divine Truth. As for Allah'sﷻ proximity to the servant, it is the Divine knowledge that Allahﷻ bestows upon him in this world and the witnessing [of Himself] that He will grant the servant in the Hereafter. The servant's proximity to Allahﷻ is not possible unless he distances himself from His creatures. This is meant for the condition of heart and does not refer to outward phenomena and empirical existence. Allah'sﷻ proximity through knowledge and power encompasses the entire human race, His proximity through kindness is limited to the believers and proximity through special intimacy is restricted to His friends. As Allahﷻ mentioned in Qurán:

> "We are nearer to him [man] than the jugular vein."
>
> [Qurán, Qaf 50:16]

And;

> "He is with you wherever you are." [Qurán, al Hadid 57:4]

And also;

> "Three men conspire not secretly together, but He is the fourth of them." [Qurán, al Mujadilah 58:7]

When the seeker fully realizes proximity to Allahﷻ, he observes and keeps a watch over himself because of the fear, reverence and humility. The feeling of intimacy in His proximity is a sign of being governed by His power, as Allahﷻ is behind all intimacy and the manifestation of the True Reality bring about bewilderment and erasure. As for the proximity to the Divine Essence, Allahﷻ is;

> "High exalted be God, the true King" (Qurán, Tá Ha 20:114)

Concept of Unity of Perception and Unity of Being
(Wahdat al-Shuhud and Wahdat al-Wujud)

At times, people try to read text of the scholars which is beyond their comprehension and instead of being beneficial, that knowledge can cause them harm. There are topics which are beyond a common person's comprehension. Despite of one's ability to comprehend those topics, people become antagonistic towards Allahﷻ and the Beloved Prophetﷺ. It is important to understand that this knowledge of the elites is not for everyone. It is related on the authority of Ali؇ that he said, "Speak to people of things they can understand. Would you like it if people started doubting Allahﷻ and His Prophetﷺ?" [Bukhari 127]

Unity of Perception and Unity of Being is one of those topics which is beyond comprehension, however, many debate about this concept. Mufti Muhammad Taqi Usmani writes about these two concepts in his book, *'Takmilah Fath al-Mulhim'*, The doctrine of Oneness of Being (*Wahdat al-Wujud*) along with its corresponding doctrine of the Oneness of Perception (*Wahdat al-Shuhud*) is not among the doctrines that are necessary in the religion to know or to believe in their validity or invalidity. Rather, it is best not to be preoccupied with it, because it is a dangerous subject, discussion of which may lead to heresy (*zandaqah*) and apostasy (*ilhad*).

It is a philosophical question which human minds are incapable of comprehending. The safest path is to follow the pious predecessors who practiced by consigning (tafwid) their reality to Allahﷻ while avoiding these philosophical discussions which have no clear ruling in the texts of the Shariáh. Since, discussions on this topic have become more frequent and many vague ideas have surfaced, it is important to explain the concept to caution people.

Mystical States and Stations

The articles of faith which are the adherents of Islam, rather the adherents of all Heavenly religions, have agreed upon that independent beginningless and eternal existence belongs to none besides Allahﷻ; that He Most High is the One who created the cosmos and originated it and that all creatures were non-existent and came into the domain of existence by the creation of Allahﷻ and His origination. However, the scholars differed in the manner in which the creatures are characterised by "existence", according to four viewpoints:

> The majority of the scholars of the Shariáh took the position that the existence of possible creatures is a real existence that is acquired, in the sense that it is dependent on the Will of Allahﷻ, His creation and His origination.
> Some of the Muslim philosophers expressed the view that their existence is relative (*idafi*).
> The adherents of the doctrine of the Oneness of Being, and the foremost of them is Shaykh Ibn 'Arabi﷫ expressed the view that their existence is purely imaginary (*khayali*).
> The adherents of the doctrine of the Oneness of Perception, and the foremost of them is Mujaddid Alf al Thani﷫ expressed the view that their existence is a shadow existence (*wujud zilli*).

As regards to the difference between real acquired existence (*al-wujud al-haqiqi al-muktasab*) and relative (*idafi*), imaginative (*khayali*) and shadow (*zilli*) existence, it can be explained with an analogy that is; if we were to put a glass before the sun, the sun would produce four changes in the glass:

The first change is that the glass would become warm due to the heat of the sun. The existence of heat and warmth in the glass in this state is a real existence different to the existence of the heat of the sun. This is proven by the fact that if the glass's opposition to the sun was removed, the heat of the glass would remain for a while. Hence, this is a proof for the difference between the reality of heat and the reality of warmth. However, the warmth of the glass is acquired from the heat of the sun and is dependent on it. This is an illustration or analogy of real acquired existence.

The scholars have taken the view that the existence of possible entities and creatures is a real acquired existence, in the sense that Allahﷻ is the One that created its existence; however, real existence is different from the existence of Allahﷻ. Moreover, the existence and existent are both complete and separate. Real existence is divided into two types: the beginningless independent existence by Itself and this existence belongs to none besides Allahﷻ and an acquired temporal existence which is a quality of all possible entities. Likewise, the existent is divided into two types: the beginningless independent existent and this is none besides Allahﷻ and a contingent created existent and this includes all possible entities.

The second change in the glass facing the sun is that it emits light due to the radiation of the sun but this light which the glass emits is not different to the light of the sun. Rather, it is the same as the light of the sun, but it is distinguished from it by a specific relation acquired by it due to the ascription of the glass to it. And the proof of it being from the light of the sun is that it disappears when the opposition between the sun and the glass is removed. This is an analogy of relative existence since the existence of the light of the glass, from

Mystical States and Stations

the perspective that it is the light of the glass, is not real, and it is only the light of the sun through which the glass acquires a specific attribution. Hence, the light of the glass is the same as the light of the sun, although it is distinguished from it by this specific relation.

Some of the Islamic philosophers have taken the position that the characterisation of possible entities by existence is similar to the description of the glass with light in this illustration. When Allahﷻ wanted to create the possible entities, He gave them a specific connection, whose true nature is unknown, to the existence that is subsisting in itself. He did not give it an existence different from that existence, but it is described as having existence by virtue of this connection which Allahﷻ gave to it. Hence, the existence according to them is real and partial, and the existent is complete and separate.

The third change in the glass facing the sun is that the disc of the sun appears in the glass as though it is located in it. However, the reality is that the image of the sun which appears in the glass does not have a real existence. Since, it is not the same as the sun, or an apparition of it or a replication of it, rather it is purely fantasy and imaginary. The reality is when the visual rays descend on the glass, it turns to the sun, so the sun appears in those visual rays. Thus, the image of the sun reflected in the glass is an illusion, generated only by visual rays. If one closes his eye, the image of the sun will no longer remain in the glass, therefore, if it had an actual existence in the glass, that existence would not disappear upon closing the eye. This is an illustration of imaginary existence.

One of the adherents of the doctrine of the Oneness of Being, and the foremost of them is Shaykh Ibn 'Arabi would say that the existence of Allah is eternal and beginningless, and there was nothing before the creation of the world besides this beginningless eternal existence along with His names and attributes, and this is what is called "external existence" (*zahir al-wujud*). All the possible entities were non-existent in the exterior but its detailed knowledge was available to Allahﷻ. These possible entities from the perspective of their being known to Allahﷻ are called in the terminology "the immutable entities" (*al-a'yan al-thabita*). Hence, when Allahﷻ intended to remove the world from pure non-existence, He manifested these immutable entities upon external existence, by different levels of manifestation and in a manner whose true nature is known only to Allah ﷻ.

Thus, the reflections of these immutable entities were manifested into external existence. These immutable entities do not acquire an existence from the outside, nor do they acquire the ability to penetrate into external existence. It only acquires an imaginary existence that appears from the outside as though it is an external existence, just as the disc of the sun acquired an imaginary existence in the glass without acquiring a real existence externally. Thus, the real existent is none other than Allahﷻ and the entire world is a reflection of the immutable entities and is nothing but pure imagination, which appears to be existent externally, but is not existent with a real existence.

Moreover, although Shaykh Ibn 'Arabi﷦ said that the existence of the world in its entirety is purely imaginary, he nevertheless believed that the imagination has different levels. Hence, from the imaginary existent there are two types; one which disappears by stepping up the imagination, thus rules do not pertain to it and another which does not disappear by stepping up the imagination, therefore, some rules pertain to

Mystical States and Stations

it. The existence of the world is from the second type of imaginary existence which does not disappear by stepping up the imagination and for that reason it is correct for the rules of the Shariáh to pertain to it. So, what some people raise as an objection to him that the view of the entire world being purely imaginary necessitates the view of the negation of laws and rules, is an objection not brought about by what Shaykh Ibn 'Arabiﷺ said.

The fourth change in the glass facing the sun is that the shadow of the glass falls on the earth. This shadow does not have a real existence. It is but an original darkness encompassed by light and by this encompassment it becomes an image from the outside called a shadow. This is an illustration of shadow existence. The adherents of the theory of the Oneness of Perception, and the foremost of them is Shaykh Mujaddid Alf Thaniﷺ say that before the creation of the world there was nothing existent besides Allahﷻ and all the possible entities were non-existent.

Thus, the names of Allahﷻ and His attributes were existent with a beginningless existence and these are an expression of the attributes of perfection. In contrast to them are the non-existent imperfect entities, like incapacity in contrast to power, and ignorance in contrast to knowledge. When Allahﷻ intended to create the world, He manifested the attributes of His perfection on these non-existents, so the image of the perfections reflected on these non-existents. By this reflection emerged the realities whose substance (*maddah*) are the non-existents and their forms (*surah*) these reflections. Thus, they are not existent with a real existence, due to originally being non-existents and imperfect entities, but they are by virtue of this reflection not considered pure non-existents. Hence, their existence is not a real existence, because the real existence is none besides Allahﷻ and not a purely imaginary existence but it has a level between the two levels, like the existence of a shadow, and is called a shadow existence.

This synopsis of the four positions on this issue is derived from the book *Bawadir al-Nawadir* by Mowlana Ashraf Ali al-Thanviؒ, "The safest position is to consign its reality to Allahﷻ. We believe that the existence of Allahﷻ is independent, complete, eternal and beginningless, while the existence of creatures in their entirety is a temporal existence dependent on the will of Allahﷻ and it is imperfect in all respects relative to the existence of Allahﷻ. As regards to the true understanding of this imperfect existence and the manner in which the creatures are characterised by it, we are not commanded to investigate this and arrive at its true nature. There is no way for us to have firm resolve in this at all.

It appears the position of the majority of the scholars corresponds to the first from the four positions we mentioned earlier, due to it being closest [in keeping] to His statement Most High:

> *"Verily, when He intends a thing, His Command is, 'be', and it is!"*
> [Qur'an 36:82]

As regards to what Shaykh Ibn 'Arabiؒ and Shaykh Mujaddid Alf Thaniؒ said, we assign its reality to Allahﷻ and we do not speak insolently about them. They spoke about these issues due to a reason they knew best and there is nothing in what they said that directly clashes with the texts. However, at the same time there is nothing in the texts which necessitate adhering to their views or being resolute about what they said. Whoever construes the texts of the Shariáh to express one of these views, then his construal is not devoid of being a distortion (*tahrif*) or extremism (*ghuluww*), or forced interpretation (*takalluf*) and an aberration (*ta'assuf*), for indeed the texts of the Shariáh are silent on these issues; the true reality of which human minds are unable to comprehend.

Whoever holds, in regards to the discourse of this topic, to the correctness of the doctrine of the Oneness of Being from the perspective that Allah's Messenger ﷺ approved the judgement of the vainness of all things besides Allah ﷻ, it is a fixation in the matter and far-off from acquiring any benefit, because it is not the intent of the poem to discuss the manner in which creation is characterised by existence. The intent is only that all things besides Allah ﷻ are imperfect and death will overtake them, whereas imperfection or death does not occur in Allah ﷻ.[12]

Chapter Eleven

GENERAL MISCONCEPTIONS

Use of Musical Instruments

The Beloved Prophetﷺ said, "Among my ummah there will certainly be people who permit zina, silk, alcohol and musical instruments........."[Bukhari 5590,al-Tabarani and al-Bayhaqi]

There is no disagreement that poems were recited before Allah's Messengerﷺ and he listened to them, without condemning those who recited them. Anas bin Malik⌐ narrated: "The Helpers (ansar) were digging the ditch, chanting: 'We have pledged our allegiance to Muhammadﷺ in [his] struggle (jihad) As long as we are alive.' The Messenger ﷺ responded to them, saying: 'O Allah, there's no life except that of the Hereafter, be benevolent to the Helpers and the Emigrants!'" [Bukhari: 2834, Muslim: 1805, Tirmidhi: 3857]

Thus, Samá should be understood to be the means to an end, where the end or objective, is worship. The abovementioned Hadith is a precedent for this practice. The digging of the Trench was the objective, while fatigue and hunger might have led to irresolution. The recitation of the rhymed and metered verses performed the function of lifting spirits and preventing indolence. In view of these factors, then, this would seem to be the wisdom behind this practice. It must be remembered, however, that to suppose Samá itself to be the objective or to practise it without concern for propriety, is tantamount to

General Misconceptions 241

tampering with religion.

As for the songs of the camel drivers (hida), all of them agreed that it was permissible. Allah's Messenger ﷺ said: "Two sounds are cursed: the sound of wailing at the time of an affliction and the sound of the flute at the time of happiness."

Regarding Sáma, Mujaddid alf Thani ﷺ wrote, "For every Tariqa, there is a way and each one has to follow its own. Khawaja Naqshband ﷺ said, 'Sáma is against our (Naqshbandi) Tariqa, neither do we engage in Sa'ma, nor deny it, however, others engage in Sáma therefore, we do not negate it."[1]

The recitation of Qur'an in a beautiful voice or the odes in the love of the Beloved Prophet ﷺ without any musical instruments and within the bounds of Shariáh are acceptable. The listener should keep his focus towards the love of Allah ﷻ and His Last Prophet ﷺ in order to attract pure visitations to the heart. This is laudable from the standpoint of religion and preferred from the viewpoint of the Divine Law. It is narrated by Abdullah bin Masud ﷺ that the Prophet ﷺ said to him, "Recite the Qur'an for me." When 'Abdullah ﷺ replied, "What? You want me to read what was revealed to you?" the Messenger of Allah ﷺ said, "It's just that I love to hear it from someone else ... " Further on, in the same narration, Ibne Masud ﷺ reports that as he was reciting for the Prophet ﷺ ".... his eyes suddenly filled with tears." [Bukhari: 4582, Muslim: 800]

It is human nature that people often derive more pleasure from listening to something recited to them than from reading or reciting the same thing themselves. For this reason, audition or Sáma is sometimes prescribed for a disciple who needs to have a particular state intensified, or to have the desire or renewed, or to attain a certain spiritual composure. Certain

General Misconceptions 242

Sufis are of the opinion that owing to circumstances of a temporary nature if the seeker becomes spiritually irresolute, lax, or contracted, listening to the recitation of Qurán and odes in the love of the Beloved Prophetﷺ provides a remedy. In this way, the aspirant's irresolution may be dispelled, and a desire to worship will be facilitated.

As far as the movements during a listening session are concerned, someone asked Ibrahim al-Maristani؇ to which he responded: "I have heard that Moses؇ was giving a sermon to the Children of Israel. One of his listeners tore up his shirt out of ecstasy. Allah؇ revealed to Moses؇: 'Tell him: "For Me, Tear your heart, not your clothing!"'"[2]

Conveying the Reward of Actions
(Eesal e Sawab)

It is a practice to convey the reward of actions to the elders and the pious of the path. One should diligently perform acts of righteousness on behalf of one's Shaykh and parents, spouses, siblings, children and other relatives, particularly those who had carried out special acts of kindness. When a believer fasts or performs *Salah*, or gives charity and conveys the reward to another person, regardless of whether the person is alive or dead, then its reward shall reach them.

This practice is substantiated by Hadith as Saa'd؇ asked, "Allah's Messengerﷺ! My mother has passed away, which form of charity [for sending her reward] is most superior?" The Prophetﷺ replied, "Water is the most superior." Upon that, Saa'd؇ had a well excavated for reward towards his mother [Malik, Abu Dawud and al-Nasa'i]. The Beloved Prophetﷺ mentioned water as it is particularly needed everywhere and there was scarcity of water in Madinah at that time.

General Misconceptions 243

Abdullah bin Buraida reported on the authority of his father: "When we were sitting with Allah's Messenger, a woman came to him and said: 'I had gifted to my mother a maid-servant, and now she (the mother) has died.' Thereupon, the Beloved Prophet said: 'There is a definite reward for you and she (the maid-servant) has been returned to you as an inheritance. That woman again said: 'Fasts of a month (of Ramadan) are due upon her, should I observe them on her behalf?' The Beloved Prophet said: 'Observe fasts on her behalf.' She said: 'She did not perform Hajj, should I perform it on her behalf?' The Beloved Prophet said: 'Perform Hajj on her behalf.'" [Sahih Muslim:2558]

In another narration, Saa'd asked the Beloved Prophet , "Allah's Messenger! When my mother was alive, she used to perform Hajj with my wealth, give charity with my wealth, maintain ties and support people. Now she has died and if we were to carry out all of these works on her behalf, then would she benefit?" The Beloved Prophet replied that they would reach her. [Al Kanz]

It is mentioned in a Hadith that a woman asked the Beloved Prophet, "My mother has suddenly passed away. If she had not passed away, she would have given some charity etc. If I were to give some charity on her behalf, then would it be from her?" The Beloved Prophet said, "Yes, give charity on her behalf." [Abu Dawood]

Salih ibn Dirham related: "We departed for the Hajj and met a person on the way who asked us: 'Is there any village near you by the name of al-Ubullah?' We replied: 'Yes.' He asked: 'Is there anyone among you who can take the responsibility of offering two or four cycles of prayer in the Masjid al-'Ashshar [which is in this village) and say that these cycles are on behalf of Abu Hurairah? I heard my friend Abu al-Qasim saying: 'On the day of Resurrection Allah will raise from the Masjid al-'Ashshar such martyrs who will rise with the martyrs of Badr. No other martyrs will rise with them. [Abu Dawud: 4308]

It is obvious that Abu Hurairah's ؓ asking someone to offer the Salah on his behalf was solely for the purpose of getting the reward. Two topics regarding the conveying of spiritual rewards are established from this Hadith; the rewards for physical worship reach the person in whose name it is carried out, secondly, just as the rewards reach the deceased, they also reach those who are alive. This is because the person who made this request was Abu Hurairah ؓ himself and he was obviously alive at the time.

It is noticed that some of those who love their Shaykh or spiritual master pay particular attention to engaging in remembrance and other acts of worship at the places where spiritual master lived or at the places where he performed his acts of worship. The blessed nature of such places is obvious and the Hadith establishes the benefit of carrying out acts of worship in such places.³

Imam Zayn ud-din Ibn Nujaim al-Misri ؒ wrote, "According to us the rewards of deeds performed by one person reaches the other, this includes praying, fasting, charity, recitation of Qurán, *Dhikr*, Tawaf, Hajj, lesser Hajj or any other good deeds. This is proven from Qurán and Sunnah.⁴

The same viewpoint is observed by Imam Ibn Abideen ash-Shami ؒ in his book Dur ul Mukhtar.⁵

Visiting the Graves of Awliya

Shirk is to affirm the special attributes of Allahﷻ for anyone besides Him. The pre-Islamic polytheists did believe in Allahﷻ, but associated partners and servants with Him. It was their false belief that Allahﷻ does not take charge of the affairs of His subjects and their particular affairs Himself, rather He delegates this to His authorities and has conferred the robe of divinity to some of His servants. As a result, they carved their images and statues, prostrated before them and slaughtered on their behalf, took oaths upon their names and sought help by their absolute power.

Shah Waliullah Dehlavi۔ wrote on this issue: "All who go to the land of Ajmer or to the grave of Salar Mas'ud or those that resemble them in order to request to fulfil a need, it is indeed a sin more grievous than murder and adultery. It is like those who worship the creation or those who call on Al-Lat and Al-'Uzza(famous idols of pre-Islamic times). However, we do not unequivocally declare disbelief [upon them] due to the absence of a text from the Lawgiver in this specific matter. All who assign life to the dead and request their needs from them, *'his heart is surely sinful'* [Qurán, 2:283], and [this act] is included as Allahﷻ says, *'that is iniquity'* [Qurán, 5:3]."[6]

In the same work, he writes: "The definition of associating (*shirk*) [partners] with Allahﷻ in worship is glorifying anyone other than Allahﷻ, intending thereby to come closer to Allahﷻ and salvation in the Final Abode. One of the greatest issues in this era is the worshipping of their Shaykh when they are alive or their graves when dead. The ignorant [Muslims] imitate the disbelievers of India [i.e., Hindus] in worshipping their idols which is amongst their rituals. The definition of associating partners with Allahﷻ in seeking help (*isti'anah*) is to seek one's need from another while believing he has the power to accomplish it by applying his powerful will (*sarf al-iradah al-nafidhah*), like curing the sick, giving life and death, giving provision and creating a child and other things that are contained in the Names of Allah. The definition of associating partners with Allah in supplication is to mention other than Allah while believing this action of his will benefit him in his afterlife or in coming closer to Allah, just as they mention their Shaykh upon waking up in the morning."[7]

After explaining the condition of the polytheists, Shah Waliullah compares them with some Muslims of his era. He writes: "If you, dear reader, are hesitant in accepting the accuracy of what was said about the beliefs of the polytheists and their deeds, look at the falsehoods of this age, especially of those who reside in the borders of the Abode of Islam [i.e. India] and what their concepts are regarding sainthood (*Walaya*); for, despite recognising the sainthood of the early saints, they believe the existence of *Walaya* in this age is impossible and they attend the graves and holy places [of the earlier ones]. Hence, they are afflicted by all kinds of *shirk*, *bid'a* and superstitions. Distortion (*tahrif*) and assimilation (*tashbih*) have taken root in their beliefs and penetrated through their minds. The tribulation and the trial are mentioned in the authentic Hadith, 'You will surely follow the ways of those who went before you...' remained but a group from amongst the groups that are Muslims by name plunged into it and became attached to it. Allah save us from that."[8]

This Hadith provides guidance in terms of supplication and how Allah's Messenger emphatically rejected it. It is narrated that a Bedouin came to Allah's Messenger and said, "People have done everything they could do, but families are hungry, fortunes (orchards and plantations) have been destroyed and

General Misconceptions 247

cattle are dying. Pray to Allahﷻ for us and ask Him to send down rain. We petition you as an intercessor before Allahﷻ and we petition Allahﷻ as an intercessor before you." Allah's Messengerﷺ became distressed by these words ("We petition Allahﷻ as an intercessor before you") and said, "Glory be to Allah, glory be to Allah, *SubhanAllah, SubhanAllah, SubhanAllah.*" He repeated these words with such intensity that their effects were seen on the faces of his Companions. Finally, he said: "Woe unto you! Allahﷻ is not to be considered an intercessor before anyone. Allah'sﷻ status is far beyond that." (In other words, an intercession entails a supplication and a need. Allahﷻ does not supplicate anyone, nor is He in need of anyone. This statement supposes Allahﷻ to have need, and is therefore repulsive). [Abu Dawud:4726]

Another common practice is to place sheets over the graves, Ibn 'Umar﷜ saw a cloth over the grave of 'Abd ar-Rahman﷜, so he said [to his attendant]: "Remove it, young man! For verily he is shaded by his deeds." [Bukhari]

Mother of the believers, Ayesha﷜ narrated, "I used to go into my house [in which the Messenger of Allahﷺ and Abu Bakr﷜ were buried]. But when 'Umar﷜ was buried with them, by Allah, I never entered that room without first covering myself properly out of modesty for 'Umar﷜."[Musnad Ahmad: 6:202]. In explanation of the Hadith, the scholars state that one may go to the grave of the deceased and accord as much respect to that person as one used to when the person was alive. This is on condition that one does not transgress the limits of the Shariáh.

The correct way to visit the graves is to convey the reward of action (*Eesal e Sawab*) by reciting Qurán or giving charity. Then, one can supplicate to Allahﷻ through the blessings which Allahﷻ had bestowed upon His pious men, Allahﷻ is the Provider and the Sustainer, therefore, supplication is to Him only.

Chapter Twelve

THE ORDERS~SILSILA

Tariqa is to take the path to transform the soul, the way of the *Tariqa* may differ but mostly it consists of uprooting the blameworthy traits of the *Nafs*, cleansing of the heart so it is pure to reach the state of *Ihsan*. A Tariqa is often named after its most prominent Shaykh or service devoted to the order, for example, the Qadiriya order is named after Shaykh Abdul Qadir Gilani ﷺ. Many orders have their own suborders, for example Naqshbandi Mujaddidi order.

Despite the existence of numerous different traditions, practice and organization, all the orders lead to the same path which is following the Shariáh and Sunnah to achieve the love of Allah ﷻ. It is also common to characterize each way as a "chain" (*silsila*), with masters and disciples constituting the links. Nearly all of these chains reach the Beloved Prophet Muhammad ﷺ through his son-in-law and cousin Ali ﷺ. A notable exception is the Naqshbandi order, which reaches the Beloved Prophet ﷺ through Abu Bakr ﷺ.

Chishtiya Order

The Chishtiya Order is known for its emphasis on love, tolerance, humility and dedication. According to the Chishtiya elders, *Nafs* is the biggest idol and its annihilation is the first stage for the wayfarer. The way of the order is to subdue *Nafs* through rigor and purification of the heart is achieved through *Dhikr*. The order took its name from the town of Chist near Herat in Afghanistan, where Abu Ishaq Shamiﷺ taught his disciples.

The order initiates from Allah's Messengerﷺ, followed by Ali ibn Abi Talibﷺ who was a cousin, son-in-law and Companion of the Beloved Prophetﷺ. He was raised under the care of the Beloved Prophetﷺ and was the first amongst young to accept Islam. He was the fourth rightly guided Caliph and known for his knowledge and wisdom, Allah's Prophetﷺ said, "I am the house of wisdom, and Aliﷺ is its door." [Tirmidhi]

Aliﷺ was followed by Al-Hasan al-Basriﷺ who was a Tabayée scholar of Hadith born in Madinah. Hasanﷺ is known as one of the most knowledgeable and pious amongst the Tabayeé. He was followed by 'Abdul Waḥid bin Zaid Abul Faḍlﷺ who was also a renowned Hadith scholar.

Masud Bin Bishr al-Tamimiﷺ also known as al-Fudaylﷺ was next in the chain. The life of al-Fudaylﷺ is inspiring as he was a bandit, before he repented. Allahﷻ enlightened his heart and he became one of the most figurative sufi Shaykh. Ibraheem bin Adhamﷺ, was the next in chain, he was a king who left his throne to lead a life of asceticism and reached a status which surpassed many other sufis of his time.

The order spread in South Asia by the efforts of Shaykh Moin ad-Din Chisthtiﷺ who was born in the province of Sijistan in eastern Persia and studied under Shaykh Uthman Hirvaniﷺ. He was a learned scholar of Qurán, Hadith and

Fiqh and travelled across to Balkh and Samarkand to be in the company of the most learned scholars of his time.

Later in his life, Moin ad-Din ﷺ moved to Lahore and then settled in Ajmer. His well-known disciples were Qutb-ad-Din Bakhtyar Kaki ﷺ and Farid ad-Din Masud known as 'Baba Farid' ﷺ. After Baba Farid ﷺ, the Chishti Order of South Asia split into two branches, named after the two successors of Baba Farid ﷺ; Nizamuddin Awliya ﷺ –the Chishti-Nizami branch and Alauddin Sabir Kaliyari ﷺ – the Chishti-Sabiri branch.

Spiritual Hierarchy of the Chistiya Order

The Last Prophet Muhammad ﷺ
Ali ibn Abi Talib ﷺ
Al-Hasan al-Basri ﷺ
'Abdul Wahid Bin Zaid Abul Fadl ﷺ
Fudayl ibn 'Iyad ﷺ
Ibrahim bin Adham ﷺ
Khwaja Sadid ad-Din Huzaifa al-Marashi ﷺ
Abu Hubayra al-Basri ﷺ
Khwaja Mumshad Uluw Al Dinawari ﷺ
Abu Ishaq Shami ﷺ
Abu Ahmad Abdal ﷺ
Abu Muhammad ﷺ
Abu Yusuf Nasar-ud-Din ﷺ
Qutb-ad-Din Maudood ﷺ
Haji Sharif Zindani ﷺ
Usman Hirvani ﷺ
Moinuddin Chishti ﷺ
Qutb-ad-Din Bakhtyar Kaki ﷺ
Farid ad-Din Masud (Baba Farid) ﷺ

Qadiriya Order

The Qadiriya order is named after Abd al-Qadir Gilaniﷺ (1077–1166), who was a scholar from Gilan, Iran. He studied Fiqh and Hadith in Baghdad. His reputation as a great scholar attracted disciples from all around and he enlightened the hearts of thousands. Hundreds of Jews and Christians also accepted Islam through his teachings. He revived the true *Tasawwuf* by denying the fake mysticism introduced by the pretend Sufis. The order strongly emphasises adherence to the fundamentals of Shariáh and Sunnah. The Qadiriya way is of rigor, self-denial and abstinence to curb the *Nafs*. The order is widespread in Turkey, Indonesia, Afghanistan, India, Bangladesh, Pakistan, the Balkans and Africa. The spiritual hierarchy of the order is as follows, although, according to historians, there are few other variations.

Spiritual Hierarchy of the Qadiriya Order

Allah's Last Prophet Muhammad ﷺ
Ali ibn Abi Talib ؓ
Husayn ibn Ali ؓ
Zayn al-Abidin ؓ
Muhammad al-Baqir ؓ
Ja'far al-Sadiq ؓ
Musa al-Kazim ؓ
Ali ar-Rida ؓ
Maruf Karkhi ؓ
Sirri Saqti ؓ
Junayd al-Baghdadi ؓ
Abu Bakr Shibli ؓ
Abu Al Fazal Abdul Wahid Yemeni Tamimi ؓ
Mohammad Yousaf Abu al-Farah Tartusi ؓ
Abu al-Hasan Hankari ؓ
Abu Sa'id al-Mubarak Makhzoomi ؓ
Abd al-Qadir Gilani ؓ

Shadhili Order

The Shadhili order takes its name from Shaykh Abu'l-Hassan ash-Shadhili (1196/1197 – 1258 CE) who was born in Ghumara, near Cueta in northern Morocco. He studied the principles of Islamic Law at the Qarawiyyin University in Fez. His Shaykh, Abu as-Salam Ibn Mashish؅, the great Moroccan spiritual master initiated him on the path. Shaykh ash-Shadhili؅ had hundreds of close followers in Alexandria and Cairo from every walk of life. The Shadhili way is of contemplation and remembrance of Allah؅ while performing the normal everyday activities of the world. The order initiates from Allah's Messenger؅ followed by Ali bin Abi Talib؅.

Spiritual Hierarchy of the Shadhili Order

The Last Prophet Muhammad ؅
Ali ibn Abi Talib ؅
Imam Hasan ؅
Abu Muhammad Jabir ibn 'Abdullah ؅
Sa'id al-Ghazawani ؅
Abu Muhammad Fath al-Su'ood ؅
Abu Muhammad Sa'eed ؅
Abul Qasim Ahmad ibn Marwani ؅
Sayyid Ishaq Ibrahim al-Basri ؅
Zayn ad-Din al-Qazwin ؅
Shams ad-Din ؅
Muhammad Taj ad-Din ؅
Nur al-Din Abul Hasan 'Ali ؅
Fakhr ad-Din ؅
Tuqayy al-Din al-Fuqayr ؅
Abd al-Rahman al-Madani al-'Attar Az Zayyat ؅
Abd as-Salam ibn Mashish ؅
Abul Hasan al-Shadhili ؅

Sohrevardi Order

The order was founded by Diya ad-Din Abu Najib al-Sohrevardi (1097–1168 CE). The order originated in Sohrevard in Zanjan province, Iran. The order spread through the Islamic world by the teachings of Shihab ad-Din Abu Hafs Umar al-Sohrevardiﷺ who was Diya ad-Din al-Sohrevard'sﷺ nephew. Shihab ad-Dinﷺ was the author of the famous book *'Awarif ul-Maarif'*, ("The Knowledge of the Spiritually Learned"). The order takes its spiritual lineage from Ali ibn Abi Talib؈. In South Asia, the order was established by the efforts of Baha-ad-Din Zakariyaﷺ (1170–1262) who chose Multan, a city in present day Pakistan as his centre of activities.

◆

Chapter Thirteen

NAQSHBANDI ORDER

Naqshbandi order takes pride in the fact that first link after the Beloved Prophetﷺ in the order is Sayeddina Abu Bakrؓ followed by Salman Farsiؓ, a feature that distinguishes this order from other orders. The order is often referred as the Golden Chain (*Silsilat adh-dhahab*) for its physical and spiritual descent from the Beloved Prophetﷺ.¹

The Naqshbandi way has a great focus on connection '*Talluq*' as Mujaddid Alf Thaniؓ wrote, "In Naqshbandi way, the benefit, *Fayd* depends on the company with the Shaykh. Articulation and writing are not enough, Khawaja Naqshbandؓ said that the Naqshbandi way is through keeping company. Due to the company with the best of the persons, *Khayr-ul-Bashr*ﷺ, the blessed Companions are superior than the friends of Allah of the nation. None of the friends of Allah (*Awliya*) can reach the rank of any Companion of Allah's Messengerﷺ, not even if he was Owais al-Qarniؓ."²

Most spiritual paths require that their adherents first purify their *Nafs* before enlightenment of the spiritual faculties and the heart. However, in Naqshbandi *Tariqa*, the seeker starts with a focus on the subtleties which enlightens and transforms the heart. This approach, known as *"Indiraj al-nihayat fi al-bidayat,"* or "in their end is our beginning", was first taught by

Khwaja Baha'uddin Naqshband ﷺ. Naqshbandi way requires less rigor and the journey is covered at a faster pace as the purification of the heart is followed by cleansing of the Nafs. The Naqshbandi Order initiates from Allah's Last Messenger, the Seal of the Prophets, Muhammad ﷺ, the Chief of both Worlds.

Allah's Last Messenger: Prophet Muhammad ﷺ

Allah and His angels bless the Prophet. Believers, invoke blessings and peace on him"

[Quran, al Ahzaab 33:56]

اَللّٰهُمَّ صَلِّ عَلٰى مُحَمَّدٍ وَعَلٰى اٰلِ مُحَمَّدٍ كَمَا صَلَّيْتَ عَلٰى اِبْرَاهِيْمَ وَعَلٰى اٰلِ اِبْرَاهِيْمَ اِنَّكَ حَمِيْدٌ مَجِيْدٌ

اَللّٰهُمَّ بَارِكْ عَلٰى مُحَمَّدٍ وَعَلٰى اٰلِ مُحَمَّدٍ كَمَا بَارَكْتَ عَلٰى اِبْرَاهِيْمَ وَعَلٰى اٰلِ اِبْرَاهِيْمَ اِنَّكَ حَمِيْدٌ مَجِيْدٌ

Allah's Last Messenger ﷺ was born in Makkah in the tribe of Quraysh, the clan of Banu Hashim to Abdullah the son of Abdul Muttalib. His respected mother was Aminah the daughter of Wahb. His blessed birth occurred in the month of Rabi al Awwal, corresponding to the year 570. This date is the most light filled and blessed date in the history of humanity. Authentic Hadith mentions that at the time of his birth, a light shone from the belly of his mother which illuminated the East and West. His father passed away when he was in his mother's womb, thus he was born an orphan. After his birth, his grandfather, Abdul Muttalib took him to Kába and named him Muhammad ﷺ.

According to Arab culture, the Last Prophet ﷺ was given to a wet nurse named Halima ﷺ from Banu Saád tribe, to be raised in the clean environment of the desert. During his stay at Halima Sa'dia ﷺ, he learnt the pure Arabic. While the Beloved Prophet ﷺ was still young, two angels appeared, opened his blessed chest and thoroughly cleansed his heart. Then, they placed the heart back and closed the chest. The marks of the sutures remained on the blessed chest. Halima☪ was scared and brought him back to his mother. His mother took him to see the maternal family in Madinah and on the return journey to Makkah, she passed away at the place called 'Abwa'. The Beloved Prophet☪ was taken in the care of his grandfather, but two years later, Abdul Muttalib also passed away. Before his demise, the grandfather gave him in the care of his son Abu Talib.

The Beloved Prophet☪ was known as the 'Honest' and 'Trustworthy' by the people of Makkah, even in his early years. Truthfulness and honesty were such an intrinsic part of his disposition, that he became known as Al-Amin (the honest). Even the non-Muslims would entrust him with their valuable possessions and would go to him as an impartial judge in their disputes.

Khadija☪, a wealthy lady known for her piety, upon hearing the account of his honesty and character, proposed to him. The Beloved Prophet☪ was twenty-five years old when he married Khadija☪. From Khadija, Allah gave the Beloved Prophet☪ four daughters and two sons. The two sons Qasim☪ and Tahir☪ passed away in childhood. The four blessed daughters were Sayedda Ruqayyah☪, Sayedda Zaynab☪, Sayedda Umme Kulthum☪ and Sayedda Fatima☪. Later, the Beloved Prophet☪ had another son named Ibraheem☪ from Mariya Qibtiyah☪ but he also passed away in his childhood.

When the Beloved Prophet☪ turned forty, Allah's Angel Gibrael☪ brought Allah's message to him. It was in the Cave of Hira where he was engaged in Allah's☪ praise and glorification that the first verses of Qurán were revealed to him. The experience was overwhelming, the Beloved Prophet ﷺ came to Khadija ؓ and asked her to cover him in blankets. The mother of the believers, Khadija ؓ consoled him in these words, "By Allah! Allah ﷻ will never humiliate you. You maintain family ties and show consideration to relatives. You lighten the burden of others and help those in need. You display hospitality to the guests and support the innocent who have been afflicted."

Later, the mother of the believers, Khadija ؓ took the Beloved Prophet ﷺ to her cousin, Waraqah bin Nofal. Waraqah was a learned scholar, well-versed with the Abrahamic religion. After listening to the Beloved Prophet ﷺ, Waraqah exclaimed, "This is the same archangel who came to Musa. If only I were young and could live until that time when your people will evict you." The Beloved Prophet ﷺ was surprised and asked him as to why would people evict him. Waraqah replied, "Whenever a prophet was appointed and he preached the Oneness of Allah ﷻ, the people reacted with hatred."

After some time, the second revelation descended and the Beloved Prophet ﷺ was commanded to convey the message of Allah's ﷻ Oneness. The first one to believe in the message of Allah ﷻ was Ummul Momineen Khadija ؓ. Then, the Beloved Prophet's cousin and Abu Talib's son Ali ؓ embraced Islam. Zayd bin Harith ؓ also believed in him from the very beginning. Another early believer was his close friend, Sayeddina Abu Bakr Siddique ؓ.

For next three years, Islam was propagated quietly until Allah ﷻ commanded to invite the people openly. In compliance to the command, Allah's Beloved Prophet ﷺ climbed Mount Sáfa and called out to each clan by name.

Once, they gathered, the Beloved Prophet ﷺ invited them to Islam. The Quraysh laughed at those words and dispersed. Later, the Beloved Prophet ﷺ organised a meeting with his close relatives and invited them to believe in the Oneness of Allah ﷻ. Only Ali ؓ supported the Beloved Prophet ﷺ while the other relatives left.

Once, the Beloved Prophet ﷺ invited the disbelievers towards oneness of Allah ﷻ, the idol worshippers saw this as a loss of honour and glory and severely persecuted him. The great chiefs and nobility would not acknowledge him as a Messenger and Prophet as they did not want to lose their position and obey him. During those days, the early Muslims used Arqam's ؓ house as a place to gather and learn from the Beloved Prophet ﷺ.

The ones who accepted Islam during those few years are known as the early believers and their status is unsurpassed by others. The Quraysh resolved upon the extermination of the Beloved Prophet ﷺ and chose every possible way to persecute the early believers. At all times, he was concerned about the welfare of his people. He never took revenge for personal matters. Allah's Prophet ﷺ said, *"Allah ﷻ will not be merciful to those who are not merciful to the people."* [Bukhari]

A delegation was appointed to approach Abu Talib and convince him to cease his support for the Beloved Prophet ﷺ. Abu Talib discussed the matter with the Beloved Prophet. The Beloved Prophet ﷺ was determined to carry on the mission till Allah's message was delivered declared to continue his efforts till his death. Abu Talib acknowledged his commitment and pledged his unconditional support for the Beloved Prophet ﷺ. The atrocities of the disbelievers increased towards the Muslims.

In the fifth year after revelation, the Beloved Prophetﷺ allowed the Muslims to migrate towards Ethiopia, which was ruled by a kind Christian king, called by the title, Negus. The disbelievers followed the Muslims to Ethiopia and attempted to turn the king against the Muslims. Negus, however, summoned the Muslims to his court, where Ja'farؓ successfully defended the Muslims and the king declared his support for them.

When the Beloved Prophetﷺ turned forty, Allah's Angel Gibrael brought Allah's message to him. It was in the Cave of Hira where he was engaged in Allah'sﷻ praise and glorification that the first verses of Qurán were revealed to him. The experience was overwhelming, the Beloved Prophetﷺ came to Khadija and asked her to cover him in blankets. The mother of the believers, Khadija consoled him in these words, "By Allah! Allahﷻ will never humiliate you. You maintain family ties and show consideration to relatives. You lighten the burden of others and help those in need. You display hospitality to the guests and support the innocent who have been afflicted."

The Beloved Prophetﷺ decided to visit another town called Taif where he invited the people to the message of Allahﷻ. The people of Taif were insolent and threw stones at the Beloved Prophetﷺ. The Beloved Prophetﷺ was heavily injured and even though the angels sought permission from him to crush the people of Taif between the mountains, the Beloved Prophetﷺ prayed and sought Allah'sﷻ mercy for them.

It was during the fourth year of revelation that Allahﷻ took the Beloved Prophetﷺ on the night journey and Ascension. An animal resembling a white horse, known as *Buraq* was brought and Gibrael ؑ took the Beloved Prophet ﷺ from Masjid al-Haram to Bait al-Muqaddas. The Beloved

Prophet ﷺ led all the Prophets in Salah and then the Ascension journey (*Mai'raj*) was undertaken. The Beloved Prophet ﷺ travelled through the Heavens, meeting the Prophets until he reached the Lote Tree known as Sidrat al-Muntaha. The Beloved Prophet ﷺ attained the exclusive Divine Proximity and was awarded the gift of the five prayers (*Salah*).

By this time, the message of Allah ﷻ reached out of Makkah and the number of people entering the folds of Islam increased. This included the tribes of Aws and Khazraj who lived in Yathrib. Meanwhile, the Quraysh organised a group of young men, appointed from each tribe to assassinate the Beloved Prophet ﷺ. Allah ﷻ informed the Beloved Prophet ﷺ about the conspiracy and permitted him to leave Makkah. The Beloved Prophet ﷺ told Abu Bakr ؓ about the plan and chose him as his companion for the migration journey, upon which Abu Bakr ؓ wept with joy.

Ali ؓ was chosen to sleep in the Beloved Prophet's ﷺ blanket, while the Beloved Prophet ﷺ left Makkah with Abu Bakr ؓ. They went to the Cave of Thawr and waited until the search parties failed in their pursuit. After a long tiring journey, they reached Quba. The people of Yathrib had heard the news that the Beloved Prophet ﷺ had left Makkah. They would come out of the city every morning to receive the Beloved Prophet ﷺ and after a long wait, they would disperse in the afternoon. On that day, they were returning, when someone called out that the Beloved Prophet ﷺ had arrived.

The people of Yathrib rushed to greet him and gathered like rays around the sun. The Beloved Prophet ﷺ spent three days at Quba where he built a masjid, which is the first Masjid in the history of Islam. On Friday, the Beloved Prophet ﷺ left Quba and performed the first Jumá prayers as congregation on the way to Yathrib. He then entered the city which was the most magnificent event in history and the city of Yathrib became *Madinatul Nabi* (The City of the Prophetﷺ).

The streets echoed with the praise to Allah; men, women and children emerged to witness the manifestation of Allah'sﷻ favour. The Beloved Prophetﷺ stayed at Abu Ayub Ansari'sؓ house. The first task was to build a Masjid; therefore, the land was bought and the construction started. The Beloved Prophetﷺ joined the Companions in the construction and a simple Masjid was built. Rooms were also constructed for the family of the Beloved Prophetﷺ so, they migrated from Makkah and joined the Beloved Prophetﷺ.

Allahﷻ had appointed Bait al-Muqaddas as the Qiblah, but sixteen months after the Migration to Madinah, Allahﷻ changed the Qiblah to Kába. The migrants from Makkah had left everything behind, their houses, belongings and all other possessions. They had no place to call home anymore. Allah's Beloved Prophetﷺ appointed each local Muslim from Madinah as a brother to a migrant Muslim. The Muslims who migrated from Makkah were called *'Muhajireen'* or the migrants. The local residents of Madinah were called the *'Ansaar'* or the helpers.

The Ansaar or the local Muslims took their brothers in with open arms and loving hearts. It was not a relationship built on words. Allah's Beloved Prophetﷺ actually implemented it. The Muslims from different caste, creed or tribes ignored all differences and became brothers in faith. It was a relationship built on love for Allah and His Last Prophetﷺ.

The migrants were in need but they did not want to be a burden on their brothers. They started working and soon established themselves. Such brotherhood had never been witnessed in history before. He emphasized that all members of society were equal and justice was of paramount importance to him. He was meticulous and resolute in administering this. The Beloved Prophetﷺ said, "Help your brother whether he is the oppressor or the oppressed one." When his companions asked him how they should help an oppressor, he replied, "By preventing him from oppressing others." [Bukhari]

There were three major tribes of Jews; Banu Qaynqa, Banu Nuzair and Banu Quraiza who had established their own strongholds in Madinah. In the very first year of migration, Allah's Beloved Prophetﷺ signed a treaty with the Jews for a peaceful co-existence. Initially, the Jews agreed to the charter but did not adhere to the conditions of the treaty. Torah and Bible had detailed descriptions of Allah's Beloved Prophetﷺ.

Over centuries, the Jewish priests had modified the contents of Torah and Bible to suit their own interests. Still, the Jews recognised the Last Prophetﷺ, just as they recognised their sons. Yet, due to their prejudice they were not ready to accept the truth. They believed that the Last Prophetﷺ was to be born from Jews.

The disbelievers of Makkah continued with their threats and found an ally in the form of Jews. The disbelievers gathered their warriors and attacked Madinah in the second year after migration. The first battle of Islam known as the Battle of Badr was fought, where three hundred and thirteen Muslims defeated a well-equipped army of a thousand warriors. Though, the disbelievers did not mourn the death of their relatives in Badr but their hearts were filled with the desire of revenge. They gathered their forces and enlisted the neighbouring tribes to assist them. In the third year after migration, the disbelievers attacked Madinah with an army of three thousand men, this battle is known as the Battle of Uhud.

Meanwhile, the Jewish tribe of Qaynqa breached the terms of treaty and created a perilous situation. They were arrogant and proud of being the greatest warriors, however, when Muslims went to fight them and laid a siege, they left their citadel without any fight. Later, Banu Nuzair Jews were also expelled with all their wealth and belongings from Madinah for their acts of treachery. Their leaders travelled far and wide and gained support from other allied tribes to muster an army with the disbelievers of Makkah. They were able to gather ten thousand men to attack Madinah.

Allah's Beloved Prophetﷺ received the news of their alliance and called a counsel where Salman Farsi؆ suggested digging a trench around the city. Due to the alliance of the disbelievers, the battle is known as the 'Battle of Ahzaab' meaning alliance and also known as the Battle of Trench. The disbelievers concluded that they would not be able to cross the trench; therefore, they decided to lay a siege. They asked the Jewish tribe Banu Quraiza to let the army in, through their stronghold.

Allah؅ sent strong winds which made the enemy retreat. After the allied army retreated, Banu Quraizah tribe was left to face the consequences of their treason and betrayal. Banu Quraiza requested Sa'ad bin Ma'az؆ to be the mediator. According to 'Torah' the punishment for treason is death; therefore, he awarded death penalty to every able man of Banu Quraiza. Banu Quraiza had no choice as they knew the rulings of Torah.

In the sixth year after migration, Allah's Beloved Prophet ﷺ decided to perform Umrah along with fourteen hundred Companions. To show the disbelievers that there was no intention of fighting, the swords were sheathed. Allah's

Beloved Prophet ﷺ conveyed the message to the disbelievers that the purpose of their visit was to perform Umrah and there was no intention to fight. The disbeleivers imprisoned Uthman bin Affan ؓ, who went as an envoy and the rumour spread that he was killed.

Once, the news reached the Beloved Prophet ﷺ, he sat under an acacia tree and called upon the Muslims to make a pledge. This is called Bait e Rizwan, Allah ﷻ mentioned this in Qur'an as a victory. The disbeleivers were scared when they received the news of the pledge. They sent one of their spokespersons as an ambassador to negotiate on their behalf.

The disbeleivers offered that the Muslims should return to Madinah, only to be allowed next year. They were not to bring any weapons except for a sheathed sword and they would be allowed to stay in Makkah for only three days. Anyone who wished to stay in Makkah would not be taken to Madinah. The Muslims already residing in Makkah would not be permitted to leave. Anyone who would go to Madinah had to be returned to Makkah and anyone from Makkah would not be permitted to go back to Madinah. The other Arab tribes were free to choose their allegiance.

From this time onwards, the disbelievers visited the city of Madinah. Most of them were so impressed by the conduct of the Muslims, that they accepted Islam. Allah's Beloved Prophet ﷺ wrote letters to the neighbouring Empires of Persia, Rome, Abyssinia and Egypt. The Persian and the Roman kings had appointed governors in the territories who would subserve the empire, letters were also sent to them, calling them to the message of Allah ﷻ.

The open threat of an attack from the disbelievers of Makkah was averted. However, there were two other groups in the region; the Bedouins and the Jews. The strength of the Jews in Madinah was diminished; however, their leaders had moved to Khyber which was a Jewish stronghold. The city of Khyber located at two hundred kilometres from Madinah served as a capital for the Jewish community. It had eight major forts, five grouped in one area and three in the other, with twenty thousand soldiers to defend their territory.

This was the early seventh year of Migration to Madinah, the year 629, the Beloved Prophet ﷺ left for Khyber with sixteen hundred men. The battle is known as the Battle of Khyber in which the Jews were defeated. A treaty was signed and the Jews were allowed to live in their homes and cultivate the lands for a share in the harvest for the Muslims. Besides the disbelievers and the Jews, there were Bedouins, who roamed the desert. They were opportunists who plundered and killed but it was hard to control them as they were nomads. News of their attack on Madinah was received, hence, the Beloved Prophet ﷺ left Madinah with five to seven hundred Companions to encounter them.

Some of the tribes embraced Islam and others were subdued. Few other skirmishes took place where Allah's beloved Prophet ﷺ sent small envoys to control the situation. As one year had passed since the Treaty of Hudaibiya, the Beloved Prophet ﷺ decided to visit Makkah with an intention to perform Umrah. The Beloved Prophet ﷺ performed Umrah with two thousand Companions and returned to Madinah.

There was a fight between the allied tribe of the Muslims and the disbelievers and in the spur of the moment the disbelievers decided to abolish the treaty. Soon, they realised their mistake and sent Abu Sufyan to discuss the matter and keep the terms of the treaty. Allah's Beloved Prophetﷺ did not give any reply to Abu Sufyan and ordered the Muslims to prepare for the journey to Makkah. This was the eighth year after migration, the Muslim convoy consisting of around ten thousand men moved towards Makkah while other tribes joined on the way.

The army camped in a valley just outside Makkah where each tribe was ordered to light their own fire at night. The whole valley lit up and looked like a constellation in the dark night.The Beloved Prophetﷺ being the most kind amongst humans granted safety to all the people of Makkah including those who conspired to kill him or ill-treated him. He granted safety to anyone who would close the doors of his house, or seek refuge in Ka'ba.

The Beloved Prophetﷺ also granted safety to those who took refuge at Abu Sufyan's house and no one was to be persecuted. After the conquest of Makkah, the Beloved Prophetﷺ organised an army against the Bani Hawazan and Bani Thaqeef tribes. During the ninth year of migration, hundreds of delegations came and embraced Islam.

It was the tenth year of Migration that the Beloved Prophetﷺ announced his intention to perform Hajj. This was the Beloved Prophet's first and the last Hajj. The Beloved Prophetﷺ delivered his sermon which is the charter for the Muslim Ummah-a proclamation of the basic principles of Islam; (Musnad :19774, Sahih al-Bukhari 1623, 1626, 6361 and Tirmidhi 1628, 2046, 2085)

The Beloved Prophetﷺ asked, "What month is this month?"

The Companions out of respect replied, "Allahﷻ and His Messengerﷺ know better."

He then asked, "What is this city called?"

The Companions again replied, "Allah ﷻ and His Messenger ﷺ know better."

The Beloved Prophet ﷺ asked, "Which month is it?"

The Companions replied, "Allah ﷻ and His Messenger ﷺ know better."

The Beloved Prophet ﷺ said, "O people! Listen to what I say. I do not know whether I will ever meet you at this place once again after this year. It is unlawful for you to shed the blood of one another or take (unlawfully) the fortunes of one another. They are as unlawful, (*haram*) as shedding blood on such a day as today and in such a month as this Haram month and in such a sanctified city as this sacred city (Makkah and the surrounding areas). Neither an Arab has any preference over non-Arab, nor white over black"

"Behold! all practices of paganism and ignorance are now under my feet. The blood-revenge of the Days of Ignorance (pre-Islamic time) are remitted. The first claim on blood I abolish is that of Ibn Rabi'a bin Harith who was fostered in the tribe of Sa'd and killed by Hudhayl. Usury is forbidden, and I make a beginning by remitting the amount of interest which 'Abbas ؓ bin 'Abdul Muttalib has to receive. Verily, it is remitted entirely."

"O people! Fear Allah ﷻ concerning women. Verily you have taken them on the security of Allah ﷻ and have made their persons lawful unto you by Words of Allah ﷻ! It is incumbent upon them to honour their conjugal rights and, not to commit acts of impropriety which, if they do, you have authority to chastise them, yet not severely. If your wives refrain from impropriety and are faithful to you, clothe and feed them suitably."

"Verily, I have left amongst you the Book of Allahﷻ and the Sunnah (Traditions) of His Messengerﷺ which if you hold fast, you shall never go astray. O' people! Know that every Muslim is another Muslim's brother, and all Muslims are brethren. It is not lawful for any man to take from his brother anything except for which he gives willingly, so do not wrong yourself."

"O people, I am not succeeded by a Prophet, and you are not succeeded by any nation. I recommend you to worship your Lord, to pray the five prayers, to fast Ramadan and to offer the Zakat (alms) of your provision willingly. I recommend you to do the pilgrimage to the Sacred House of your Lord and to obey those who are in charge of you then, you will be awarded to enter the Paradise of your Lord. And if you were asked about me, what would you say?"

The Companions replied, "We bear witness that you have conveyed the message and discharged your ministry."

The Beloved Prophetﷺ then said three times, "O Allahﷻ, Bear witness."

The same day the following verses of Qurán were revealed:

"This day I have perfected your religion for you, completed my favour to you and have chosen Islam as your religion."

[Qurán, al Ma'idah 5:3]

In the eleventh year after migration, the Beloved Prophet ﷺ came home, and suffered from headache and fever. The Beloved Prophetﷺ said, "Indeed a slave is given the choice by Allahﷻ between having anything that he desired from the worldly attractions and what was with Allahﷻ and he chose that which was with Allahﷻ." Ummul Momineen Ayesha﷜ upon hearing these words understood that the slave was no

Naqshbandi Order

other than himself and the Beloved Prophet ﷺ was about to leave them. Throughout his life, the Beloved Prophet's character imbued virtue and righteousness. Allah ﷻ approved of his character as:

"Verily, you have in the Messenger of Allah an excellent example, for him who fears Allah and the Last Day, and who remembers Allah much."

[Qura'n, al Ahzaab 33:21]

When Ayesha ؓ, the Mother of the believers, the wife of the Prophet ﷺ, was asked regarding his character, she answered, "His character was the Qurán." [Muslim]

Few days later, when it was time for Salah, the Beloved Prophet ﷺ felt better and asked Ali ؓ and Fadal bin Abbas ؓ to take him to Masjid. Ali ؓ and Fadal bin Abbas ؓ held him from the sides and carried him. Ayesha ؓ narrated that the Beloved Prophet ﷺ had no strength and his legs dragged. When the Beloved Prophet ﷺ entered Masjid e Nabwi, the Companions were rejoiced to see him. Abu Bakr ؓ moved from the *Musalla* for the Beloved Prophet ﷺ to lead the prayers. The Beloved Prophet ﷺ told him to continue and sat in front of him. Abu Bakr ؓ led the Ummah and the Beloved Prophet ﷺ led him in the prayers. When the prayers finished, the Beloved Prophet ﷺ asked him as to why he did not follow the orders. Abu Bakr ؓ replied, "Son of Abu Qahafa ؓ does not have the courage in him to stand on *Musallah* in front of Allah's Messenger ﷺ."

The Beloved Prophet ﷺ motioned to be seated on the pulpit and delivered a short sermon. After that the Beloved Prophet ﷺ returned home, he felt frail so Ummul Momineen Ayesha ؓ rested his head against herself. That's when, Izrael ؈ came with Gibrael ؈ and sought permission. Ummul

Momineen Ayesha's home is where the Beloved Prophet's grave was made and till eternity Allah, His angels and the Muslims would keep sending their blessings upon the Beloved Prophet.

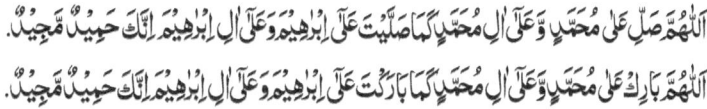

The First Caliph- Abu Bakr Siddique

The next in the chain is Sayeddina Abu Bakr who was chosen to be the companion of the Beloved Prophet before his birth. He was the first man to accept Islam and given the title of 'Siddique', 'the truthful' for his acceptance of truth without a question. After the prophets, Sayeddina Abu Bakr has the greatest status amongst all believers. The Beloved Prophet said, "No wealth ever benefited me as did the wealth of Abu Bakr." Sayyedina Abu Bakr wept and said, "Allah's Messenger! My wealth and I are for you." [Tirmidhi] Hafiz ibn Kathir states that Abu Bakr was the most knowledgeable of the Companions as the Beloved Prophet appointed him as the imam. It is narrated in *Siratus Siddique* that the Beloved Prophet said, "Allah has not poured anything into my heart, except that I have poured it into the heart of Abu Bakr."

Sayeddina Abu Bakr used to say, "We discovered piety in abstinence, wealth in conviction and honour in humility." He also said, "O people! Weep out of fear of Allah, if you are unable to weep, then pretend as if you are weeping."

Sayeddina Salman Farsi ؓ

The next link in the chain, Salman al-Farsi ؓ came from an affluent Persian family. He was a seeker of truth who himself narrated that he was sold as a slave by one master to another for more than ten times. [Bukhari 3946] He had the honour to be released from his master by the Beloved Prophet ﷺ and he remained amongst the Companions of the Suffa. The Beloved Prophet ﷺ said that Salman ؓ was from *Ahle Bayt* meaning family of the Prophet ﷺ. It is narrated by Ibne Jawzi ؒ in his book *'Sifatus Safwah'* that Salman ؓ said, "When Allah's slave prays unto Him when times and conditions are good, then the angels recognise his voice when he prays at the time of difficulty and intercede for him. When he does not pray unto Him when times and conditions are good, then the angels do not recognise his voice, when he prays at the time of difficulty and do not intercede for him."

Salman ؓ said to Hudhaifa ؓ, "O brother of Banu Abs, there is no limit to knowledge but age is very limited. So, strive to acquire that much knowledge required to enact your religious dealings, and leave what is besides that." Salman Farsi ؓ passed away during the caliphate of Uthman ؓ in the city of Madain in the 36th year after migration.

Imam Qasim ؒ

The next in chain is Imam Qasim ؒ who was Abu Bakr's ؓ grandson and a Tábayee, known for his piety and knowledge of Deen. His personality was very similar to Sayeddina Abu Bakr ؓ. His father Muhammad bin Abu Bakr ؓ was martyred in a battle, so Ummul Momineen Ayesha ؓ took him in his care and he was raised by her. He learnt Qurán and Hadith from many Companions of the Beloved Prophet ﷺ, therefore considered as one of the greatest scholars of Qurán and

Hadith. He also specialised in Islamic Jurisprudence and was regarded as one of the seven great Jurists of Madinah.

Imam Jáfar as-Sadiq ؓ

Imam Qasim ؓ was followed by Imam Jáfar as-Sadiq ؓ, who was a great Hadith scholar. Imam Malik ؓ and Imam Abu Hanifa ؓ had narrated Hadith from him. He was born in the 80th year after migration, in the city of Madinah and passed away in the year 148 Hijri. It was as if knowledge was the rightful inheritance of Imam Jáfar aṣ-Ṣadiq ؓ. As for his other virtues, he was the Imam of his era and one of the foremost leaders. Even amongst the noble family of the Prophet ﷺ, his knowledge was unsurpassed. Ibn Ḥibban ؓ stated that he was amongst the leaders in Fiqh and virtuous amongst the family of the Beloved Prophet ﷺ.

Imam Nawawi ؓ said that all agree upon his leadership and august personality. He said, "When Allah ﷻ grants you a bounty and you wish to retain it, then thank Allah ﷻ abundantly for it, for Allah ﷻ says in His Book, 'If you are grateful, I shall certainly increase for you.' When there is a delay in receiving sustenance, then seek forgiveness. He who remains content with the share, fate has allotted him, will remain independent. He who gazes at the wealth of others will die poor. He who is not pleased with Allah's ﷻ allocation has doubt in that decision of Allah ﷻ. If one exposes others, Allah ﷻ will expose him in the privacy of his own home. The one who digs a hole for his brother, will fall in it himself. The one who sits in the company of foolish becomes worthless and the one who sits in the company of scholars becomes honoured. He who goes to places of ill repute gains ill repute."

Bayazid Bustami ؓ

Sultan al-Arifeen, Bayazid al-Bastami ؓ, born in 136 Hijri and lived to the age of 73. He was completely annihilated in the Divine Love. His esteemed mother narrated that when she was pregnant with him, whenever she ate a doubtful morsel, she felt so ill that she would feel no peace until she vomited. He used to say that the company of the pious is better than pious deeds and the company of the evil is worse than the evil deeds. Somebody told him about a saint residing in a certain place. When he arrived there, the saint spat in the direction of the Qiblah, Bayazid ؓ remarked, "If that man had the slightest inkling of *Tariqa*, he would not have perpetrated such a disrespectful act." He was asked as to when one reaches the border of being a true man. He replied, "When one recognises the defects of his ego, he reaches the border of true men."

Shaykh Abu al-Hassan al-Kharqani ؓ

Shaykh Abu al-Hassan al-Kharqani ؓ was known for his love of Sunnah of the Beloved Prophet ﷺ. One day he asked his followers, "What is the most excellent thing?" "O Shaykh," they replied, "You tell us." He said, "That heart in which there is only His remembrance." Some people asked him, "Who is a Sufi?" He replied, "A robe, turban or prayer-mat does not make one a Sufi, nor do rituals and tradition make a Sufi. Sufi is the one who considers himself as nothing."

Shaykh Abi Al Qasim Gurgani ؓ

Shaykh Abi Al Qasim Gurgani ؓ was born in Gurgan, Iran. He studied the religious sciences at an early age. He lived in Baghdad and Makkah and finally settled in Nishapur in the

North east of Iran. Shaykh Gurgani﷫ authored a book named 'Fusul al-Tariqah wa Fusul al-Haqiqah'. Ali Hujwiri﷫ also benefitted from him and mentioned him in his book, *Kashful Mahjub*. One of his famous quotes is mentioned in the book is, "Whenever anyone prefers company of rich rather than poor, Allahﷻ afflicts him with spiritual death."

Shaykh Abu al-Farmadi ﷫

The next in the chain is Shaykh Abu al-Farmadi﷫ who was also the Shaykh of Imam Ghazali﷫. He was a well-known scholar in Khorasan, an outstanding personality of his era who held a special position of mastery within his school of thought. He was the student of Abul Qasim al-Qushayri﷫.

Abi Yusuf Hamadani ﷫

The first of the Khwajagan, Abi Yusuf Hamadani﷫ was a well-respected scholar of Hadith and Fiqh in Baghdad. Shaykh Abd al-Qadir Gilani﷫ used to visit him frequently, Khawaja Moen ad din Chishti﷫ also spent some time with him and benefitted from him. Later in his life, Khawaja Yusuf al-Hamdani﷫ left Baghdad and moved to Merv, where he spent the rest of his days.

Khawaja 'Abd al-Khaliq Ghajdawani ﷫

Khawaja 'Abd al-Khaliq Ghajdawani﷫, the next link in the Naqshbandi order was born in a small town known as Ghajdawan, near Bukhara. He studied Islamic Shariáh law and Jurisprudence and during one of those sessions asked his teacher about the significance of vocal and the silent *Dhikr*, which the teacher was unable to explain. It is narrated that Allahﷻ sent Khidrﷷ who instructed Abd al-Khaliq Ghajdawani﷫ to submerge himself in water to avoid movement of the lips and recite the *Dhikr* silently in his heart. Abd al-Khaliq's ﷺ was further trained by Yousuf al-Hamdani ﷺ who practised both silent and vocal *Dhikr*. In addition to the normative practice of silent *Dhikr*, Abd al-Khaliq ﷺ also bequeathed the principles of Naqshbandi Order. He said, "One traversing the spiritual path should take care of every breath, inhaled and exhaled. So, that not a single breath is exhaled in negligence of Allah ﷻ nor should one inhale in forgetfulness."

Khawaja Muhammad Arif al-Riyogari ﷺ

Khawaja Muhammad Arif al-Riyogari's ﷺ, heart was submerged in the Divine Reality. Perfection of his character made him one of the greatest *Awliya* of all times. He remained in the company of his Shaykh throughout his entire life. He held a high status in qualities as forbearance, abstention and following the Sunnah. He passed away in 616 Hijri and is buried in the city of Bukhara.

Khawaja Mahmood al-Faghnawi ﷺ

Khawaja Mahmood al-Faghnawi, the next in the chain was born in a town close to Bukhara. He was amongst the best and most accomplished disciple of Khawaja Arif Riyogari ﷺ. He took up residence at Rahkand where he practiced the spiritual upbringing of many followers.

Khawaja Ali al-Ramitini ﷺ

The next in the golden chain is Khawaja Ali al-Ramitini ﷺ who was also known as Azeezan as he used to call himself by this name. He also wrote an epistle on *Tasawwuf*, it is said that the seekers reached *Maárfa* in a day in his company. He said, "Keep Allah's ﷻ company, if that is not possible, then keep company with the one who keeps Allah's company." He was a weaver by profession and it is narrated that Rumi wrote the verse for him;

> If it were not that knowledge of the state is superior to traditional knowledge;
> How then do the great personalities of Bukhara become slaves to a weaver?

Khawaja Muhammad Samasi

The next in the golden chain is Khawaja Muhammad Samasi, it is said that Samasi, when passing by Qasr-i Hinduvan used to remark that he could smell the scent of spirituality rising from its soil; the scent became perceptibly stronger when Baha ad-Din Naqshband was born.

Syed Shams ud din Amir Kulal

Syed Shams ud din Amir Kulal was a strong wrestler and it was during one of those feats that Baba Samasi stopped and said that the man would bring great benefit to others. Amir Kulal spent thirty years in his Shaykh's company.

Baha ad-Din Naqshband

The Khawajagan become the Naqshbandi with Baha ad-Din Naqshband, born in 1318 in the village of Qasr-i Hinduvan, later renamed Qasr-i Arifan near Bukhara. Most of his life was spent in Bukhara, in keeping with the principle of "journeying within the homeland," with the exception of two long journeys for the performance of the Hajj. He came into early contact with the Khawajagan through Baba Muhammad Samasi, while still an infant. It was from Amir Kulal who was Baba Samasi's spiritual descendant that Baha ad-Din received his training on the path.

The eight principles were further elaborated by Baha ad-Din Naqshband ﷺ, and taken together summarize the essential spirit of the Naqshbandi order. Baha ad-Din ﷺ entered the highest ranks of *Awliya*, and known as Shah-i Naqshband over a vast area extending from the Balkans to China.

There are few narratives regarding the word 'Naqshband' meaning engrave; at times the reference is made to various trades followed by Baha ad-Din ﷺ in his early years as a weaver or as an engraver where he is said to have weaved or engraved the Supreme Divine name 'Allah'. However, more appropriately, it is an epithet he acquired as a spiritual master, where the true meaning consists of engraving the Supreme Divine name 'Allah', upon the hearts.

He said, "*La ilaha*' is the negation of worshipping the self and '*Illallahu*' is affirmation of the true Being worthy of worship. '*Muhammadur Rasulullah* ﷺ' is to bind oneself to the command of Qurán where it orders the believers to follow the Beloved Prophet ﷺ. The reality of the declaration of monotheism is absolute negation of all besides Allah ﷻ."

He also said, "Our order is that of *Urwatul Wuthqa* (the Firm Handle), meaning holding onto the garment of the Beloved Prophet ﷺ and following the way of the Noble Companions. This method ensures more achievement through less deeds. There is immense reward in following the Sunnah and the one who turns away from this way puts his faith in danger."

Khawaja Ala ad-Din Attar ﷺ

During the life of Ala ad-Din Attar ﷺ, the Naqshbandi order was established in Asia minor. He said, "The aim of rigor is to negate bodily links and focus completely on the world of souls. If a man detects within himself an inclination to Allah's ﷻ pleasure, then let him express gratitude. If the heart does not incline to Allah's ﷻ pleasure, then show humility and fear Allah's ﷻ quality of not needing anyone."

Khawaja Ya'qub Charkhi ☼

He was originally from a town in Ghazni known as Charkh. He studied in Herat and then Egypt. His immense love for Allah ﷻ drew him to Khawaja Baha ad-Din ☼, who instructed him in *Wuquf e Adadi* meaning performing *Dhikr* in odd numbers. After some time, he was instructed to travel and spread what he had learnt from Khawaja Baha ad-Din ☼. As he received the news of Khawaja Baha ad-Din's departure from this world, Khawaja Yáqub ☼ was struck with immense grief. However, he received a letter from Khawaja Ala ad-Din ☼ reminding him of his Shayk's instructions. Khawaja Yáqub ☼ went to Khawaja Ala-ad-Din ☼ and remained with him till he passed away. One of his blessed sayings is, "The student who comes into the company of his Shaykh should behave like Khawaja Ubaydullah. His lamp was ready, wick prepared. All that was required was to set it alight."

Khawaja Ubaydullah al-Ahrar ☼

He was born in Tashkent, his grandfather Khawaja Shahab ad-Din ☼ was the well-known Wali of his era. Before his departure from this world, he took his grandson in his lap and gave the glad tidings that he will be a great spiritual mentor. He exercised the Naqshbandi principle, 'solitude en-masse' (*khalwat dar anjuman*), which pertains to intense devotion to Allah ﷻ within the context of society. When recounting a certain instance of his spiritual influence, Khawaja Ahrar ☼ said, "If we acted only as the Shaykh in this age, no other Shaykh would find a disciple."

He advised his disciples, "Deeds and character affect inanimate objects as well. Thus, if a person performs Salah at such a place where deeds and character are frowned upon, then it will not have the same blessings and light as if performed at such a place where the effects of the Masters of union﷽ have reached. This is the reason why Salah in Masjid al-Haram equals 100,000 Salah."

His spiritual successors and disciples came from distant regions of Iran, Isfahan, Afghanistan, Samarkand and Anatolia. The famous poet Jami﷽ heard of Khawaja Ubaydullah﷽ and went to see him. Allah﷽ had blessed Khawaja﷽ with plenty of wealth and so Jami﷽ noticed the lavish gathering. He was disappointed and assumed that Khawaja﷽ was a worldly person so, Jami﷽ left the place reciting the couplet;

The friend of the world is never a true man [of Allah]

He went to the mosque and slept there. In his dream he saw that it was the Day of Judgement and someone asked him to fulfil the rights owed to him. Jami﷽ replied that he had nothing, so the man asked him to give away his good deeds. As he grew worried, Jami﷽ saw Ubaydullah﷽ riding a horse. Khawaja Ubaydullahr﷽ stopped by and asked Jami﷽ as to why he was troubled. When Jami﷽ told him about the situation, Khawaja Ubaydullah﷽ said, "There is no need to worry. You can take whatever from my treasury."

Jami﷽ was struck by awe and understood that Khawaja Ubaydullah﷽ was not a worldly man, rather he was a man with such qualities that he remembered Allah﷽ despite being surrounded by the worldly treasures. Jami﷽ went to see Khawaja﷽ and begged for forgiveness. Khawaja﷽ laughed and said that dreams should not be relied upon. This convinced Jami﷽ even more as he had not even shared his dream with anyone. Khawaja﷽ asked him to repeat the couplet, but

Jami﷽ was embarrassed to do so. However, Khawaja Ubaydullah﷽ insisted and when Jami﷽ said; (The beauty of this couplet is in Persian, however, for the sake of understanding, it is translated in English)

The friend of the world is never a true man [of Allah]

Khawaja Ubaydullah﷽ replied;

Only if he keeps the friend for the sake of the Friend [Allah]

Khawaja Muhammad Zahid ﷽

It is narrated that Muhammad Zahid﷽ was related to Khawaja Yáqub Charkhi﷽. He took to seclusion and rigor at an early age and then presented himself to Khawaja Ubaydullah﷽. He performed Báya and told Khawaja Ubaydullah﷽ his states. Khawaja﷽ casted his attention towards him and in the same meeting authorised him as his successor.

Khawaja Darvaish Muhammad ﷽

It is narrated that he engaged in abstention and rigor for fifteen years before presenting himself to his Shaykh. He lived in isolation in the wilderness, spent days fasting and performing *Dhikr* of Allahﷻ. After the demise of his Shaykh, Khawaja Muhammad Zahid﷽, he became the mentor for hundreds. He displayed remarkable resolve in piety and forbearance, yet kept a very low profile.

Khawaja Muhammad al-Amkanki ﷽

He was Khawaja Muhammad Zahid's﷽ son, therefore, brought up in a way that he attained a great status in piety at a very young age. He succeeded to his father's position as Shaykh for thirty years. He continued on the path helping thousands to purify their hearts. He used to serve the visitors personally, despite his advanced age and frail state. He was very assiduous in regards to the Naqshbandi ways and famous for his ability to enlighten the hearts. His disciples came from all parts of Anatolia and Asia minor. Scholars and rulers presented themselves to benefit from him.

Khawaja Baqibillah ؓ

He was born in Kabul to Abdus Salam ؓ who was known for his knowledge and virtues. Khawaja Baqibillah ؓ was accomplished in the knowledge of Hadith and Islamic Jurisprudence. Following the orders of his Shaykh, Khawaja Baqibillah ؓ left his homeland and settled in India. It was during the reign of Akbar, that he moved from Lahore to Delhi. Despite the prevalence of Akbar's pseudo religion at the Moghul court, Baqibillah ؓ initiated various courtiers and army commanders into the Naqshbandi order. Even though, he lived a short life, his *Fayd* reached far and wide.

He disliked claiming any status for himself and liked to serve visitors to put them at ease. He had great spiritual states and stations and his mere glance was sufficient to change a person's life. One who spent time in his company for the first time would acquire spiritual zeal and get absorbed in Divine Love. His very first focus on a follower and instruction would set his heart flowing with *Dhikr*. His affection for all creation was all-encompassing; as narrated that a young man lived in his neighbourhood who was involved in many forms of sin.

Despite knowing this, Khawaja ؓ always overlooked, however, one of his disciples complained to the authorities. The young man was apprehended and sent to jail. When Khawaja ؓ found out he was very upset and questioned the disciple. The disciple replied that the young man was an open sinner, hence, he reported him to the authorities. Khawajaﷺ took a deep breath and said, "Yes, you are people of piety and Taqwa, hence you could perceive his sin and evil. I do not consider myself any better than him, hence, I could not ignore myself and complain to the authorities."

Khawajaﷺ then, interceded and got the young man released from jail. Upon release, the man repented and became one of the pious disciples. The effects of his attention and focus were immense. One night, Mujaddid Alf Thaniﷺ sent an attendant with some desert for Khawaja Baqibillahﷺ. The man knocked on the door and Khawajaﷺ opened the door himself. Khawajaﷺ asked his name and said, "You are Shaykh Ahmad'sﷺ servant, indeed you are ours."

The man was submerged in the state of Sukr (spiritual intoxication) and returned to Shaykh Ahmadﷺ stumbling and screaming. Mujaddid Alf Thaniﷺ asked him as to what had transpired. He told him that the earth, trees, stones and everything else was shining. Mujaddid Alf Thaniﷺ exclaimed, "When Khawaja Baqibillahﷺ appeared, a ray of his sun befell on the man."

Shaykh Ahmad Sirhindi-Mujaddid Alf Thani ﷺ

Khawaja Baqibillah'sﷺ most significant disciple was, Shaykh Ahmad Sirhindiﷺ, known by the titles of Imam-i Rabbani and Mujaddid Alf Thani meaning, 'the Divinely appointed Imam', and 'Revivor of the second millennium'. He memorised Qurán at a very young age and gained the knowledge of Qurán and Hadith. He attained his certification of the Hadith knowledge from the famous Hadith teacher Shaykh Yáqub Kashmiriﷺ and Qadi Bahlul Badakhshaniﷺ. Initially, he rendered Báya to his father in Chishti and Qadri order and traversed the path under his guidance. After the demise of his father, he rendered Báya with Khawaja Baqibillah ﷺ in Naqshbandi Order.

Mujaddid Alf Thani ﷺ is known to be the revivor for his immense efforts to rid the innovations and the misconceptions caused by Akbar's purported *deen i-illahi*. Mujaddid Alf Thani ﷺ gives his tribute to the *Mashaikh*; "The one who does not show gratitude towards people is ungrateful to Allah ﷻ as well. The favours of the scholars and elders (Mashaikh) of the *'Mawara-an-Nahr'* [the region of Uzbekistan, Tajikistan, southern Kyrgyzstan, and southwest Kazakhstan] upon us who are destitute and even upon all the Muslims of India are too immense to be contained within the domain of words. With the research and the sound judgement of these elders, we attained the correction in the articles of faith, may Allah ﷻ increase the *Ahle Sunna wal Jama* in these areas. According to Hanafi scholars, the correction of deeds is also achieved from their deepest knowledge. In the Indian region, the wayfaring (suluk) of this spiritual grand method is also through the blessings of that blessed magnificent land. The station of passion and wayfaring (jazba-o-suluk), "annihilation and abiding" (fana-o-baqa), the "journey towards Allah ﷻ (sair ilallah), journey within Allah ﷻ (sair fillah) which is uniquely linked with the Sacred level (walayat-e-martaba-e-khasa) is transmitted to us through the blessings of the grand noble elders of that region. In short, the external reformation and the internal success is achieved from that region."[3]

Mujaddid Alf Thani ﷺ fought the battle against the profane ideology created by king Akbar through his writings. The letters he wrote to his disciples became a movement and brought the revolution in the society. He was imprisoned by Akbar's successor. The influential disciples of Shaykh Mujaddid Alf

Thani﷽ planned a coup but he advised them against any action. Later, Jehnagir was cautioned in his dream and released Mujaddid Alf Thani﷽ from the prison. Shaykh Mujaddid Alf Thani﷽ initiated thousands of successors who helped cleanse the society of the innovations created in Deen by the Moghul emperor.

Khawaja Muhammad Masoom ﷽

Mujaddid Alf Thani's﷽ son Khawaja Muhammad Masoom﷽ was one of the most prominent successors, followed by a million disciples. He was against any innovation in religion and even if it was the king, he advised him against any innovation. His letters possess world of knowledge and secrets. They are an explanation and clarification of the mystic knowledge of Mujaddid Alf Thani﷽. One of his letters, written to Mulla Qasim﷽ narrates, "Honoured sir! Salah is the ascension of the believer. The state that you perform your Salah is like the state of your ascension and is superior to all spiritual states. Other states compared to Salah are like a picture compared to reality. For example, consider the reflection in the mirror; What comparison does it have to the original form other than similarities in shape and image? The extent that one perfects Salah is the extent to which one will draw blessings from it. Salah is perfected through consideration of the Sunnah, making an effort on the etiquettes, lengthy recitation, bowing and prostrating according to the Sunnah. The beauty and perfection of Salah will become more apparent."

Another letter written to a seeker narrates, "Fill your time with *Dhikr* and concern. Try to fill your inside with light. For that is the spot, the Lord gazes upon. Understand that enlightening the inside is through perpetual *Dhikr*, meditation, implementing the duties of your slavery - which means that you fulfil every obligatory action, Sunnah, non-obligatory obligation (*Wajib*) and avoid every innovation, prohibition and disliked act."

Khawaja Saifuddin ؓ

Khawaja Muhammad Masoom's ؓ son, Khawaja Saifuddin ؓ is next in chain who followed the way of his ancestors and continued with the work of cleansing the society of the innovations. He memorised Qurán at a very young age and acquired the knowledge of Qurán and Hadith. At the tender age of eleven years, his heart was annihilated in the Divine Love. King Aurengzeb used to benefit from the company of Khawaja Saifuddin.

Khawaja Muhammad Mohsin ad-Dehlavi ؓ

He was from the children of Shaykh Abdul Haq Muhaddith Dehlavi ؓ and excelled in piety. He lived in Delhi where he first met Khawaja Muhammad Saifuddin ؓ who was sent there by his blessed father for the spiritual guidance of Emperor Aurangzeb and the others. Muhammad Mohsin ؓ used to communicate with his Shaykh through letters when he was away; letter 67 in volume 2 of the letters of Imam Muhammad Masoom ؓ is addressed to him. The collection of letters from Shaykh Saifuddin ؓ contains two letters mentioning Muhammad Mohsin ؓ and his spiritual status (letter 170 and 172) and two letters directly addressed to him (letter 179 and 180).

Khawaja Nur Muhammad al-Badayoni ؓ

It is narrated that he was so deeply annihilated in the Divine Love that for fifteen years he was in a state of *sukr* where he only remembered to perform Salah. He was extremely cautious of food cooked by anyone, therefore, he used to cook himself and ate very little. There are many narrations regarding his *Karamah* where he could tell the state of the person and the person left that particular sin. Once King

Aurengzeb asked about his age and Khawaja Nur﷽ replied, "The years which I spent in the company of my Shaykh are the years' worth remembering, rest all are thorns."

Mirza Mazhar Janejana ﷽

Mirza Mazhar﷽, the next link in the chain was a great Wali, Shah Muhaddith Dehlavi﷽ was also his devotee. His poetry is a living tribute to his devotion. His father and forefathers were extremely learned men, hence at a young age he was also educated in most branches of religious sciences. Although, the elite and the wealthy of the time attended his company, yet he led a very simple life. He never accepted any gifts from the rich, however, if any of his poor disciples brought anything insignificant, he would accept it. He preferred a very basic life. He was assassinated by a Rafzi on the tenth of Muharram.

Khawaja Ghulam Ali ad-Dehlavi ﷽

Khawaja Ghulam Ali﷽ spent two decades in the company of his Shaykh Mirza Mazhar Janejana﷽. He was first initiated in Qadiriya order but later traversed the path the Naqshbandi Order. He acquired the knowledge of Hadith from his Shaykh and Shah Waliullah Muhaddith's﷽ son. Hundreds of people attended his *Dhikr* gatherings; therefore, *Dhikr* gatherings were conducted few times a day. His disciple Mowlana Khalid﷽ came from Kurdistan to learn from him and initiated a branch known as Naqshbandi Khalidiya in the region of Anatolia.

Khawaja Abu Sa'eed Ahmad ﷽

The next in the chain, Abu Saeed Ahmad﷽ was a great scholar and the author of the book 'Hidayat al-Talibeen' which has been translated in many languages. He memorised Qurán at the age of ten and learnt the religious sciences from Shah Abdul Aziz Muhaddith﷽ and Shah Ghulam Ali﷽. He had hundreds of spiritual successors from Indo-Pak to Turkistan.

Khawaja Ahmad Saeed nil Madani ﷽

He was Abu Saeed Ahmad's﷽ son, who settled in Madinah for good and established the Naqshbandi Order in Hejaz. He is blessed to be buried next to the Companion of the Messenger ﷺ and the third Caliph Syeddina Uthman bin Affan ﷺ.

Dost Muhammad al-Qandhari ﷽

The next in the chain is Dost Muhammad al-Qandhari﷽ who travelled from Qandhar to Kurdistan and later to India in search of a Shaykh. Finally, he reached Shaykh Ahmad Saeed﷽ and stayed in his company for almost year and a half. Shaykh Ahmad Saeed﷽ appointed him as his successor and sent him to settle in Dera Ismail Khan where he lived till his demise. He is buried in Musa Zai Shareef near Dera Ismail Khan in Pakistan.

Muhammad Uthman ad Daamani ﷽

The next in the golden chain, Muhammad Uthman ad Daamani﷽ was also a great scholar of Islamic jurisprudence and Hadith. He used to travel forty miles every day for eighteen years to visit his Shaykh and learnt Hadith and *Tasawwuf* from him. When he went for Hajj and made a visit to Madinah, he stopped eating many weeks before his visit, to keep his stomach empty.

Shaykh Muhammad Sirajuddin ﷽

His son Shaykh Muhammad Sirajuddin﷽ is the next in chain. He was born in Musa Zai. He was also a renowned scholar of Fiqh and Hadith. His disciples came from Khorasan, Herat,

Bukhara and South India to learn from him and benefit from his company. He was given *Khilafah* (succession) in four orders at the age of fourteen. He passed away at the age of thirty-five, yet thousands of people benefitted from him.

Shaykh Muhammad Fazal Ali Qureshi

His disciple, Shaykh Muhammad Fazal Ali Qureshi was born in Mianwali and later established the town of Miskeenpur. He was also a Hadith scholar and used to earn his living by farming. He used to perform *Dhikr* of the Divine Supreme Name 'Allah' while tilling the land. It is said, that he used to serve the plain bread with curd milk produced from his farmlands to the seekers. Due to constant *Dhikr*, the food had immense blessings and the hearts of the seekers were illuminated in days. He used to stay in the hometown for six months and travelled the rest of the year. He was extremely modest; he never took a ride to Musa Zai Shareef and used to walk for two hundred and fifty kilometres to visit his Shaykh's hometown.

Once, Syed Ataullah Shah Bukhari, emir of *'Tahaffuz e Khatm e Nubuwat'* (Safeguarding the belief of finality of Prophethood of Muhammad) went to see Shaykh Fazal Ali and found him tilling the fields. Shah Ataullah requested to pray for him, Shaykh placed his finger on the heart of Shah Bukhari and his heart started *Dhikr* Allah. Once, Shah Bukhari was going to Multan for a special congregation to condemn Qadiyaniat, he requested Shaykh Fazal Ali to bless him with his company and pray for him. Shaykh Fazal Ali accompanied him and Shah Ataullah Bukhari delivered a great speech against Qadiyaniat. When Shaykh Fazal Ali was about to leave, Shah requested him to stay and said that the words from him were the spiritual blessing of Shaykh Fazal Ali Qureshi.

Shaykh Mohammad Abdul Ghafoor al-Madni al-Abbassi ؓ

Shaykh Abdul Ghafoor al-Madni al-Abbasi ؓ, is known to be a strict follower of Sunnah from his early age. He lost his father at a very young age and worked hard to look after his younger siblings. He spent many years in the company of Shaykh Fazal Ali ؓ and looked after the guests. Miskeenpur was a remote village without any electricity or water supply. For years, he worked arduously bringing wood and pulling water out of the well. Shaykh Abdul Ghafoor ؓ was from northern areas, people of the town used to mock him and call him out for his hard toil. He used to say that he loved it when people called him names as he felt the affinity even stronger. Once, initiated, he was ordered by his Shaykh to travel through Northern India. Later, whenever he used to visit his Shaykh, he still performed those tasks himself.

During his stay in Delhi, he visited Hejaz three times and had a strong urge to permanently settle in Madinah. Finally, he moved to Madinah and started teaching Hadith and other Islamic sciences from his home. *Dhikr* gatherings were conducted and thousands of people took the pledge from him. Till his health permitted, he used to perform Hajj every year and did the trips on foot. Allah ﷻ had blessed him with immense knowledge, *ilm al-Ladunni*, *Kashf* and *Karamah*. He passed away in Madinah and blessed to be buried in Jannat al-Baqí next to the Companions of the Beloved Prophet ﷺ.

Shaykh Abdul Haq al-Madni al-Abbasi ؓ

The next in the golden chain is the son of Shaykh Abdul Ghafoor al-Madni al-Abbasi ؓ. He completed his education from 'Jamia al-Islamia al-Madinah'. He was known for his modesty and generosity. His community kitchen was open to all the pilgrims and free meals were provided every day. When walking through the streets of Madinah, he used to carry a bag to pick up any scraps or left-over food on the path. Once, a companion asked him the wisdom behind the act and he told him that he fed those to his sheep rather than being trampled over. He said, "When the servant is ungrateful of the blessings of Allahﷻ, then Allahﷻ takes that blessing away. I am afraid, that people waste a lot of food in Madinah and Allahﷻ may censure us. I try to pick any left-over food from the streets and supplicate to Allahﷻ to forgive us for this wastage and lack of gratitude."

Shaykh Shamsur Rehman Al Abbasi مدظله العالی

My Shaykh is a born Wali, his grandmother was told in her dream by Shaykh Abd al-Qadir Gilani﷫ to name him Shamsur Rehman. Even as a child, instead of wasting time playing with his friends, he used to sit in the Masjid and recite 'Salawat'. He studied at Jamia al Uloom Binori under the tutelage of the best scholars. Shaykh Shamsur Rehman Al Abbasi (Daamut Barakaatuhu) is counted amongst the luminaries of this time and day. His first mentor was Shaykh Abdul Ghafoor al Abbasi al-Madni﷫. After his demise he joined the counsel of Syed Zawwar Hussain Shah﷫. After the demise of Syed Zawwar Hussein Shah﷫, he followed a series of teachers namely Shaykh Mustajaab Khan﷫ and Shaykh Abdul Haq al-Abbasi﷫.

In 2003, he established the Khanqah Ghafooria Haqqania Naqshbandia (khanqah is a centre for training and *Dhikr*). He started the *Dhikr* gatherings on the instruction of Sufi Mohammad Iqbal﷫, who was the spiritual successor of Shaykh-ul-Hadith Mowlana Zakariya﷫. He has devoted all his life trying to inculcate love for Allahﷻ and infusing a desire to follow Sunnah in the masses. His resolute and unwavering commitment to Shariáh has attracted the hearts of thousands of people to follow him.[4]

Chapter Fourteen

NAQSHBANDI PRINCIPLES

The following phrases by Abdul Khaliq al-Ghajdawani ﷺ are considered the principles of the Naqshbandi Sufi Order;

Conscious Breathing (Hosh dar Dam)

The literal meaning of the term Hosh Dar Dam is mindful breathing. It requires the seeker to safeguard each breath from negligence and be constant watchful of the Divine Presence. Each breath should revive *Iman* and connect to Allah ﷻ as any neglectful breath is a disconnection from the Divine Presence.

Ubaidullah al-Ahrar ﷺ said that the most important mission for the seeker in this Order is to safeguard his breath, and he who cannot safeguard his breath is lost. Shah Naqshband ﷺ said that Naqshbandi order is based on breath, each inhale, exhale and the interval in between demands the awareness of the Divine Presence, also known as *'Paas Anfaas'*. [1]

Watch the Step (Nazar bar Qadam)

It means that the seeker must keep his eyes on his feet, while walking. The glance must follow the feet to avoid undue wavering of the sight. The heart gets tainted by the sights of the worldly things and those sights can get imprinted on the mind. The worldly images can act as a barrier between the manifestations of the Divine Light. Therefore, it is greatly emphasised to keep the glance low and avoid any other reflection on the heart, except for the Divine Presence. This is the reason during *Salah*, the gaze is kept at the place of *Sajdah* while standing, on the feet while in *Ruku* and on the lap while sitting. As Qurán commands:

"O Prophet! Tell the believing men to lower their gaze and guard their chastity"

[Quran, An Nur 24:30]

A higher gaze is a sign of egotism, whereas keeping the gaze low is a sign of humility and the seeker can keep the arrogance at bay. As the Qurán commands:

"And do not walk on the earth arrogantly. Surely you can neither crack the earth nor stretch to the height of the mountains."

[Qurán, al Isra 17:37]

Fazl Ali Shahﷺ said the term requires the seeker to keep the gaze on the footsteps of the Beloved Prophetﷺ, and represents following the path of Sunnah. Mujaddid Alf Thaniﷺ states,

"The gaze precedes the step and the step follows the gaze. The ascension to the high state is first by the vision, followed by the step. When the step reaches the level of the ascension of the gaze, then the gaze will be lifted up to another state, to which the step follows in its turn. The gaze then will be lifted even higher and the step will follow and so on until the gaze reaches a state of perfection to which it will pull the step. We say, 'When the step follows the gaze, the seeker has reached the state of readiness in approaching the footsteps of the Beloved Prophetﷺ, therefore, the footsteps of the Prophetﷺ are considered the origin of all steps."[2]

Journey Homeward (Safar dar Watan)

The phrase refers to the journey of the soul towards Divine. It is journey of the seeker leaving behind the blameworthy traits towards the praise worthy traits. The Naqshbandi Sufi Order divides the journey into external and internal. External travel is meant for finding the guide who could take the seeker on the inward journey. The internal journey begins when the seeker finds the Shaykh who initiates the journey from low morals to high morals, culminating the worldly desires and sowing the seeds of *Ma'arfa*. In the internal journey, the seeker travels through various status and rankings of *Walaya*, reaching his destination of the Divine love.

Solitude en masse (Khalwat dar Anjuman)

The phrase refers to a state where the heart of the seeker is engaged in *Dhikr* of Allahﷻ while the seeker is engaged outwardly with others. The denotes to the seclusion of the heart from others and being present with Allahﷻ while the seeker is engaged in the worldly affairs. As Qurán mentions:

> "Men whom neither commerce nor sale distracts from the remembrance of Allah"
>
> [Qurán, an Nur 24:37]

It is when the seeker is so immersed in the manifestations of the Divine Presence that nothing can distract him. It is said that the believer who is with people and carry on with the burdens of life is better than the one who shuns from them. True *Tasawwuf* does not support monasticism. Mujaddid Alf Thaniﷺ explained the concept that the seeker at the beginning might use the external seclusion to isolate himself from people, worshipping and concentrating on Allahﷻ, until he reaches a higher state. In the words of Sayyed al-Kharrazﷺ,

'Perfection is not in exhibitions of miraculous powers, but perfection is to sit among people, sell and buy, marry and have children; and yet never leave the presence of Allahﷻ even for one moment.'

Remembrance (Yad Kard)

The phrase refers to *Dhikr* and remembrance of Allahﷻ and requires the seeker to perform it extensively, until he reaches a state where except for the Divine Presence everything else '*ghair*' is negated. *Dhikr* can be 'negation affirmation', silent *Dhikr* or by the tongue, it must be done until the seeker reaches the state of the contemplation of his heart. The heart should be cleansed to reflect the Divine manifestations and that is the concept of vital remembrance. Bayazid؆ said, "Abundance of *Dhikr* is not by way of numbers, it is awareness without negligence."

Resonate (Baaz Gasht)

The meaning of the phrase "*baaz gasht*" is returning to Allah ﷻ by showing complete surrender and submission to His Will and complete humbleness in giving Him all due praise. This is a state where the seeker, who makes *Dhikr* by negation and affirmation, comes to understand the meanings of the phrase, "O my Allahﷻ, You are my Goal and Your Good Pleasure is my aim, award me Your love and '*Márafa*'." The recitation of this phrase increases the awareness of '*Wahdaniyat*' (Oneness of Allah) and the creations cease to exist in the heart of the seeker. The seeker only covers the stages of '*Márafa*' through Allah'sﷻ special blessings '*inaya*' and the seeker must recognise that he is only capable of remembering Allahﷻ through Hisﷻ '*Taufeeq*'.

Diligence (Nigah Dasht)

The phrase implies that the seeker must watch his heart and safeguard it by preventing bad thoughts. Bad inclinations tarnish the heart and lead to heedlessness; therefore, the seeker must keep the heart in constant remembrance of Allahﷻ and safeguard it. As and when any evil thought occurs, the seeker should busy himself in *Dhikr* which would nullify the effects of the thought.

Recollection (Yad Dasht)

It requires the seeker to keep his heart in Allah's Divine Presence continuously, which allows the seeker to realize and manifest the Light of the Unique Essence. This leads the seeker to the highest state of perfection by discarding all his inclinations and embracing only the True Reality. As Allahﷻ mentioned in Qurán:

> "And He [Allah] is with you wherever you are"
>
> [Qurán, al Hadid 57:4]

Awareness of Time (Wuqoof e Zamani)

The phrase refers to reprising one's thoughts and actions, where the seeker is responsible for his time. The seeker is accountable for every moment of his life, whether it was spent in accordance with Shariáh and Sunnah or not. This keeps the seeker vigilant at all times and in case of forgetfulness or mistakes urges the seeker to repent and return to Allahﷻ.

Awareness of Number (Wuqoof e Adadi)

This refers to keeping the *Dhikr* '*nafi athbat*' or 'negation affirmation' in odd numbers as the Beloved Prophet ﷺ said, 'Allah is One and Prefers odd' [Muslim 2677 Book 48]

Awareness of Heart (Wuqoof e Qalbi)

This principle requires the seeker to be vigilant towards his heart and keep the attention towards the Divine Presence. The place of the spiritual heart is two fingers below the left nipple towards the arm. The vigilance is to be exercised to an extent that the heart is free of everything else '*ghair*' and remains in the constant remembrance of Allah ﷻ. Khawaja Naqshband ﷺ considered '*Wuqoof-e-Qalbi*' as vital as meditation and communication with one's Shaykh. The essence of *Dhikr* is to keep the heart vigilant towards the Divine Presence to absorb the manifestations of the True Reality. [3]

Chapter Fifteen

SUBTLETIES AND MANIFESTATIONS

Subtleties

The Realm of Command came into existence instantaneously with the command "*Kun*" (*be*), as indicated in the following Quranic verse:

"... *and when He decrees an affair, He only says to it, Be, so there it is.*"

[Quran, al Baqarah 2:117]

The Realm of Creation was created in gradual stages, as indicated in the following Quranic verse:

"*Surely your Lord is Allah, Who created the heavens and the earth in six days (periods of time).*"

[Quran, al Aáraf 7:54]

The Realm of Command is infinite and interminable, whereas the Realm of Creation is defined and limited. The combination of the two is known as the Greater Universe or *Aalam al-Kabeer*. The Circle of Possibility (*Dairah al-Imkan*) is a combination of these two realms. The '*Arsh* which is Allah's Throne is at the middle of the Circle of Possibility and divides it in two; the Realm of Command is the higher half, which is above the Throne and the Realm of Creation is the lower half, below the Throne.

The beings of matter as Sun, moon and stars belong to the Realm of Creation whereas, souls and subtleties (*Lataif*) belong to the Realm of Command. There is another realm called,

'Aalam al-Misaal' also known as Intermediate Realm, which is quantitative yet without matter. Therefore, Intermediate Realm simulates Realm of Command for its lack of matter and the Realm of Creation for being quantitative. The soul belongs to both realms, while awake it has a stronger connection with the material body whereas in sleep or being unconscious it inclines towards the Intermediate Realm or *Aalam al-Misaal*. The souls are kept in this realm till the Day of Judgement.[1]

The literal translation of *'Lataif'* is subtleties. The *Lata'if* are faculties which can be explained just as senses or experience. As an example, even though the physiological aspects of memory can be explained, yet the description fails to convey all the dimensions of memory. Similarly, the *lata'if* cannot be adequately defined in words, but as they are enlightened, the seeker can comprehend their existence. Through practice, training and due concentration on *lata'if* the seeker becomes able to use them as means to greater awareness of the Divine Presence.

According to Imam Rabbani Mujaddid Alf Thaniﷺ, a human being is formed from ten *Lata'if* (plural of Latifa), which are centres of perception or inner senses. The innermost self serves as a repository of vision, while the innermost of the innermost self is that which is known to no one but Allahﷻ alone. According to Imam al Qushayriﷺ, the innermost selves or *'Latáif'* are free from the bondage of all things other than Allahﷻ. The word "innermost self" denotes the mystical states that are kept secret between Allahﷻ and the servant.[2]

Five of these subtleties belong to the Realm of Command known as *Aalam al-Amr* and five to the Realm of Creation called *Aalam al-Khalq*. The five from the Realm of Command are *Qalb, Ruh, Sirr, Khafi* and *Akhfa*. The five from the Realm of Creation are *Nafs*, and the four elements, fire, air, water and earth. The combination of these ten subtleties forms the human known as the Smaller Universe or *Aalam al-Sagheer*. Different orders have associated *lata'if* with various locations on the body, however, the Naqshbandi order places the five centres of the Realm of Command in the chest.[3]

> The heart or *qalb* is on the left side of the body, two inches below the nipple and its light or colour is yellow.
> The spirit, *ruh*, is in the corresponding position on the right side of the chest and its light is golden.
> The subtle centre known as secret, or *sirr*, is on the left side of the chest but towards the right of the heart and its light is white in colour.
> Hidden or *khafi* is two fingers on the left side of the right breast and its light is black.
> Most hidden or *akhfa* is in the middle of the chest, between the heart and its colour is green.

When Allah ﷻ created *lata'if*, they were luminous, however, when they were connected to the material body, the influence of the blameworthy traits of the physical world diminished them, as in Qurán;

> "Surely, We created the human being of the best stature, then We reduced him to the lowest of the low, except those who believe and do good works, for they shall have a reward unfailing."
>
> [Surat At-Tin Qur'an 95:4-6]

Latifa e Qalb is tainted with lust which drags the servant towards the worldly pleasures and away from the true Beloved. Anger immersed through *Latifa e Ruh* to draw it towards the bestial nature. *Latifa e Sir* was contaminated by greed which filled it with the love of worldly riches. The pure black light of *Latifa e Khafi* is tainted by the darkness of jealousy which hinders the vision of the servant to look beyond the physical aspects. Pride and arrogance corrupted *Latifa e Akhfa* and pushed it away from the grace.

The five subtleties of the Realm of Command are accorded to five Resolute Prophets, with each level deriving *Fayd* accordingly. Each level is a shadow of the status of the *Walaya* of the Prophet and called *Mashrab*. For instance, the first level which is Qalb is accorded to Adam ﷺ, the second is Ruh which is rendered to Ibraheem ﷺ and Nuh ﷺ. The third is *Sirr* which is accorded Musa ﷺ and the fourth is *Khafi* which is accorded to Eesa ﷺ. The fifth level is under the Last Prophet ﷺ and the seeker derives the *Fayd of Shan e Jamiá*.

When the seeker travels through the path and performs meditation on the Latáif, they are illuminated and return to their origin. At this stage, the seeker attains the Divine Love according to his capacity and the journey is called *Sair Qadmi* or procuration. After procuration, the infinite journey of acquisition called *Sair Nazri*, begins.

Divine Manifestations (Tajalliat)

It is related on the authority of Abu Ayyub ﷺ that Allah's Messenger ﷺ said, 'Were it not for your wrongdoing, Allah ﷻ would have done away with you and created creatures to whom He could grant forgiveness." In another version, on the authority of Abu Hurairah ﷺ the last sentence is as follows; "He would have created creatures who seek forgiveness, so that He could forgive them." [Muslim: 2748, Tirmidhi: 3539]

Subtleties and Manifestations

The Hadith emphasises the need for the occurrence of wrongdoing and the words, "to whom He could grant forgiveness;' relates to wisdom or the secret behind His creation of evil, which is to do with forgiveness. From the perspective of *Shari'ah*, faith and righteousness are of significance in this world, however, from the perspective of creation, disbelief and wrongdoing are also of significance. Among the names of Allahﷻ is *al-Ghaffar* or The Forgiving, which can only be manifested in connection with the occurrence of wrongdoing.

The scholars assert that all the names of Allahﷻ are manifested. The manifestation of each name or attribute then becomes the cause for the occurrence of different proceedings. To summarise, therefore, since among the names of Allah is *Al-Muntaqim* or The Avenger, the manifestation of the same requires the occurrence of disbelief, and rebellion.

It should be remembered that "requiring" in connection with Allahﷻ is not in literal terms because Allahﷻ is far above being required to do anything. Nor do we encourage anyone to do wrong because we refer to this as something "required" or "necessary'. The texts of the Qur'an and Hadith are clearly in opposition to such a notion.

It often happens that after any wrongdoing, the seeker becomes extremely depressed and dejected, therefore may lose hope. It is essential that he understands the need for repentance, seek forgiveness from Allahﷻ and have hope in Allah'sﷻ Mercy.[4]

Chapter Sixteen

DAILY ROUTINES IN THE NAQSHBANDI ORDER

Remembrance (Tasbeehat)

The following remembrance must be performed 100 times each, twice daily. The set of three must be performed once after *Fajr* and to be repeated after *Maghrib*.

① اَسْتَغْفِرُ اللّٰهَ تَعَالٰى رَبِّى مِنْ كُلِّ ذَنْبٍ وَّاَتُوْبُ اِلَيْهِ.

② اَللّٰهُمَّ صَلِّ عَلٰى سَيِّدِنَا مُحَمَّدٍ وَّعَلٰى اٰلِ سَيِّدِنَا مُحَمَّدٍ وَّبَارِكْ وَسَلِّمْ.

③ سُبْحَانَ اللّٰهِ وَالْحَمْدُ لِلّٰهِ وَلَا اِلٰهَ اِلَّا اللّٰهُ وَاللّٰهُ اَكْبَرُ.

وَلَا حَوْلَ وَلَا قُوَّةَ اِلَّا بِاللّٰهِ الْعَلِىِّ الْعَظِيْمِ. at the hundredth time recite

Meditation (Muraqabah in the Naqshbandi Order)

Meditation is called *Muraqabah* in Arabic, derived from the word *Raqibun*, meaning, the watchful one or the vigilant. *Ar Raqib* is one of Allah's ﷻ attributes meaning, 'the One Who is Ever Watchful'. Therefore, Muraqabah means an act of guarding the heart and mind. *Muraqabah* in Naqshbandi order means to watch over or to keep a vigil.

It implies that the seeker takes care of his spiritual heart and truly believes that he is under the constant watch of the 'Ever watchful One', that is Allah ﷻ. The origin of *muraqabah* lies in the Hadith, *"Adore Allah as if you are seeing Him, and if you do not see Him, know that He is seeing you."* [Sahih Muslim, 1.37: Hadith 8]

Daily Routines in the Naqshbandi Order

It is narrated by Ibn Abbas﷛, "I was sitting behind Allah's Messengerﷺ on the back of the same animal when he said: 'O son! Remain constantly aware of Allahﷻ and you will find Him before you.'" [Hannad ibn al-Sariy's Kittab az-Zuhd: 1:304]

The meaning of the words "Remain constantly aware of Allah" is the essence of *muraqabah* which is from among the essential practices of the Naqshbandi order. The fruits of *muraqabah* are closeness and proximity to Allahﷻ as the phrase "you will find Him before you" are the consequence of "Remain constantly aware of Allah". In *Tasawwuf*, *muraqabah* or meditation means to detach from worldly pursuits for a period of time with the intention of nurturing the spiritual guidance that the seeker has received from his Shaykh. *Muraqabah* purifies and reforms the *subtleties* and the seeker attains the love of Allahﷻ.

The basic method of *muraqabah* is to clear one's mind of all thoughts and wait for the Divine Light or *Fayd* from Allahﷻ. At the beginning of the particular *muraqabah*, the seeker recites the intention of that *muraqabah* and keeps that intention in the heart. It is advised to choose a specific time and sit in a quiet place free from any distractions. It is recommended to meditate with an empty stomach or few hours after a meal. The seeker should perform *Wudu* and sit as per Sunnah or cross legged, facing *Qiblah*, with eyes closed and breathe through the nose.

The seeker should reflect on Allahﷻ; the Almighty with all His attributes, free from any flaws. With these thoughts in mind, one is to imagine that the light is emanating from Allahﷻ to the blessed heart of Allah's Last Prophetﷺ and through the hearts of the *Naqshbandi Mashaikh* towards his heart. This is to be visualized for a few seconds only, then, the seeker just imagines that the heart is performing the 'Dhikr Allah' and he is listening to it. The *Dhikr* is not performed through the tongue.

At the initiation of the journey, a novice may find it hard to focus, but over time, the whisperings or thoughts calm down and focus is achieved. The essence of this treatment is that a person should not be troubled by whisperings as Allahﷻ spared one the sort of tribulations that are worse than whisperings.

Ibn 'Abbasﷺ related that someone said, "Allah's Messenger ﷺ! We occasionally have such thoughts in our hearts and experience such things that we would rather burn and become coal than express them verbally." The Messenger of Allahﷺ [became pleased and said]: "Allah is Greatest! All thanks are due to Allahﷻ Who turned Satan's trap into nothing more than whisperings [and did not permit them to go beyond that]." [Dawood: 5112]

Envisage (Tasawwur-e-Shaykh)

Tasawwur-e-Shaykh is the concept of envisioning the figure of the Shaykh in one's mind. Numerous Hadith refer to the concept, therefore, the concept is not unconditionally impermissible. Ibne Masud ﷺ narrated, "It is as though I can picture the Messenger of Allahﷺ relating the story of one of the previous Prophets, whose people had beat him and caused blood to flow from his body. He was wiping the blood off his face and saying: 'O Allah! Forgive my people because they do not know what they do.'" [Bukhari: 3477, Muslim: 1792]

There are numerous Hadiths when Allah's Messengerﷺ described the appearance of the prophets and their features. It is narrated on the authority of Ibn 'Abbasﷺ that Allah's

Messengerﷺ passed through the valley of Azraq, and he asked, 'Which valley is this?' They said, 'This is the valley of Azraq,' and he observed, '(I perceive) as if I am seeing Musa ؑ coming down from the mountain track, and he is calling upon Allahﷻ loudly (saying: Here I am! at your service!)'. Then, he came to the mountain track of Harsha. Allah's Messengerﷺ said, 'Which Mountain track is this?' They said, 'It is the mountain track of Harsha.' Allah's Messengerﷺ said, '(I feel) as If I am seeing Yunus ؑ (Jonah) son of Matta on a well- built red dromedary, with a cloak of wool around him and the rein of his dromedary is made of the fibres of date-palm, and he is calling upon Allahﷻ (saying: Here I am! at your service, my Lord!)'. [Sahih Muslim 166a]

Awn Ibn Abu Juhayfah ؓ narrated from his father who said: "I saw the Prophetﷺ and on him was a red garb and it is as if I am seeing the lustre of his shins." Abu Juhayfah ؓ said, "According to my understanding the clothing was printed red." [Tirmidhi and Al-Bajuri's commentary of *Al-Shamail*]

Anas ؓ said that when Allah's Messengerﷺ intended to write to the non-Arabs it was said to him: 'Indeed, the *'ajam* only accept letters that are sealed.' He had a ring made; it is as if I can see its shine in his palm." [Al-Tirmidhi has mentioned this *Hadith* in his *Al-Shamail*]

There is also the Hadith narrated by 'Ali ؓ that Allah's Messengerﷺ said to him: "Say, 'O Allahﷻ, guide me and make me adhere to the straight path,' and when you mention 'guide' (*hidayah*), keep in mind the right path, and when you mention the straight (path), keep in mind the straightness of the arrow.'" [Sahih Muslim 2725a]

Mowlana Khalil Ahmad Saharanpuri ؓ, wrote in the commentary of this in *Badhl al-Majhud* that: "In other words, when mentioning 'guide' keep in your heart the right path. In the same way that a path is tread in its middle and the person walking does not turn right or left, and if he were to turn then, he would not reach the goal. Likewise, when mentioning 'guide' keep in mind that reaching the goal is dependent on remaining firm on the path. Similarly, keep in mind the straightness of an arrow when mentioning 'adhere to the straight path', in other words its straightness and firmness in that. So, may Allahﷻ guide one to the correct and straight path and there remains no crookedness in the way as there is none in the arrow."

There is an indication for the permissibility of *Tasawwur-e-Shaykh* because the rank of the Shaykh is no less in front of Allahﷻ than the arrow and the path. It is not an issue if, during the envision, the love of the Shaykh enters one's heart. For removing thoughts (*khawatir*), or for those who are afflicted with metaphorical love (*al-'ishq al-majazi*), it is an elixir. It is a practice which is done with caution. A disciple of Mujaddid Alif Thaniﷺ wrote him a letter that contemplation of Shaykh had dominated him. The experience had reached to an extent that he could feel the presence even during Salah and could not negate it. Mujaddid Alif Thaniﷺ replied to his letter;

"O the portrayal of love! This wealth is a longing and desire of true seekers. Only one in millions may become fortunate to achieve it. A disciple experiencing such state is man of ability and in full accordance to his Shaykh. It is likely to be attributed with all the attributes of spiritual guide through his sacred company. There is no need to negate the contemplation of the spiritual guide. Shaykh is not the one to be prostrated (as prostration is done only for Allahﷻ), he is the one who directs. One does not negate pulpit and the masjid (in the state of Salah, the mosque, minaret, mihrab walls etc. are there, yet Salah is not ruined). Only the ones who are fortunate achieve the blessings of such manifestation. This is so that they always make their spiritual guide a medium in all states (to reach Allahﷻ and gain His gnosis) and remain engrossed in Allahﷻ. This blessing is not for any unfortunate who considers himself independent of such medium and turns away from his spiritual guide.[1]

However, if *Tasawur-e-Shaykh* leads one to something that is not permitted in Shariáh then it would be considered impermissible. It would be harmful if during the envisioning one considers the Shaykh to have the power of disposal or believes that the Shaykh is present (*hadir*) or that the Shaykh understands his situation. Although, the practice of envisioning the Shaykh has its benefits in gaining focus but the practice had been taken out of context by the ignorant through excessive exalting of the concept. The wrongdoers altered it with forbidden and impermissible practices as believing that the Shaykh is omnipresent or began worshipping the image. When the scholars noted this concept leading to the corruption of tenets of faith amongst masses, then they unconditionally forbade it, which is correct according to the situation.

Mowlana Ashraf Ali Thanvi﷫ wrote, "It is mentioned in the books of this science that the plentiful envisioning of the image of the Shaykh and his perfect traits gives birth to his love and strengthens the spiritual connection (*nisbah*); it is through a strong *nisbah* that many types of blessings can be gained. Some researchers say that the only benefit of *Tasawwur-e-Shaykh* is that one thought removes another, something that allows one to focus and removes thoughts (*khawatir*). This exercise is of benefit to the Elite and extremely harmful for the general masses as it can take them to the level of worshipping images. It is on account of this that Imam al-Ghazali﷫ and other researchers forbade instructing the general masses and the ignorant from undertaking such exercises that cause *Kashf* etc. For this reason, general masses should be kept away from this exercise and if the Elite do perform this then it should be done with caution: No one should not assume that the Shaykh is omnipresent or their aide and helper, as a 'similitude form' (*al-surah al-mithaliyyah*) or present himself."[2]

Hierarchy of the Spiritual Order (Shajrah)

The Shajrah is to be read daily. It is common practice in the path to supplicate Allahﷻ through intercession. The legitimacy of this practice is established through Hadith as Anas ؓ narrated that, "When we experienced draught, Umar ؓ used to supplicate for rain through Abbas ibn Muttalib ؓ saying, 'O Allahﷻ! We used to supplicate through our Prophet ﷺ and you sent rain to us, now we supplicate you through the uncle of the Prophet ﷺ, so send us rain.' Rain would then come. [Bukhari 1010]

As narrated by Umayyah ibn Khalid ؓ that the Messenger ﷺ used to supplicate for victory through the poor migrants. [Sharh as-Sunnah Al Baghawi 7:303]

It is narrated by Sulaym ibn 'Amir ؓ, "The sky withheld rain, so Mu'awiyah ibn Abi Sufyan and the people of Damascus sought prayers for rain. When Mu'awiyah ؓ sat upon the pulpit, he said, "Where is Yazid ibn al-Aswad al-Jurashi?" Then, the people called for him and he came forward

Daily Routines in the Naqshbandi Order

through the crowd. Mu'awiyah ordered him to ascend the pulpit and Yazid sat by his feet. Mu'awiyah said, "O Allah, we seek intercession with You today by the best of us and most virtuous of us! O Allah, we seek intercession with You today by Yazid ibn al-Aswad al-Jurashi. O Yazid, raise your hands to Allah". Yazid raised his hands and the people raised their hands. The clouds in the west soon began to stir, a wind began to rush, and we were given rain until the people almost could not pray but in their houses." [al-Tabaqāt al-Kubrá 7/444 Sahih]

The permissibility of intercession is proved by Hadith, Allah's Messenger supplicated through the poor emigrants. The statement of Umar and Sulaym show that intercession is permissible through people other than Prophets as well. According to *ahle Sunnah wal Jamáh* taking a means in supplications through Prophets and the righteous, martyrs and truthful, is permissible during their lifetime and after their death, in that one says: "O Allah! I take so-and-so as a means to You that you accept my supplication and You accomplish my need." The concept is clarified by Shaykh Shah Muhammad Ishaq al-Dehlawi al-Muhajir al-Makki and Shaykh Rashid Ahmad al-Gangohi in Fatawa in 'Al-Muhannad 'ala al-Mufannad-The Sword on the Disproved' [3]

Spiritual Hierarchy of the Naqshbandi Mujaddidi Order

Bismillah hirRahman nirRaheem

Allahumma salee a'la Sayyedina Muhammadin wa'laa aali sayyidina muhammadin wabaarik wasalim bi'adadi kulli shayin ma'loomin lak.

Elahi behurmate Shafi ul Muznebeena Rahmatul lil aalameena Sayyedena Muhammad ir Rasulilah sallal lahu Alaihi Wassalam ﷺ

Elahi behurmate Khaleefat e Rasul Allah, Sayyedena Ameer ul Momineen Abi Bakr nis Siddique ؓ

Elahi behurmate Sayyedena Sahib e Rasul Allah Hazrat Salman Farsi ؓ

Elahi behurmate Sayyedena Al Imam al Qasim ؒ

Elahi behurmate Sayyedena Imam Al jafar Sadiq ؒ

Elahi behurmate Sayyedena Bayazeed nil Bustami ؒ

Elahi behurmate Sayyedena Abi Al Hasan Kharqani ؒ

Elahi behurmate Sayyedena Abi Al Qasim Gorgani ؒ

Elahi behurmate Sayyedena Abu Ali nil Farmadi ؒ

Elahi behurmate Sayyedena Abi Yusuf al Hamdani ؒ

Elahi behurmate Sayyedena Khawaja Abdul Khaliq Gajadwani ؒ

Elahi behurmate Sayyedena Khawaja Muhammad Arif nir Riogri ؒ

Elahi behurmate Sayyedena Khawaja Mehmood nil Faghnavi ؒ

Elahi behurmate Sayyedena Khawaja Azizane Ali Raamitni ؒ

Elahi behurmate Sayeddena Khawaja Baba As Samasi ؒ

Elahi behurmate Sayyedena Ameer nil Kulaal ﷺ
Elahi behurmate Sayyedena Shaykh al Mashaikh Bahauddin Naqshband Bukhari ﷺ
Elahi behurmate Ala'uddin al Attar ﷺ
Elahi behurmate Sayyedena Khawaja Yaqoob Sarkhi ﷺ
Elahi behurmate Sayyedena Khawaja Ubaidullah Al Ahrar ﷺ
Elahi behurmate Sayyedena Muhammad niz Zahid ﷺ
Elahi behurmate Sayyedena Darvaish Muhammad ﷺ
Elahi behurmate Sayyedena Khawaja Muhammad nil Amkangi ﷺ
Elahi behurmate Syyedena Khawaja Muhammad nil Baqibillah ﷺ
Elahi behurmate Sayyedena o Mowlana Ahmad Al-Faruqi as Sirhindi ﷺ
Elahi behurmate Sayyedena Muhammad nil Masoom ﷺ
Elahi behurmate Sayyedena Khawaja Saifuddin ﷺ
Elahi behurmate Sayyedena Muhammad Mohsin Ad Dahalvi ﷺ
Elahi behurmate Sayyedena Nur Muhammad Al Badayoni ﷺ
Elahi behurmate Sayyedena Mirza Mazhar Janejana ﷺ
Elahi behurmate Sayyedena Ghulam Ali Ad Dahalvi ﷺ
Elahi behurmate Sayyedena Abu Sa'eed nil Ahmad ﷺ
Elahi behurmate Sayyedena Ahmad Saeed nil Madani ﷺ
Elahi behurmate Sayyedena Dost Muhammad nil Qandhari ﷺ
Elahi behurmate Sayyedena Muhammad Usman ad Daamani ﷺ
Elahi behurmate Sayyedena Muhammad Sirajuddin ﷺ
Elahi behurmate Sayyedena Muhammad Fazal Ali Qureshi ﷺ

Elahi behurmate Sayyedena Mohammad Abdul Ghafoor al Madni al Abbassi ﷺ

Elahi behurmate Sayyedena Abdul Haq al Madni al Abbassi ﷺ

Elahi behurmate Hazrat Mowlana Shamsur Rehman Al Abbasi مدظله العالی

Elahi behurmate Hazrat Shaykh Humayun Hanif مدظله العالی Irham al haqeer al faqeer (your own name) al Naqshbandi al Mujjadadi al ghafoori war zuqni kamala fi martabatil ehsaan behurmate Sayyed Bani Adnan wa behurmate Saadaat hadehis Silsilatish shareefati min Sayyedena Abi Bakr nis Siddique Radhi Allah Taala Anhu I'la ash Shaykh Humayun Hanif Naqshbandi Mudazillahu aali wa sallal lahu Taala Ala' khair e khalqihi Muhammadin wa Alihi wa Ashabihi ajmaeen bi Rahmatihi wa howa Arham Ar Raheemeen.

Daily Routines in the Naqshbandi Order

اَلسِّلْسِلَةُ الشَّرِيفَةُ بِلِسَانٍ عَرَبِيٍّ مُبِينٍ

بِسْمِ اللهِ الرَّحْمٰنِ الرَّحِيمِ

اَللّٰهُمَّ صَلِّ عَلٰى سَيِّدِنَا مُحَمَّدٍ وَّعَلٰى اٰلِ سَيِّدِنَا مُحَمَّدٍ وَّبَارِكْ وَسَلِّمْ بِعَدَدِ كُلِّ شَىْءٍ مَعْلُومٍ لَّكَ

①. اِلٰهِى بِحُرْمَةِ شَفِيعِ الْمُذْنِبِينَ رَحْمَةٍ لِّلْعَالَمِينَ سَيِّدِنَا مُحَمَّدٍ رَّسُولِ اللهِ صَلَّى اللهُ عَلَيْهِ وَعَلٰى اٰلِهِ وَسَلَّمَ

②. اِلٰهِى بِحُرْمَةِ سَيِّدِنَا أَمِيرِ الْمُؤْمِنِينَ أَبِي بَكْرٍ الصِّدِّيقِ رَضِيَ اللهُ تَعَالٰى عَنْهُ

③. اِلٰهِى بِحُرْمَةِ سَيِّدِنَا صَاحِبِ رَسُولِ اللهِ سَلْمَانَ الْفَارِسِيِّ رَضِيَ اللهُ تَعَالٰى عَنْهُ

④. اِلٰهِى بِحُرْمَةِ سَيِّدِنَا الْإِمَامِ الْقَاسِمِ رَحْمَةُ اللهِ تَعَالٰى عَلَيْهِ

⑤. اِلٰهِى بِحُرْمَةِ سَيِّدِنَا الْإِمَامِ الْجَعْفَرِ الصَّادِقِ رَحْمَةُ اللهِ تَعَالٰى عَلَيْهِ

⑥. اِلٰهِى بِحُرْمَةِ سَيِّدِنَا بَايَزِيدٍ الْبَسْطَامِيّ رَحْمَةُ اللهِ تَعَالٰى عَلَيْهِ

⑦. اِلٰهِى بِحُرْمَةِ سَيِّدِنَا أَبِي الْحَسَنِ الْخَرَقَانِيّ رَحْمَةُ اللهِ تَعَالٰى عَلَيْهِ

⑧. اِلٰهِى بِحُرْمَةِ سَيِّدِنَا أَبِي الْقَاسِمِ الْجُرْجَانِيّ رَحْمَةُ اللهِ تَعَالٰى عَلَيْهِ

⑨. اِلٰهِى بِحُرْمَةِ سَيِّدِنَا أَبُو عَلِيٍّ الْفَارَمَدِيّ رَحْمَةُ اللهِ تَعَالٰى عَلَيْهِ

⑩. اِلٰهِى بِحُرْمَةِ سَيِّدِنَا أَبِي يُوسُفَ الْهَمَدَانِيّ رَحْمَةُ اللهِ تَعَالٰى عَلَيْهِ

⑪. اِلٰهِى بِحُرْمَةِ سَيِّدِنَا عَبْدِ الْخَالِقِ الْغُجْدَوَانِيّ رَحْمَةُ اللهِ تَعَالٰى عَلَيْهِ

⑫. اِلٰهِى بِحُرْمَةِ سَيِّدِنَا مُحَمَّدٍ عَارِفٍ الرَّيُوجَرِيّ رَحْمَةُ اللهِ تَعَالٰى عَلَيْهِ

⑬. اِلٰهِى بِحُرْمَةِ سَيِّدِنَا مَحْمُودٍ الْفَغْنَوِيّ رَحْمَةُ اللهِ تَعَالٰى عَلَيْهِ

⑭. اِلٰهِى بِحُرْمَةِ سَيِّدِنَا عَزِيزَانِ عَلِيٍّ الرَّامَيْتِنِيّ رَحْمَةُ اللهِ تَعَالٰى عَلَيْهِ

⑮. اِلٰهِى بِحُرْمَةِ سَيِّدِنَا بَابَا السَّمَاسِيّ رَحْمَةُ اللهِ تَعَالٰى عَلَيْهِ

⑯. اِلٰهِى بِحُرْمَةِ سَيِّدِنَا أَمِيرٍ الْكُلَالِ رَحْمَةُ اللهِ تَعَالٰى عَلَيْهِ

⑰. اِلٰهِى بِحُرْمَةِ سَيِّدِنَا شَيْخِ الْمَشَايِخِ مُحَمَّدٍ بَهَاءِ الدِّينِ الْبُخَارِيّ رَحْمَةُ اللهِ تَعَالٰى عَلَيْهِ

⑱. اِلٰهِى بِحُرْمَةِ سَيِّدِنَا عَلَاءِ الدِّينِ الْعَطَّارِ رَحْمَةُ اللهِ تَعَالٰى عَلَيْهِ

⑲. اِلٰهِى بِحُرْمَةِ سَيِّدِنَا يَعْقُوبَ الصَّرْخِيّ رَحْمَةُ اللهِ تَعَالٰى عَلَيْهِ

⑳. اِلٰهِى بِحُرْمَةِ سَيِّدِنَا عُبَيْدِ اللهِ الْأَحْرَارِ رَحْمَةُ اللهِ تَعَالٰى عَلَيْهِ

㉑. اِلٰهِى بِحُرْمَةِ سَيِّدِنَا مُحَمَّدٍ الزَّاهِدِ رَحْمَةُ اللهِ تَعَالٰى عَلَيْهِ

㉒. اِلٰهِى بِحُرْمَةِ سَيِّدِنَا دَرْوِيشُ مُحَمَّدٍ رَحْمَةُ اللهِ تَعَالٰى عَلَيْهِ

٧٢. اِلٰهِى بِحُرْمَةِ سَيِّدِنَا مُحَمَّدٍ الْاَمْكَنْكِى رَحْمَةُ اللهِ تَعَالىٰ عَلَيْهِ
٧٣. اِلٰهِى بِحُرْمَةِ سَيِّدِنَا مُحَمَّدٍ الْبَاقِى بِاللهِ رَحْمَةُ اللهِ تَعَالىٰ عَلَيْهِ
٧٤. اِلٰهِى بِحُرْمَةِ سَيِّدِنَا وَ مَوْلَانَا اَحْمَدَ الْفَارُوقِ السِّرْهِنْدِىِّ رَحْمَةُ اللهِ تَعَالىٰ عَلَيْهِ
٧٥. اِلٰهِى بِحُرْمَةِ سَيِّدِنَا مُحَمَّدٍ الْمَعْصُومِ رَحْمَةُ اللهِ تَعَالىٰ عَلَيْهِ
٧٦. اِلٰهِى بِحُرْمَةِ سَيِّدِنَا مُحَمَّدٍ سَيْفِ الدِّيْنِ رَحْمَةُ اللهِ تَعَالىٰ عَلَيْهِ
٧٧. اِلٰهِى بِحُرْمَةِ سَيِّدِنَا مُحَمَّدٍ مُحْسِنِ الدِّهْلَوِىِّ رَحْمَةُ اللهِ تَعَالىٰ عَلَيْهِ
٧٨. اِلٰهِى بِحُرْمَةِ سَيِّدِنَا نُورِ مُحَمَّدٍ الْبَدَايُوْنِى رَحْمَةُ اللهِ تَعَالىٰ عَلَيْهِ
٧٩. اِلٰهِى بِحُرْمَةِ سَيِّدِنَا مَظْهَرِ جَانِ جَانَانَ رَحْمَةُ اللهِ تَعَالىٰ عَلَيْهِ
٨٠. اِلٰهِى بِحُرْمَةِ سَيِّدِنَا غُلَامِ عَلِىٍّ رَحْمَةُ اللهِ تَعَالىٰ عَلَيْهِ
٨١. اِلٰهِى بِحُرْمَةِ سَيِّدِنَا اَبِى سَعِيْدٍ الْاَحْمَدِ رَحْمَةُ اللهِ تَعَالىٰ عَلَيْهِ
٨٢. اِلٰهِى بِحُرْمَةِ سَيِّدِنَا اَحْمَدَ سَعِيْدٍ الْمَدَنِى رَحْمَةُ اللهِ تَعَالىٰ عَلَيْهِ
٨٣. اِلٰهِى بِحُرْمَةِ سَيِّدِنَا دَوْسْتِ مُحَمَّدٍ الْقَنْدَهَارِىِّ رَحْمَةُ اللهِ تَعَالىٰ عَلَيْهِ
٨٤. اِلٰهِى بِحُرْمَةِ سَيِّدِنَا مُحَمَّدٍ عُثْمَانَ الدَّامَانِى رَحْمَةُ اللهِ تَعَالىٰ عَلَيْهِ
٨٥. اِلٰهِى بِحُرْمَةِ سَيِّدِنَا مُحَمَّدٍ سِرَاجِ الدِّيْنِ رَحْمَةُ اللهِ تَعَالىٰ عَلَيْهِ
٨٦. اِلٰهِى بِحُرْمَةِ سَيِّدِنَا مُحَمَّدٍ فَضْلِ عَلِىٍّ الْقُرَيْشِى رَحْمَةُ اللهِ تَعَالىٰ عَلَيْهِ
٨٧. اِلٰهِى بِحُرْمَةِ سَيِّدِنَا مُحَمَّدٍ عَبْدِ الْغَفُوْرِ الْعَبَّاسِى الْمَدَنِى رَحْمَةُ اللهِ تَعَالىٰ عَلَيْهِ

وَنَوِّرْ اللهُ مَرْقَدَهُ وَاَعْلِ اللهُ دَرَجَاتِهِ وَنَفَعْنَا اللهُ بِعُلُوْمِهِ وَاَفَاضَ عَلَيْنَا مِنْ بَرَكَاتِهِ وَفُيُوْضَاتِهِ فِى الدُّنْيَا وَالْاٰخِرَةِ اٰمِيْن يَا رَبَّ الْعٰلَمِيْن.

٨٨. اِلٰهِى بِحُرْمَةِ مَوْلَانَا عَبْدِ الْحَقِّ الْمَدَنِى الْعَبَّاسِى رَحْمَةُ اللهِ تَعَالىٰ عَلَيْهِ
٨٩. اِلٰهِى بِحُرْمَةِ مَوْلَانَا شَمْسِ الرَّحْمٰنِ الْعَبَّاسِى مَدَّظِلُّهُ الْعَالِى،
٩٠. اِلٰهِى بِحُرْمَةِ الشَّيخِ هُمَايُون حَنِيْف مَدَّظِلُّهُ الْعَالِى

٩١. اِرْحَمِ الْحَقِيْرَ الْفَقِيْرَ (your own name) التَّقَشْبَنْدِىَّ الْمُجَدِّدِىَّ الْغَفُوْرِىَّ وَارْزُقْنِى كَمَالاً فِى مَرْتَبَةِ الْاِحْسَانِ بِحُرْمَةِ سَيِّدَيْنِى عَدْنَانَ وَبِحُرْمَةِ سَادَاتِ هٰذِهِ السِّلْسِلَةِ الشَّرِيْفَةِ مِنْ سَيِّدِنَا اَبِى بَكْرٍ الصِّدِّيْقِ رَضِى اللهُ عَنْهُ اِلَى الشَّيْخِ هُمَايُون حَنِيْف مَدَّظِلُّهُ الْعَالِى وَصَلَّى اللهُ عَلَى خَيْرِ خَلْقِهِ مُحَمَّدٍ وَاٰلِهِ وَاَصْحَابِهِ اَجْمَعِيْن بِرَحْمَتِهِ وَهُوَ اَرْحَمُ الرَّاحِمِيْن.

Chapter Seventeen

LESSONS OF THE NAQSHBANDI ORDER

Shaykhs of the Naqshbandi order guide the seeker in enlightening the *lata'if* of *Qalb, Ruh, Sirr, Khafi* and *Ikhfaa* which are the subtleties of the Realm of Command. Once, the seeker is able to cleanse these subtleties and attains enlightenment, then the Shaykh guides him through the lessons which deal with the subtleties associated with the Realm of Creation. Out of the subtle centres connected with the Realm of Creation, only the self or *Nafs* located in the middle of the forehead, is regarded as corresponding to a particular point on the human body.

The seeker undertakes lessons accorded by the Shaykh and with due communication, practice and dedication, one travels the path. Shaykh would assess and move the seeker to the next lesson when he deems that the seeker has achieved the station. There is a width and a breadth for each lesson which the seeker has to cover. Due to his states, a seeker may think that he has attained a particular station, but only the Shaykh would know whether the seeker has achieved the station or not.

A lesson is not something to ask for as only the Shaykh identifies when the seeker has completed the lesson and attained the particular station. It is important to perform Bayá and follow the instructions of the Shaykh to perform these lessons. The lessons shall never be practiced without the guidance or approval of the Shaykh. Anyone trying to perform these lessons without due guidance or according to his own prerogative would suffer immensely. Through *Dhikr*, Muraqabah, keeping the vigil on the heart and keeping the communication with one's Shaykh, the seeker progresses on the path.

Lesson 1: Dhikr in Latifa e Qalb - Heart Subtlety

The *Qalb* (spiritual heart) is located two finger-widths below the left nipple in the chest, somewhat oriented towards the side. At times, when the Shaykh teaches this lesson to a new seeker, he places his right index finger on this place and says "Allah, Allah, Allah", while exerting his spiritual *Tawajjuh* on his heart (this method is only for men, women are taught verbally).

Daily Muraqabah for at least half an hour is suggested in a quiet place, away from any distractions. It is recommended to make a fixed time in the daily routine to make it a habit. The seeker shall sit cross legged or both legs folded, keeping the body relaxed and free from tension and bow the neck. The tongue is to be kept to the palette to avoid moving as it is a silent *Dhikr*.

The seeker then, makes the intention that the light of Allah's *Dhikr* is coming to his Qalb from the blessed heart of the Beloved Prophet and through the hearts of the Naqshbandi *Mashaikh*, purifying his heart from the filth of sin and disobedience. The seeker must concentrate that his heart is calling out to Allah and eliminate any other thoughts. In the beginning, one may not be able to focus, but with due practice, it becomes easy to concentrate. The purpose of the Muraqabah is to kindle the heart with love and desire for Allah.

At the completion of this lesson, the heart of the seeker is purified from lust and overcomes gluttony. The aspiration for worldly possessions is reduced and passion to follow Sunnah and Shariáh is achieved. As this subtlety is associated with the negative emotions of excessive appetite and lust, it becomes easier to control these emotions.

Lesson 2: Dhikr Latifa e Ruh - Soul Subtlety

Laṭifah e Ruh (soul subtlety) is located two finger-widths below the right nipple in the chest, somewhat oriented towards the side. The seeker should perform the intention that the light of Allah's ﷻ *Dhikr* is coming to his *Latifa e Ruh* from the blessed heart of the Beloved Prophet ﷺ and through the hearts of the Naqshbandi *Mashaikh*, purifying his *Latifa e Ruh* from the filth of sin and disobedience.

The Nur of this *Latifah* is glittering red or gold. This subtlety is associated with the negative emotions of anger and rage. The sign of completion of this lesson is that the seeker can control his anger and develops patience. He becomes steadfast in following the path of Sunnah and Shariáh.

Lesson 3: Dhikr in Latifa e Sirr - Secret Subtlety

Latifa e Sirr is located at a distance of two finger-widths from the left nipple towards the centre of the chest. *Dhikr* is achieved in this *Latifa* by making the intention that the light of Allah's Dhikr is coming to his *Latifa e Sirr* from the blessed heart of the Beloved Prophet ﷺ and through the hearts of the Naqshbandi Mashaikh, purifying his *Latifa e Sirr* from the filth of sin and disobedience. The seeker must concentrate that his Latifa e Sirr is calling out to Allah ﷻ and eliminate any other thoughts.

The Nur or light of this Latifah is pure white. This subtlety is associated with the spiritual disease of greed. The sign of completion is that frugality is diminished, the seeker finds it easier to spend for the sake of Allah ﷻ and loves to help the poor and the needy. The love of Sunnah and Shariáh becomes stronger than before.

Lesson 4: Dhikr of Latifa e Khafi - Hidden Subtlety

Latifa e Khafi is located at a distance of two finger-width from the right nipple towards the centre of the chest. This *Latifa* also attains *Dhikr* with practice and Shaykh's *tawajjuh*. The seeker makes the intention that the light of Allah's *Dhikr* is coming to his *Latifa e Khafi* from the blessed heart of the Beloved Prophet ﷺ and through the hearts of the Naqshbandi *Mashaikh*, purifying his *Latifa e Khafi* from the filth of sin and disobedience. The seeker must concentrate that his *Latifa e Khafi* is calling out to Allah ﷻ. and eliminate any other thoughts.

The light of this *Latifah* is pure black and this subtlety is associated with the spiritual disease of jealousy. The sign of its completion is that jealousy and envy are diminished.

Lesson 5: Dhikr of Latifa e Akhfa - Hidden-most Subtlety

This Latifa is the place of *Walayat-e-Muhammad* ﷺ and the highest spiritual faculty of a human being. The *Latifah of Akhfa* is located in the centre of the chest between the two breasts. With due practice, *Dhikr* is achieved by remembering the name Allah ﷻ at this location. The seeker makes the intention that the light of Allah's *Dhikr* is coming to his *Latifa e Akhfa* from the blessed heart of the Beloved Prophet ﷺ and through the hearts of the Naqshbandi Mashaikh, purifying his *Latifa e Akhfa* from the filth of sin and disobedience. The seeker must concentrate that his *Latifa e Akhfa* is calling out to Allah ﷻ. and eliminate any other thoughts.

The light of this subtlety is green and it is associated with the spiritual diseases of pride and arrogance. The sign of its completion is that arrogance and pride are diminished and the seeker becomes humble and selfless.

Lesson 6: Dhikr in Laṭifa e *Nafs* - Carnal-soul Subtlety

In Tariqa, other than Naqshbandi, the carnal self is controlled before purifying the subtleties whereas, in Naqshbandi Tariqa, the carnal *Nafs* is controlled after purifying the subtleties of the Realm of Command. Once, the subtleties of the Realm of Command are purified, it becomes easy to control the carnal *Nafs*. Under the spiritual attractions (*jazba*) acquired in earlier lessons, the seeker does not need excessive exercises and drills for cleansing his *Nafs*.

According to some *Mashaikh, Latifa e Nafs* is located two finger-widths below the navel. But, according to Mujaddid Alf Thaniﷺ, it is located in the centre of the forehead between the two eyebrows. The seeker makes the intention that the light of Allah'sﷻ *Dhikr* is coming to his Latifa e *Nafs* from the Beloved Prophetﷺ and through the hearts of the Naqshbandi *Mashaikh*, purifying his *Latifa e Nafs* from the filth of sin and disobedience. The seeker must concentrate that his *Latifa e Nafs* is calling out to Allahﷻ and eliminate any other thoughts. Dhikr at this location removes the arrogance and defiance of *Nafs*.

Lesson 7: Dhikr in Laṭifa e Qalbiya - Physical Body

Latifa e Qalbiya denotes the whole body and represents the four elements; fire, air, water and earth. The Sufi Shaykhs teach this lesson in the centre of the head. This lesson is also called Sulṭan *al-Adhkaar* (the chief *Dhikr*). The seeker makes the intention that the light of Allah'sﷻ *Dhikr* is coming to his *Latifa e Qalbiya* from the Beloved Prophetﷺ and through the hearts of the Naqshbandi *Mashaikh*, purifying his *Latifa e Qalbiya* from the filth of sin and disobedience.

The seeker must concentrate that his *Latifa e Qalibiya* is calling out to Allahﷻ and eliminate any other thoughts. The sign of its completion is that the entire body including flesh, blood, bones and hair is engaged in constant *Dhikr*, remembering the Creator with His Personal Name Allahﷻ. At times, the seeker may feel any part of the body quiver or the whole body may enjoin *Dhikr*.

Lesson 8: Dhikr Nafi Athbat-Negation Affirmation

This *Dhikr* is also known as *Habs e Dam*. As taught by the masters of this noble Path, Habs e Dam is the recitation of *La Ilaha IllAllah* (لا اله الّا الله) silently and without breathing. *Nafi* means negation and refers to the first part which is *La Ilaha* meaning there is no god, and *Athbat* means affirmation and refers to the second part which is *Illallah* (but Allah).

To perform this *Dhikr,* one need to sit with eyes closed and hold the breath below the navel. In imagination, the seeker has to visualize the word 'La' is going from the navel to the centre of the skull and '*Ilah*' touches the right shoulder, finally *Illalah* touching upon the five *lataif* hits on the heart. When *Illallah* hits the heart, the effect resonates through the five lataif as ripples in the water. This *Dhikr* is done silently, without any body movements and the tongue is not moved. At the release of the breath, the seeker is to say, '*Mohammad ur Rasoolulah*ﷺ'.

It is necessary to focus on the meaning of these noble words, such that while saying *La Ilaha*, one should imagine that nothing exists, and while saying *Illallah*, one should direct the attention to Allahﷻ. In the beginning, this *Dhikr* can be done in any odd number in a breath. After sufficient practice, this is increased up to twenty-one times in a single breath. The odd number for this lesson is called *Wuquf-i Adadi*. After every few times, the seeker should remind himself that his ultimate goal is the pleasure of his Lord and nothing else.

If one wants to rid of any particular spiritual disease as back biting, then during this *Dhikr*, imagine cutting that spiritual disease with the sword of *La* and with *Ilah* throw it to the right shoulder and with *Illallah* the beat is felt on the heart and reverberates through the *lataif*. The seeker can imagine and perform this *Dhikr* for any evil habits or for carnal self and Shaytan.

This *Dhikr* is known as the essence of *Dhikr*, it is said that this was the *Dhikr* which Khizar ﷺ taught Ghajdawani ﷺ and he used to perform this while standing in the river. Syed Zawwar Hussain Shah ﷺ said that by the time, seeker would reach up to twenty-one, he should feel the unveiling and if not then, start all over again. These days, it is hard to achieve that state because of the impure foods and the evils.

Lesson 9: Dhikr Tahlil Lisani- Negation-Affirmation through Tongue

This is the recitation of *"La Ilaha Illallah"* in the same method as previous lesson, but with the tongue and without holding the breath. The daily minimum is 1200 and the recommended number is 5000 or more. This *Dhikr* can be done any time of the day with or without wudu, but keeping the wudu is much more preferred. This *Dhikr* brings the seeker closer to Allah ﷻ.

Lesson 10: Muraqabah Aḥadiyyat - Meditation of Oneness

The following lessons relate to higher spiritual advancements and the seeker shall not perform these without being permitted by the Shaykh. The meditation is called 'Muraqabah Ahadiyyat'

(Meditation of Oneness). The receiver of *Fayd* or emanation in this meditation is *Latifa e Qalb*, the heart subtlety. This meditation helps the seeker get rid of excessive thoughts and to permanently fix his attention towards Allah. The sign of completion of this meditation is that the no thought enters the heart for about twelve hours. The intention of Muraqabah Aḥadiyyat (meditation of oneness) is as follows;

Fayd (emanation) is coming to my *Qalb* from the Being that is comprehensive of all Attributes and Perfections, free from all defects and deficiencies, and is named by the Supreme name "Allah".

When Muraqabah Ahadiyyat is completed, the seeker follows a sequence of meditations, each pertaining to one Latifah. It should be noted that the seeker should not start a new meditation before the previous meditation is completed. Otherwise, he will not reach the stage of *Fana* or annihilation. During these Meditation lessons, the seeker should imagine to place his heart in front of the heart of the Beloved Prophet and imagine as if the hearts of the great masters of the Silsila are like mirrors reflecting the emanation to his *Latifa*.

Lesson 11: Muraqabah Tajalliyat e Afáliya -Meditation of the Divine Manifestation of Action

The receiver of emanation in this meditation is *Latifah e Qalb*. The seeker is to imagine as his heart is placed in front of the heart of Allah's Last Messenger, and then make the intention;

"Ya Allah! The Fayd (emanation) of the Divine Manifestation of Action [tajalliyat e afáliya] that you have manifested from Latifa e Qalb (the heart subtlety) of Prophet Muhammad to the Qalb of the Prophet Adam, kindly manifest that (Fayd) to my Qalb by the sanctity of my grand masters."

Latifa e Qalb has special association with the formation (Takwin) Attribute that is an attribute of Allahﷻ that gives existence to the non-existent and is the source of creation, invention, actions and events. *Latifa e Qalb* is under the feet of the first Prophet Adamؑ. This meditation leads to the *Fana* (annihilation) of *Latifa e Qalb* and the seeker acquires the sainthood or *Walaya of Qalb*, which is the lowest in the stations of sainthood. When the seeker achieves this noble stage, he finds that his actions and the actions of all the creation are rays or echoes of the actions of the Creator. He does not attribute the actions to anyone other than his Lord. Thus, his heart is not affected by the changes and events or the pleasures and sorrows. As he considers those sorrows and pleasures from his Beloved then, everything that is from the Beloved is also beloved.

Lesson 12: Muraqabah Tajjaliyat e Sifat e Thubutiyya- Meditation of the Subsistent Attributes

Latifah Ruh is accorded to the Prophet Ibraheemؑ and Prophet Nuhؑ. It is associated with the Subsistent Attributes [*Sifat ath-thubutiyya*]. The seeker is to imagine as his *Latifa e Ruh* is placed in front of the *Latifa e Ruh* of Allah's Last Messengerﷺ and make the following intention;

"Ya Allah! the *Fayd* (emanation) of the of Subsistent Attributes [*tajalliyat e sifaat e thubutiya*] that you have manifested from the *Latifa e Ruh* (the Soul subtlety) of Prophet Muhammadﷺ to *Latifa e Ruh* of Prophet Nuhؑ and Prophet Ibraheemؑ; kindly manifest that emanation to my *Latifa e Ruh* by the sanctity of my grand masters."

At this stage, the attributes are exonerated and absolved from the creations to the Creator and the seeker acknowledges *Tawheed e Wujudi*.

Lesson 13: Muraqabah Tajalliyat-e Shuyun e Zatiya- Meditation of the Divine Manifestation of the Essential Splendours

Shuyun is the plural of *shaan* which is the Theophany of Essential Splendour which signifies as;

> "Day in and day out He has something to bring about."
>
> [Qurán, Ar Rahman 55:29]

The receiver of *Fayd or* emanation in this meditation is *Latifa e Sirr*. The seeker imagines to place his *Latifa e Sirr* in front of the *Latifa e Sirr* of Allah's Last Messengerﷺ with the intention;

"*Ya Allah*! the *Fayd* (emanation) of the Divine Manifestation of the Essential Splendours [*tajalliyat e shuyun e Zatiya*] that you have manifested from the *Latifa e Sirr* (the Secret subtlety) of Prophet Muhammadﷺ to the *Latifa e Sirr* of Prophet Musa عليه السلام, kindly manifest that *Fayd* to my *Latifa e Sirr*, by the sanctity of my grand masters."

At the completion of this lesson, the seeker feels absorbed in the Divine Love and appreciation or criticism hold no value to him.

Lesson 14: Muraqabah Tajalliyat e Sifat e Salbiya- Meditation of the Divine Manifestation of the Privative Attributes

Divine Manifestation of the Privative Attributes mean that Allahﷻ is free from any imperfections, flaws or deficiencies. Allahﷻ is free of space, time, body, direction or any other limitations. Allahﷻ is not born of anyone neither does Allahﷻ have any children. All attributes and qualities are for Him only and any limitations or imperfections are privative to

Him. At the completion of this lesson, the seeker holds the Divine Unique and Exceptional. The receiver of *Fayd* or emanation in this meditation is *Latifa e Khafi*. The seeker is to imagine to place his *Latifa e Khafi* (hidden subtlety) in front of the *Latifa e Khafi* of Allah's Last Prophetﷺ, and then make the following intention;

"Ya Allah! the *Fayd* (emanation) of the Divine Manifestation of the Privative Attributes [*tajalliyat e sifat e salbiya*] that you have manifested from the *Latifa e Khafi* (the Hidden subtlety) of Prophet Muhammadﷺ to the *Latifa e Khafi* of Prophet Eesa ؑ, also manifest that *Fayd* to my *Latifa e Khafi* by the sanctity of my grand masters."

Lesson 15: Muraqabah Tajalliyat e Shan e Jamiá-Meditation of Divine Manifestation of the Comprehensive Splendour

The receiver of *Fayd* or emanation in this meditation is *Latifa e Akhfa*. The seeker imagines to place his *Latifa e Akhfa* (hidden-most subtlety) in front of *Latifa e Akhfa* of Allah's Last Messengerﷺ with the following intention;

"Ya Allah! the *Fayd* (emanation) of the Divine Manifestation of the Comprehensive Splendour [*tajalliyat e Shan e Jamiá*] that you have manifested on the *Latifa e Akhfa* (the Hidden-most subtlety) of Prophet Muhammadﷺ, manifest that *Fayd* to my *Latifa e Akhfa*, by the sanctity of my grand masters."

At the completion of this lesson, the conduct of the seeker improves and true morality is achieved; with more refinements to follow in the next stages. At this stage, it is important to follow the Sunnah of the Prophetﷺ to the best.

The journey through *Da'irat al-Imkan* or the Circle of Possibility is completed after these meditations.

Lesson 16: Muraqabah Ma'iyyat- Meditation of Co-Presence

This is the meditation on the meaning of the following verse of the Holy Qur'ān:

"He is with you, wherever you are" [Quran, al Hadid 57:4]

وَهُوَمَعَكُمْ أَيْنَ مَا كُنْتُمْ ۞

During this meditation, the seeker should focus on the meaning of the verse that Allahﷻ is with him and make the intention as follows;

"*Fayd* is emanating from Allahﷻ who is with me and every particle of the universe and Allahﷻ alone knows the state of that closeness. *Fayd* is emanating to my *Latifa e Qalb*, the source of the *Fayd* is the circle of *Walayat-e-Sughra* (Minor sainthood), which is the Walaya of Awliya e Azzaam and the shadow of Supreme attributes."

This meditation marks the completion of the Circle of Possibilities and the seeker accomplishes the annihilation of the heart. All other connections to the worldly affairs are debilitated and the heart is entirely absorbed in the Divine love. This is the first step towards Walaya and all other stations are dependent on it. *Dhikr* of Nafi-Athbat "*La Ilaha IllAllah*" is very helpful at this stage, such that the attention of the seeker is towards the Qalb and attention of the Qalb is towards Allahﷻ while the tongue is reciting "*La Ilaha IllAllah*".

The Naqshbandi *Sulook* by Khawaja Naqshbandﷺ is accomplished at the completion of these lessons. Allahﷻ revealed the next lessons to Mujaddid Alf Thaniﷺ. *Walayat-e-Kubra* or the major sainthood is the sainthood of Prophets, and it consists of three circles and one arc. This is the stage where *Nafs* fully surrenders to the Commands of the Divine.

Lesson 17: Muraqabah Da'irat al-Ulā- Meditation of the First Circle

In the first circle, the meditation is performed keeping in mind the meaning of the verse:

"We are nearer to him than his jugular vein". [Quran, Qaf 50:16]

وَنَحْنُ أَقْرَبُ إِلَيْهِ مِنْ حَبْلِ الْوَرِيدِ ۝

This meditation is also called the meditation of nearness [Aqrabiya], the intention of the meditation is; "Fayd or emanation is coming to my *Nafs* subtlety and my five subtleties of the Realm of Command (Aalam al-Amr) from the Being Who is nearer to me than my jugular vein. The source of the Fayd is the First Circle of Major Sainthood, which is the Walaya of Prophets and the quintessence of the circle of *Walayat-e-Sughra*"

The lower semi-circle consists of Divine Manifestation of Supreme attributes and the upper semi-circle consists of Divine Manifestation of Essential Splendour. Perpetual state of attention towards Allahﷻ, special modalities of the heart and elimination of worldly temptations is achieved. The seeker finds his whole being engulfed in a state of absorption called *Injazab*. When the connection or *Nisbah* of this station is firmly established in the *Nafs* subtlety, the heart subtlety is forgotten. Compared to the heart subtlety, the modalities and states in this station are colour-less and taste-less.

Lesson 18: Muraqabah Ad-Da'irat ath-Thaniya-Meditation of the Second Circle

In the second circle, the meditation of love is performed keeping in mind the meaning of the verse:

"He loves them and they love Him." [Qurán, Al-Ma'ida 5:54]

The intention of the meditation is: "Fayd or emanation is coming to my *Nafs* subtlety, from the Being who holds me dear and I hold him dear. The source (origin) of the Fayd is the Second Circle of Major Sainthood, which is the quintessence of the first circle of major sainthood and the Walaya of the Resolute Prophets."

Lesson 19: Muraqabah Ad-Da'irat ath-Thalitha Meditation of the Third Circle

The meditation in the third circle is also the meditation of love on the meaning of the same verse:

"*He loves them and they love Him.*" [Qurán Al-Ma'ida, 5:54]

The meditation is done by focusing on the meaning of this verse, with the intention: "Fayd or emanation is coming to my *Nafs* subtlety from the Being who holds me dear and I hold him dear. The source (origin) of the Fayd is the third circle of Major Sainthood, which is the quintessence of the second circle of major sainthood and the Walaya of the Prophets."

Lesson 20: Muraqabah Al-Qaws- Meditation of the Arc

The half-circle or arc also comprises of the meditation of love, on the meaning of the same verse:

"*He loves them and they love Him.*" [Qurán Al-Ma'ida, 5:54]

The intention is made before the meditation: "Fayd or emanation is coming to my *Nafs* subtlety, from the Being who holds me dear and I hold him dear. The source (origin) of the Fayd is the arc of Major Sainthood, which is the quintessence of the third circle of major sainthood and the Walaya of Resolute Prophets."

At this stage, the stations of patience, gratitude and serenity are achieved, such that the seeker does not argue in the affairs of fate. The seeker no more requires the evidence to accept the commandments of Shariáh and perfect certainty on the promises of Allahﷻ is achieved. The carnal self gets consumed, similar to ice that melt in the sun and becomes *Nafs e Mutmainna*. The ego of the *Nafs* is dead, the seeker considers his existence as a ray of the existence of the Supreme Divine. When he uses the word "I" for himself, he considers it as a figurative statement. He considers his intentions offensive and his actions defective. Good ethics are induced, and vice ethics such as greed, parsimony, jealousy, hatred and false pride are cleansed.

The circle of *Walayat-e-Sughra* or the minor sainthood is the manifestation of the Supreme Name and Attributes, where annihilation of Qalb within the concept of *Tawheed e Wujudi* is attained. The circle of *Walayat-e-Kubra* or the Major sainthood is the manifestation of Supreme Name, Attributes and Divine Manifestation of Essential splendour which brings the seeker to achieve the annihilation of the carnal self, therefore, *Tawheed e Shuhudi* is manifested. Both *Walayat-e-Sughra* and *Walayat-e-Kubra* are manifestations of the Supreme name '*Az-Zahir*' (the Manifest), hence conclude on the Muraqabah of '*Ism Az-Zahir*'.

Lesson 21: Muraqabah of the Name az-Zahir-Meditation of the Name 'The Manifest'

While the seeker travels through the higher circle, greater perfection is attained and the seeker cuts through his carnal self as if with a sword. *Fayd* emanates on *Latifa e Nafs* as greenish white in colour. Tranquillity, calmness and perfect focus is achieved. At this stage, *Tahleel e Lisani* with sheer focus is beneficial. The following intention is made at the beginning of meditation:

"Fayd or emanation is coming to my *Nafs* (carnal-soul) and also on the five *Lataif* of *Aalam al-Amr* (subtleties of the Realm of Command, i.e., *Qalb, Ruh, Sirr, Khafi* and *Akhfa*) from the Being who is named by the Name '*Az-Zahir*' (the Apparent, the Manifest)."

In this muraqabah, the Fayd arrives on the *Nafs* subtlety and also on the five subtleties of the Realm of Command. As the name *Az-Zahir*' means the Manifest, the seeker, in this station, sees Divine Manifestation of Allahﷻ in everything. These Manifestations are only to the exoteric or *zahir* of the seeker, whereas, his inner-being is not affected by these outer Manifestations.

This muraqabah completes the station of *Walayat-e-Kubra* and the seeker begins the journey through the next station which is called *Walayat al-Ulya*, meaning the Highest Sainthood, which is the sainthood of angels and angelic world.

Lesson 22: Muraqabah of the Name al-Batin-Meditation of the Name 'The Innermost'

The muraqabah in this sublime spiritual station is of the Divine name 'Al-Batin' (the Innermost), which is done by reciting the intention:

"Fayd or emanation is arriving on three elements; air, water and fire, from the Being who is named by the Name 'Al-Batin' (the Innermost). The source of the Fayd is the Circle of Angelic Sainthood, '*Dairah Walayat al-Ulya*', which is the sainthood of the Higher-Order angels."

The receiver of Fayd in this station are the basic elements of air, water and fire excluding earth. The seeker develops angelic qualities and the human traits are less observant. Seeker may even witness the angels and see their hidden secrets. Again,

Tehleel-e-Lisani, reciting "*La Ilaha IllAllah*", offering optional Salah with extensive recitation of Qurán are beneficial. As devotion is the quality of the angels, utter dedication and conviction is required to follow Shariáh. At this stage the inner most of the seeker is affected by the manifestations of the Innermost, therefore, those secrets are not to be revealed.

The sainthood of angels is the highest sainthood, yet this station is permanent, unlike Prophets who can progress beyond the stations of angels. Therefore, stations of Prophets are regarded higher than angels in absolute priority in the creed of Ahle Sunnah. The stations from here onwards are additions to the journey by Imam Rabbani Shaykh Ahmad Faruq Sirhindi. There was no defined way through these stations, however, Allah unfolded these exalted stations through him. These spiritual stations are not found in any other Sufi order, past or present and the only way to achieve these sublime stations is by Allah's *inaya* (the special Grace of Allah).

Lesson 23: Muraqabah Kamalat-e-Nabuwwat-Meditation of the Perfections of Prophethood

Meditation starts with the intention:

"*Fayd* is arriving on my Earth Element subtlety from that All-Pure Being [Dhat] Who is the source of the perfections of Prophethood."

At this station, the seeker achieves a state where all the states from the previous stations are insignificant. The seeker feels himself worse than an infidel, yet affirms in the state of *Ayn ul Yaqeen*. At this stage, the knowledge of *Huroof e Muqattát* may be imparted to some. It is important to continue with the extensive obligatory Salah, recitation of Qurán and follow the Sunnah with complete dedication.

Lesson 24: Muraqabah Kamalat-e-Risalat-Meditation of the Perfections of Messengerhood

From this meditation onwards, the receiver of *Fayd* is an entity called *"Haiyat-e-Wahdani"*, translated as the Singular Form. The Singular Form is a unified form of the all subtleties: earth, water, air, fire, *Nafs, qalb, ruh, sirr, khafi and akhfa*. The intention before this meditation is as follows;

"*Fayd* is arriving on my Singular Form [Haiyat-e-Wahdani] from the All-Pure Being [Dhat] Who is the source of the perfections of Messengerhood."

Lesson 25: Muraqabah Kamalat-e-Ulul-Azm-Meditation of Perfections of the Resolute Prophets

The intention before starting the meditation is;

"*Fayd* is arriving on my Singular Form [Haiyat-e-Wahdani] from the All-Pure Being [Dhat] Who is the source of the perfections of the Resolute Prophets."

The secrets of these station can only be experienced and the states are beyond writing. From this station onwards, there are two paths to continue the journey. It depends on the Shaykh as to which path he chooses for the seeker. One is called the path of Divine Realities, *Haqaiq al-Ilahiyah* which has three circles; *Haqiqat e Ka'ba, Haqiqat e Qurán and Haqiqat e Salah*. The other path is through the Circle of *Haqaiq al-Anbiya*.

Lesson 26: Muraqabah Haqiqat-e-Ka'ba-Meditation of the Reality of Ka'ba

The intention before this meditation is; "*Fayd* is arriving on my Singular Form [Haiyat-e-Wahdani] from the All-Pure Being [Dhat] Who is the Bowed-to [*Masjood Ilaihi*] by all Possibles (creations) and is the source of the Reality of Divine Ka'ba."

Lesson 27: Muraqabah Haqiqat-e-Qurán-Meditation of the Reality of Qurán

The intention before this meditation is, "*Fayd* is arriving on my Singular Form [Haiyat-e-Wahdani] from the source of Inconceivable Vastness, the Venerable Being [Dhat], Who is the source of the Reality of glorious Qurán."

Lesson 28: Muraqabah Haqiqat-e-Salah-Meditation of the Reality of Prayer

The intention before the Muraqabah is, "*Fayd* is arriving on my Singular Form [Haiyat-e-Wahdani] from a Perfectly Inconceivable Vastness, the Venerable Being [Dhat], Who is the source of the Reality of Salah."

Lesson 29: Muraqabah Ma'budiyyat-e-Sirfah-Meditation of the Pure Worship Worthiness

Intention of this Muraqabah is, "*Fayd* is arriving on my Singular Form [Haiyat-e-Wahdani] from the Being [Dhat] Who is the source of the Pure worship worthiness."

The last part was related to the Divine Realities, in which the progress is dependent on the Grace of Allah. The final part of this noble spiritual path relates to the realities of the Prophets. Progress in the realities of Prophets is dependent on the love of Allah's Last Messenger. Allah loves His 'Dhat', the Being and His Attributes and Actions. Thus, love is of two types: *Muhibbiyyah* meaning from the lover and *Mahbubiyyah* meaning from the Beloved.

Lesson 30: Muraqabah Haqiqat-e-Ibraheemi-Meditation of the Abrahamic Reality

This is the circle of the Reality of Prophet Ibraheemﷺ. It is the first circle among the circles of realities of Prophets. The reality of Sayyidina Ibraheemﷺ is the station of *Khullah* (intimacy) of Allahﷻ. As Ibraheemﷺ was Khalil Allah (intimate of Allahﷻ), this meditation helps the seeker travel through the sublime station of *Mahbubiyyah Sifatiyah*, meaning the manifestation of Belovedness of Attributes. The Muhammadanﷺ and Ahmadanﷺ realities are the manifestations of *Mahbubiyyah Zatiyah* meaning Belovedness of Being. Intention when starting the meditation:

"*Fayd* is arriving on my Singular Form [Haiyat e Wahdani] from the Being [Dhat] Who is the source of the Ibraheemi (Abrahamic) Reality."

In this noble station, other Prophets are followers of Sayyidina Ibraheem,ﷺ as mentioned in Qurán:

"*Follow the ways of Ibraheem, the True in Faith.*"

[Qurán An-Nahl 16:23]

In this station, the *Salawat e Ibraheemi* that is often recited during Salah is helpful for progress:

اَللّٰهُمَّ صَلِّ عَلٰى مُحَمَّدٍ وَّعَلٰى اٰلِ مُحَمَّدٍ كَمَا صَلَّيْتَ عَلٰى اِبْرٰهِيْمَ وَعَلٰى اٰلِ اِبْرٰهِيْمَ اِنَّكَ حَمِيْدٌ مَّجِيْدٌ

اَللّٰهُمَّ بَارِكْ عَلٰى مُحَمَّدٍ وَّعَلٰى اٰلِ مُحَمَّدٍ كَمَا بَارَكْتَ عَلٰى اِبْرٰهِيْمَ وَعَلٰى اٰلِ اِبْرٰهِيْمَ اِنَّكَ حَمِيْدٌ مَّجِيْدٌ

Lesson 31: Muraqabah Haqiqat-e-Musavi- Meditation of the Moses Reality

This is the second circle among the circles of realities of Prophets. It is the station of the Reality of Musaﷺ (Moses) in the circle of *Muhibbiyyat e Sirfah*. The intention before the meditation is,

"*Fayd* is arriving on my Singular Form [Haiyat-e-Wahdani] from the Being [Dhat] Who is Self-Lover and is the source of the Musavi Reality."

In this station, the following *Salawat Kaleemiyah* is helpful for progress:

اَللّٰهُمَّ صَلِّ عَلَىٰ سَيِّدِنَا مُحَمَّدٍ وَّاٰلِهِ وَاَصْحَابِهِ وَعَلَىٰ جَمِيْعِ الْاَنْبِيَآءِ وَالْمُرْسَلِيْنَ خُصُوْصاً عَلَىٰ كَلِيْمِكَ مُوْسَىٰ عَلَيْهِ السَّلَامُ.

Lesson 32: Muraqabah Haqiqat-e-Muhammadi- Meditation of the Muhammadan ﷺ reality

This is the third circle among the circle of realities of Prophets. It is the circle of Muhammadan ﷺ Reality, also called the Reality of Realities [Haqiqat al-Haqaiq]. The Muhammadan Reality is the first manifestation, known as the Reality of Realities, because all other realities, including the realities of Prophets and the realities of angels, are the shadows of this Reality. The following intention is made before the Muraqabah;

"*Fayd* is arriving on my Singular Form [Haiyat-e-Wahdani] from the Being [Dhat] Who is Self-Lover and Self-Beloved and is the source of the Muhammadan ﷺ Reality."

In this station, the seeker acquires such an extreme love for Allah's Last Messenger ﷺ that the meaning of the following quote of Imam Rabbani Mujaddid Alf Thani ﷺ becomes apparent:

"I love Allah ﷻ only because he is the Lord of Muhammad ﷺ."

In this station, reciting the *Salawat* on the Beloved Prophet ﷺ is beneficial for progress, especially the following Salawat:

اَللّٰهُمَّ صَلِّ عَلَىٰ سَيِّدِنَا مُحَمَّدٍ وَّاٰلِهِ وَاَصْحَابِهِ اَفْضَلَ صَلَوَاتِكَ عَدَدَ مَعْلُوْمَاتِكَ وَبَارِكْ وَسَلِّمْ.

Lesson 33: Muraqabah Haqiqat e Ahmadiﷺ- Meditation of the Ahmadanﷺ reality

In this station, *Mahbubiyat-i Dhatiya Sarfiya* is manifested, meaning that the Supreme Being or the Beloved is loved regardless of His fine attributes. The following intention is made before the Muraqabah;

"*Fayd* is arriving on my Singular Form [Haiyat-e-Wahdani] from the Being [Dhat] Who is Self-Beloved and is the source of the Ahmadanﷺ Reality."

The *Salawat* or benediction mentioned in the Muhammadan ﷺ Reality is helpful for progress in this station and recitation of the following *Salawat* is also beneficial:

اَللّٰهُمَّ صَلِّ عَلٰى سَيِّدِنَا مُحَمَّدٍ وَعَلٰى اٰلِ سَيِّدِنَا مُحَمَّدٍ وَّأَصْحَابِ سَيِّدِنَا مُحَمَّدٍ أَفْضَلَ صَلَوَاتِكَ عَدَدَ مَعْلُوْمَاتِكَ وَبَارِكْ وَسَلِّمْ.

Lesson 34: Muraqabah Hubb-e-Sarf- Meditation of the Pure Love

Hubb e Sarf means the Pure Love of which Muhammadanﷺ Reality is a shadow. The intention before the Muraqabah is,

"*Fayd* is coming from the Being [Dhat] who is the source of Pure Love on my Singular Form [Haiyat-e-Wahdani]."

This stage involves travelling with discernment, even the perception is deficient, incapable and inadequate. Reciting the *Salawat* mentioned in the Meditation for Muhammadanﷺ Reality is also beneficial for progress in this stage. This stage is very close to the Absolute Being and the Non-Determination, because the very first manifestation was Love that is the origin of all manifestations and the source of creation. This is indicated from the following Hadith e Qudsi: "I was a hidden treasure; I wished (loved) to be known; thus, I created the creations so that I may be known."

This stage is specific to the Seal of the Prophets, the Master of the Universe ﷺ, who is the cause of creation, as mentioned in the following Hadith e Qudsi: '(O Muhammad! ﷺ) If you did not exist, I would not have created the Heavens; if you did not exist, neither would I have manifested my Lordship."

Lesson 35: Muraqabah La-Ta'ayyun- Meditation of the Non-Peripheral

La-Ta'ayyun means non-peripheral, although, there is no end of progression towards Allahﷻ as the path of His love is endless and infinite, this is the last lesson of the Naqshbandi Mujaddidi path. The intention before the Muraqabah is, "*Fayd* is coming from the Pure Being who is the source of *Fayd* of the Circle of Non-Peripheral, to my Singular Form [Haiyat-e-Wahdani]."

This meditation is done to receive the *Fayd* of the Being [Dhat] that is higher than all determinations. Among the Prophets, this station is specific to the Seal of the Prophets, the Last Messenger Sayyedina Muhammad ﷺ With extreme humbleness and humiliation, a seeker does not reach this most sublime spiritual station, rather only travels perceptually through it. "The (assertion of) incompetence of cognizance is the essence of cognition, the claim of cognizance is the essence of Shirk."[1]

Works Cited

Ajiba, Ibn. *Iqaz al-himam fi sharh al-Hikam*. Translated by Ahmad ibn Muhammad and Ahmad ibn Muhammad ibn Ata Illah. Cairo: Mustafa al-Babi al-Halabi wa Awladuhu, 1972.

Al-Buzidi, Imam Muhammad Ibn Ahmad. *The Adab of the True Seeker*. Translated by Mokrane Guezzou. Viator Books, 2006.

Algar, Hamid. "The Naqshbandī Order: A Preliminary Survey of Its History and Significance." (Maisonneuve & Larose) 44 (1976).

al-Ghazali, Abu Hamid. Deliverance from Error- Al-Munqidh Min Al-Dalal. Fons Vitae, 2004.

—. Ihya Ulum id Din- Revival of relegious Learnings Vol-III. Translated by Fazl ul Karim. Dar ul Ishaat, 1993.

al-Ízz, Ibn abi. *Commentary on the Creed of At-Tahawi by Ibn abi al-Ízz*. Translated by Muhammad Abdul Haqq. Ibn e Saud Islamic University, Riyadh Saudi Arabia, 2000.

Al-Jawziyyah, Muhammad Ibn Qayyim. *Al-Wabil al-Sayyib: min al-Kalim al-Tayyib*. Al-matba'ah al-muniriyyah bi al-Azhar, 1952.

—. Ighaathat Al- Lahfaan min Masaa'id Ash-Shaytaan). Beirut, Lebanon: Dar Ibn Jawziyyah, 1998.

—. Zad al-Maad- Provisions for the Hereafter. El-Farouq Publishers, 2018.

'Arabi, Muhiyy ad-Din Ibn. *What the seeker needs*. Translated by Tosun Bayrak. Threshold Books, 1992.

Athir, Shaykh ibne. *Usudul Ghabah fi Marifat us Sahabah*. Translated by Shaykh Muhammad Abdush Shakoor Farouqi.

Works Cited

Al Meezan Publishers, 2006.

Dehalvi, Shah Waliullah. *Altaf al-Quds*. Tasawwuf Foundation, 1998.

Gilani, Shaykh Abd al Qadir. *The Revelations of the Unseen-Futuh al-Ghaib*. Translated by Muhtar Holland. Al Baz Publishing, 2007.

Hakeem, Muhammad Abdul. *Tajjaliat Imam Rabbani*. Maktabah Nabwiya, 1975.

Hujwiri, Ali bin Usman Al. *Kashf Al Mahjub*. Translated by Reynold A Nicholson. Lahore: Luzac and Company, 1976.

ImamRabbani, Mujaddid Alf Thani. *Maktoobat Imam Rabbani*. Translated by Muhammad Saeed. Madinah Publishing Company, 1972.

Iskandari, Ibn Ataullah. *Ikmaalush shiyam-Perfection of Morals*. Translated by Mujlisul Ulama of South Africa. NMUSBA Press, 2006.

Kandhalwi, Mawlana Muhammad Zakariyya. "Deoband.org." n.d. https://www.deoband.org/2009/05/theology-rulings/tasawwur-al-shaykh/ (accessed October 23, 2021).

—. Shari'ah wa Tariqah ka Talazum. Maktabahtush Sheikh, 1979.

—. The inseperability of Sharia and Tariqa. Madania Publications, 2011.

Keller, Nuh Ha Mim. *Sea without Shore: A Manual of the Sufi Path*. Amana Publications, 2011.

—. *Sufism and Islam*. Amman, Jordan: Wakeel Books, 2002.

Keller, Nuh Ha Mim. "The Place of Tasawwuf in Traditional Islamic Sciences." Lecture Jan, 1995.

Works Cited

Khaldun, Abd Ar Rahman bin Muhammed ibn. *Muqadimmah*. Mecca: Dar al-Baz, 1978.

Louis, Franklin. Rumi Past and Present, East and West. 2000.

Makki, Abu Talib Muhammad ibn 'Ali. Qut al-qulub fi mu'amalat al-mahbub wa wf tariq almurid ila maqam al-tawhid. Beirut: Dar Sadir, 1995.

Murad, Mahmoud R. *The articles of Faith*. Cooperative Office of Call and Guidance at Sulay, 2006.

Nadwi, Abdul Bari. *Tajdeed Tasawwuf o Sulook*. Maktaba e Ashrafia, 1947.

Nadwi, Abu al Hassan Ali. *Tarikh Dawat o Azeemat-Biographies: Saviours of Islamic Spirit*. Lucknow, India: Majlis Tehqeeqat o Nashariyat Islam, 2006.

Qadri, Allama Masood. Junaid Baghdadi Rematullah ke Waqiat page 65. 2000.

Qushayry, Abu al-Qasim. *Al Risala al-Qushayriyya fi ilm al-Tasawwuf - Epistle on Tasawwuf*. Translated by Professor Alexander D Knysh. Garnet Publishing Limited, 2007.

Roohullah, Muhammad. Silsila Naqshbandi ki Roshan Kirnen- The Rays of the Naqshbandi Order. Karachi: HM Saeed Company Publishers, 2018.

Shafi, Mufti Muhammad. *Ahkam al-Qurán*. Idarat al-Qurán wa al-Ulum al-Islamiyyah , 2007 .

Shah, Syed Zawwar Hussain. "Umdatul Sulook." Zawwar Academy Publications, 2009.

Sina, Ibn. Al-Isharat Wa-Tanbihat[on Metaphysics] Part 4. Orientalistica, 2019.

Sirhindi, Shaykh Ahmad. *Maktoobat Imam Rabbani.* Madinah Publishing Company, 1974.

Thanvi, Mowlana Ashraf Ali. *Haqiqat al-Tariqa min as-Sunna al-Aniqa Translated as A Sufi study of Hadith,.* Translated by Shaykh Yusuf Talal Delorenzo. London: Turath Publishing, 2010.

—. *Living as a True Muslim.* Al Qamar Publications, Maktaba Darul Maarif, 2018.

—. *Shariah and Tariqa.* Adam Publishers and Distributors, 2010.

—. *Ta'lim al-Deen.* Karachi: Dar ul Isahát, 1986.

—. *The Road to Allah.* Mujlisul Ulama of South Africa, 2014.

Usmani, Mufti Muhammad Taqi. "Deoband.org." *Deoband.org.* n.d. https://www.deoband.org/2010/05/theology-rulings/wahdat-al-wujud-wahdat-al-shuhud-and-the-safest-position/ (accessed October 15, 2021).

Usmani, Mufti Taqi. *Takmilat Fatḥ al-mulhim bi-sharh Ṣaḥīḥ al-Imam Muslim* . Beirut: Dar Ehia Al-Tourath Al-Arabi, 2006.

Wajid, Sufi Ashfaqullah. *Fayzan e Masoomia.* Lahore: MJM Printers, 2007.

Section Index

About the Author 1

Foreword 4

Chapter 1: THE PROPHETIC MISSION 7

Definition of Sufism or Tasawwuf 12

Chapter 2: MISCONCETIONS REGARDING SUFISM 20

Sufism and Monasticism 20

Modern Sufism 22

Sufism and Ahmadiyat (Qadiyaniat) 25

Sufi versus Yogi 27

Are Sufis part of the Mainstream Society? 28

Is Tassawuf a Reprehensible Innovation (Bid'a)? 30

Chapter 3: ELEMENTS OF TASAWWUF 37

The Internal State 37

Significance of Heart 43

Purification of the Carnal Self (Tazkiyah e Nafs) 45

Path (Tariqa) 49

Definition of Suluk 52

Chapter 4: THE GUIDE-SHAYKH 56

Following a Teacher (Ittiba) 58

Attributes of the Shaykh 63

Fake Sufis 68

Reality of the Pledge (Bayá) 72

Connection (Tálluq) 76

Communication (Raabta) 80

Etiquettes with the Shaykh (Adab) 82

Section Index

Attention (Tawajjuh)	88
Affinity (Nisbah)	91
Benefit from One's Shaykh (Tauheed e Matlab)	94
Succession (Khilafah)	95
Women on the Path	96

Chapter 5: ARTICLES OF FAITH (AQAID) 99

Belief in Allah	99
Belief in Angels	104
Belief in Scriptures	105
Belief in the Messengers	106
Belief in the Day of Judgement	110
Belief in Predestination (Qadr)	114
Life of the Prophet ﷺ after Death (Hayat un-Nabi)	115

Chapter 6: REMEMBRANCE (DHIKR) 119

Assemblies of Dhikr (Halqah)	125
Silent Dhikr	128

Chapter 7: PURIFICATION OF THE SOUL (TAZKIYAH) 129

Lack of Sincerity (Riya)	129
Pride	131
Unnecessary Talking	132
Unrestrained Glances	134
Backbiting (Ghiba)	135
Envy	136
Anger	136
Gluttony	138
Bad Company	139
Stinginess	141

Section Index

Chapter 8: JOURNEY OF THE SEEKER.................................143

    Three Essentials 145

    Love of Allah... 148

    Fear of Allah (Taqwa) 151

    Hope in Allah.. 154

    Reliance on Allah (Tawakkul) 155

    Love of the Beloved Prophet ﷺ 156

    Virtuous Character (Ikhlaq) 162

    Repentance (Tawba)... 163

    Striving (Mujahida) 166

    Gratitude (*Shukr*) 167

    Patience (Sabr) 170

    Abstinence (Tabattul) 171

    Generosity (Sakha) 171

    Chastity.. 173

    Preach (Tableegh) 174

    Humility (Tawadu) 175

    Contentment (Qaná) 177

    Lawful Sustenance 178

    Time Management.. 180

Chapter 9: DIVINE LAW AND THE REALITY 182

    The Concept of Ihsan.. 182

    Divine Law and The Reality (Shariáh and Haqiqa) 186

    Maárfa 190

    Level of Certitude.. 194

    Walaya 198

Section Index

True Knowledge (Ilm e Haqeeqi) 202

Bestowed Knowledge (Ilm al-Ladunni) 203

Fana fil-Shaykh, Fana fir-Rasool and Fana Fillah 205

Journey towards Allah (Sair I'lallah and Sair Fillah) 208

Chapter 10: MYSTICAL STATES AND STATIONS 209

Contraction and Elation (Qabd and Bast) 214

Awe and Intimacy (Hayba and Uns) 216

Ecstatic Behaviour, Rapture and Ecstatic Finding 217

Unification and Separation (Jam and Farq) 220

Unification of Unification (jam al-jamá) 221

Annihilation and Subsistence (Faná and Baqá) 222

Absence and Presence (Ghayba and Hudur) 224

Tasting and Drinking (Dhawq and Shurb) 225

Sobriety and drunkenness (Sahw and Sukr) 226

Erasure and affirmation (Mahw and Ithbat) 227

Concealment and Manifestation (Satr and Tajalli) 229

Presence, Unveiling and Witnessing 229

Proximity and Distance (Qurb and Buád) 230

Concept of Unity of Perception and Unity of Being 232

Chapter 11: GENERAL MISCONCEPTIONS 240

Use of Musical Instruments 240

Conveying the Reward of Actions 242

Visiting the Graves of Awliya 245

Chapter 12: THE ORDERS-SILSILA 248

Chishtiya Order 249

Spiritual Heirarchy of the Chishtiya Order 251

Section Index

Qadiriya Order 251

Spiritual Heirarchy of the Qadiriya Order 251

Shadhili Order 251

Spiritual Heirarchy of the Shadhili Order 252

Sohrevardi Order 253

Chapter 13: NAQSHBANDI ORDER 254

    Allah's Last Messenger: Prophet Muhammad ﷺ 255

    The First Caliph- Abu Bakr Siddique ؓ 270

    Sayeddina Salman Farsi ؓ 271

    Imam Qasim ؒ 271

    Imam Jáfar as-Sadiq ؒ 272

    Bayazid Bustami ؒ 273

    Shaykh Abu al-Hassan al-Kharqani ؒ 273

    Shaykh Abi Al Qasim Gurgani ؒ 273

    Shaykh Abu al-Farmadi ؒ 274

    Abi Yusuf Hamadani ؒ 274

    Khawaja 'Abd al-Khaliq Ghajdawani ؒ 274

    Khawaja Muhammad Arif al-Riyogari ؒ 275

    Khawaja Mahmood al-Faghnawi ؒ 275

    Khawaja Ali al-Ramitini ؒ 275

    Khawaja Muhammad Samasi ؒ 276

    Syed Shams ud din Amir Kulal ؒ 276

    Baha ad-Din Naqshband ؒ 276

    Khawaja Ala ad-Din Attar ؒ 277

    Khawaja Ya'qub Charkhi ؒ 278

    Khawaja Ubaydullah al-Ahrar ؒ 278

    Khawaja Muhammad Zahid ؒ 280

    Khawaja Darvaish Muhammad ؒ 280

    Khawaja Muhammad al-Amkanki ؒ 280

    Khawaja Baqibillah ؒ 281

    Shaykh Ahmad Sirhindi-Mujaddid Alf Thani ؒ 282

    Khawaja Muhammad Masoom ؒ 284

    Khawaja Saifuddin ؒ 285

    Khawaja Muhammad Mohsin ad-Dehlavi ؒ 285

    Khawaja Nur Muhammad al-Badayoni ؒ 285

    Mirza Mazhar Janejana ؒ 286

Section Index

Khawaja Ghulam Ali ad-Dehlavi ؒ 286
Khawaja Abu Sa'eed Ahmad ؒ 286
Khawaja Ahmad Saeed nil Madani ؒ 287
Dost Muhammad al-Qandhari ؒ 287
Muhammad Uthman ad Daamani ؒ 287
Shaykh Muhammad Sirajuddin ؒ 287
Shaykh Muhammad Fazal Ali Qureshi ؒ 288
Shaykh Mohammad Abdul Ghafoor al-Madni al-Abbassi ؒ 289
Shaykh Abdul Haq al-Madni al-Abbasi ؒ 289
Shaykh Shamsur Rehman Al Abbasi مدظلہ العالی 290

Chapter 14: NAQSHBANDI PRINCIPLES..................291

Conscious Breathing (Hosh dar Dam) 291

Watch the Step (Nazar bar Qadam) 292

Journey Homeward (Safar dar Watan) 293

Solitude en masse (Khalwat dar Anjuman) 293

Remembrance (Yad Kard) 294

Resonate (Baaz Gasht) 294

Diligence (Nigah Dasht) 295

Recollection (Yad Dasht) 295

Awareness of Time (Wuqoof e Zamani) 295

Awareness of Number (Wuqoof e Adadi) 296

Awareness of Heart (Wuqoof e Qalbi) 296

Chapter 15: SUBTLETIES AND MANIFESTATIONS 297

Subtleties 297

Divine Manifestations (Tajalliat) 300

Chapter 16: DAILY ROUTINES IN THE NAQSHBANDI ORDER ... 302

Remembrance (Tasbeehat) 302

Meditation (Muraqabah in the Naqshbandi Order) 302

Envisage (Tasawwur-e-Shaykh) 304

Hierarchy of the Spiritual Order (Shajrah) 308

Section Index

Chapter 17: LESSONS OF THE NAQSHBANDI ORDER 315

Diagram for Muraqabah...

Lesson 1:
Dhikr in Latifa e Qalb–Heart Subtlety.. 316

Lesson 2:
Dhikr Latifa e Ruh-Soul Subtlety... 317

Lesson 3:
Dhikr in Latifa e Sirr–Secret Subtlety.. 317

Lesson 4:
Dhikr of Latifa e Khafi–Hidden Subtlety.. 318

Lesson 5:
Dhikr of Latifa e Akhfa–Hidden-most Subtlety............................... 318

Lesson 6:
Dhikr in Latifah e Nafs–Carnal-soul Subtlety.................................. 319

Lesson 7:
Dhikr in Latifa e Qalib–Physical Body... 319

Lesson 8:
Dhikr Nafi Athbat–Negation Affirmation... 320

Lesson 9:
Dhikr Tahlil Lisani–Negation Affirmation through Tongue..................... 321

Lesson 10:
Muraqabah Ahadiyyat–Meditation of Oneness.. 321

Lesson 11:
Muraqabah Tajalliyat e Afáliya–Meditation of the Divine Manifestation of Action... 322

Lesson 12:
Muraqabah Tajjaliyat–e–Sifat–e–Thubutiyya–Meditation of the Subsistent Attributes.. 323

Lesson 13:
Muraqabah Tajalliyat-e-Shuyun e Zatiya–Meditation of the Divine Manifestation of the Essential Splendours.. 324

Lesson 14:
Muraqabah Tajalliyat e Sifat e Salbiya–Meditation of the Divine Manifestation of the Privative Attributes.. 324

Lesson 15:
Muraqabah Tajalliyat e Shan e Jamiá–Meditation of Divine Manifestation of the Comprehensive Splendour.. 325

Lesson 16:
Muraqabah Ma'iyyat–Meditation of Co-Presence.................................. 326

Lesson 17:
Muraqabah Da'irat al–Ula–Meditation of the First Circle.................... 327

Lesson 18:
Muraqabah Ad–Da'irat ath–Thaniya–Meditation of the Second Circle......... 327

Lesson 19:
Muraqabah Ad–Da'irat ath–Thalitha–Meditation of the Third Circle........... 328

Lesson 20:
Muraqabah Al–Qaws- Meditation of the Arc... 328

Section Index

Lesson 21:
Muraqabah of the Name az-Zahir–Meditation of the Name 'The Manifest....... 329
Lesson 22:
Muraqabah of the Name al-Batin–Meditation of the Name 'The Innermost... 330
Lesson 23:
Muraqabah Kamalat-e-Nabuwwat–Meditation of the Perfections of Prophethood.. 331
Lesson 24:
Muraqabah Kamalat-e-Risalat–Meditation of the Perfections of Messengerhood.. 332
Lesson 25:
Muraqabah Kamalat-e-Ulul-Azm–Meditation of Perfections of the Resolute Prophets.. 332
Lesson 26:
Muraqabah Haqiqat-e-Ka'ba–Meditation of the Reality of Ka'ba................ 332
Lesson 27:
Muraqabah Haqiqat-e-Qurán–Meditation of the Reality of Qurán............ 333
Lesson 28:
Muraqabah Haqiqat-e-Salah–Meditation of the Reality of Prayer................ 333
Lesson 29:
Muraqabah Ma'budiyyat-e-Sirfah-Meditation of the Pure Worship Worthiness... 333
Lesson 30:
Muraqabah Haqiqat-e-Ibraheemi–Meditation of the Abrahamic Reality........ 334
Lesson 31:
Muraqabah Haqiqat-e-Musavi–Meditation of the Moses Reality................ 334
Lesson 32:
Muraqabah Haqiqat-e-Muhammadi ﷺ -Meditation of the Muhammadan ﷺ reality... 335
Lesson 33:
Muraqabah Haqiqat e Ahmadi ﷺ -Meditation of the Ahmadan ﷺ reality......... 336
Lesson 34:
Muraqabah Hubb-e-Sarf–Meditation of the Pure Love................................ 336
Lesson 35:
Muraqabah La-Ta'ayyun–Meditation of the Non-Peripheral...................... 337
Works Cited... 338
Section Index... 342

www.ingramcontent.com/pod-product-compliance
Lightning Source LLC
Chambersburg PA
CBHW020912020526
44107CB00075B/1663